AMERICA — 1603-1789

BOOKS BY LAWRENCE H. LEDER

The Livingston Indian Records, 1666-1723 (1956), editor
Robert Livingston, 1654-1728, and the Politics of Colonial New York (1961)
The Glorious Revolution in America: Documents on the Colonial Crisis of 1689 (1964), coeditor
Liberty and Authority: Early American Political Ideology, 1689-1763 (1968)
The Meaning of the American Revolution (1969), editor
The Colonial Legacy, Vol. I: Loyalist Historians (1971), editor
The Colonial Legacy, Vol. II: Some Eighteenth Century Commentators (1971), editor
America — 1603-1789: Prelude to a Nation (1972)
Dimensions of Change: Problems and Issues of American Colonial History (1972), editor

America—1603-1789
Prelude to a Nation

by Lawrence H. Leder
Lehigh University

BURGESS PUBLISHING COMPANY • MINNEAPOLIS, MINNESOTA

Copyright © 1972 by Burgess Publishing Company
Printed in the United States of America
Library of Congress Catalog Card Number 72-183684
SBN 8087-1219-5

All rights reserved. No part of this book may be reproduced in any form whatsoever, by photograph or mimeograph or by any other means, by broadcast or transmission, by translation into any kind of language, nor by recording electronically or otherwise, without permission in writing from the publisher, except by a reviewer, who may quote brief passages in critical articles and reviews.

1 2 3 4 5 6 7 8 9 0

PREFACE

In synthesizing the colonial experience in a brief and hopefully useful volume, I have attempted to explain the developments that led to the formation of the American nation by 1789. In doing so, I have been aware of the prejudices that normally surround the historian's judgment. Although I, as a mere mortal, have been unable to avoid them, I have assiduously sought to moderate them. Thus in studying the events and personalities of past times, I have tried to avoid judgments based on future consequences, preferring instead to look at the events and figures from the vantage point of their own times.

As a volume designed for those interested in the origins of our nation, this is merely an introduction. To describe fully all of the events, to analyze thoroughly all of the themes, to explore extensively all of the personalities would require a much larger work and would defeat the purpose of this one. By offering a structure and a basic analysis, this volume may encourage some students to dig more deeply into the exciting literature of colonial America. To aid them, brief selected bibliographies are appended to each chapter. Those who teach the course in colonial history will undoubtedly want to supplement those lists with additional readings for their students.

The writing of any history is a challenging experience, and it is one laden with pitfalls. Sir Walter Raleigh, when writing *The History of the World*, warned: "I know that it will bee said by many, that I might have beene more pleasing to the Reader, if I had written the Story of mine owne times; having been permitted to draw water as neare the Well-head as another. To this I answer, that who-so-ever in writing a modern Historie, shall follow truth too neare the heeles, it may happily strike out his teeth. There is no Mistresses or Guide, that hath led her followers and servants into greater miseries."

Every student of history should know that he is threatened by the same dangers mentioned by Sir Walter, no matter how distant the time about which he writes. In trying to avoid having my teeth struck out, I have gained immensely from a number of people who have generously read the manuscript in its several stages and who have offered judicious comments and suggestions. Among them are Robert F. Byrnes of Indiana University, Robert D. Cross of Swarthmore College, Norman K. Risjord of the University of Wisconsin, Darrett B. Rutman of the University of New Hampshire, R. Don Higginbotham of the University of North Carolina, Peter N. Carroll of The University of Minnesota, Paul S. Conkin of the University of Wisconsin, and John R. Howe, Jr. of the University of Minnesota. There are others, I know, to whom I am equally indebted, and the absence of their names from this list reflects my oversight, not my ingratitude. I hope they will all be pleased with the result, but the full responsibility for its shape and dimension rests with me alone.

Several people must be singled out for special mention. Mrs. Theresa Racosky and Mrs. Virginia L. Frey of the Lehigh University History Department have done yeoman work on the manuscript in its several stages. My special thanks go to Alexander K. Fraser of Burgess Publishing Company, both for his faith that this volume would materialize and for his generous labors in its behalf. Finally, my wife and children have my appreciation for restraining their enthusiastic and delightful interruptions during the gestation of the book. To them it is dedicated.

FEBRUARY 23, 1972　　　　　　　　　　　　　　LAWRENCE H. LEDER

CONTENTS

CHAPTER 1: PROLOGUE: PERVASIVE PATTERNS   1

    The Christian Heritage / 3
    The Nation-State / 6
    England's Baroque Political System / 8
    England's Social Structure / 12
    The Old Life-Style: English Agriculture / 14
    The New Life-Style: English Commerce / 16
    Emergence of Urban Values / 18
    England's Intellectual Life / 19
    The Purpose and Shape of Adventure / 21
    Selected Bibliography / 23
    DOCUMENTS
    Description of Elizabeth, 1558-1603 / 8
    Parliament in Action, 1583 / 10
    The Impact of the Enclosure Movement / 16

CHAPTER 2: THE EMPIRES FOUNDED, 1603-1640   25
    Spain's Crusade for Empire / 26
    France's Hesitant Adventure / 28
    The Dutch Search for Profit / 30
    England's Brave Experiment / 32
    Virginia: Foothold of Empire / 34
    Maryland: Feudalism Revisited / 43
    Southern Society / 45
    Escape to Plymouth / 48
    Massachusetts Bay: The New Jerusalem / 53
    The Overflow of Grace / 60
    Selected Bibliography / 64
    DOCUMENTS
    The Successful Plantation, 1625 / 42
    Bishop of Durham Clause / 44
    An Indentured Servant's Complaint, 1620's / 46
    Persecution of Puritans, 1591 / 49
    Description of James I, 1603-1625 / 51
    A Church Covenant, 1630 / 55
    Planting a Town: Woburn, Mass., 1640 / 56
    John Winthrop's Definition of Liberty, 1645 / 58
    Roger Williams on Liberty and Restraint, 1655 / 60

CHAPTER 3: UNSETTLED HUMORS, 1640-1705   67
    England's Turmoil / 68
    Colonial Reactions / 68
    Stuart Imperialism / 77
    The English and New Netherland / 80
    The Confusion of New Jersey / 82
    Penn's Holy Experiment / 84
    Spillover into the Carolinas / 86
    Strains within the Empire / 87
    Stability of Imperial Forms / 97
    Selected Bibliography / 98
    DOCUMENTS
    Problems of Private Colonies, 1701 / 78
    Nathaniel Bacon's Manifesto, 1676 / 88

Governor Berkeley's Apologia, 1676 / 91
The New England Primer, c. 1687 / 93

CHAPTER 4: THE AMERICANIZATION OF THE EMPIRE, 1705-1763 — 101

New Ethnic Streams / 103
The Philanthropic Experiment: Georgia / 110
Growing Economic Sophistication / 111
Intellectual and Cultural Growth / 116
Religious Variations / 120
Political Ideas and Attitudes / 124
The Web of Empire / 127
The Imperial Wars / 130
End of an Era / 137

Selected Bibliography / 141

DOCUMENTS

A Virginian Explains Slavery, 1757 / 105
Quakers Oppose Slavery, 1688 / 107
The Status of Blacks, 1750's / 108
William Fitzhugh's Estate in Virginia, 1686 / 114
Criminal Punishments in Boston, 1740 / 117
B. Franklin on Felons and Rattlesnakes / 119
John Adams on the Purpose of Government / 126
Virginia's Place in the Empire, 1764 / 128
The Blessings of Peace, 1763 / 138

CHAPTER 5: A BROODING VIGILANCE, 1763-1776 — 143

British Policy Revised / 146
Stamp Act / 149
Stamp Act Congress / 153
English Reactions / 154
Pitt and Townshend / 155
Enforcing the Townshend Duties / 160
The Tea Duty / 161
The Boston Massacre / 162
False Calm / 164
The Gaspée Incident / 165

Tea and the East India Company / 167
English Reactions / 170
Economic Warfare / 171
The Intolerable Acts / 172
First Continental Congress / 174
Lexington and Concord / 176
Siege of Boston / 180
Second Continental Congress / 183
British Reactions / 184
American Acceptance of Independence / 185
Selected Bibliography / 189
DOCUMENTS
The Declaratory Act, March 18, 1766 / 154
Thomas Paine on the English Monarchy / 186
Declaration of Independence, July 4, 1776 / 188

CHAPTER 6: THE WORLD TURNED UPSIDE DOWN, 1776-1783   191

American Unity / 193
Central Government / 194
State Governments / 196
Conduct of the War / 201
Diplomacy of the Revolution / 213
Diplomacy of Peace / 217
Unresolved Problems / 221
The Application of Revolutionary Ideals / 223
Black Slavery / 227
Legal Reforms / 230
The Nation in 1783 / 231
Selected Bibliography / 234
DOCUMENTS
This Unfortunate Revolution / 192
Adam Smith Questions the Concept of Empire / 198
The Dance, 1781 / 210
The Treatment of Blacks, 1774 / 228
Jefferson on Depravity of Slavery, 1784 / 230
The Indian Condemned, 1782 / 232

CONTENTS

CHAPTER 7: THE CIRCLE TURNED FULL, 1783-1789   237

Emergence of a Bureaucracy / 238
Governing the West / 239
Lack of a Mercantilist System / 241
Diplomatic Inadequacy / 242
Financial Incompetence / 244
Public Disorder / 246
Conservative Responses / 248
The Philadelphia Convention / 249
Ratification / 255
Completing the Constitution / 264
End of a Political Experiment / 266
An American Identity and Elan / 267
Selected Bibliography / 270

DOCUMENTS

Madison on Factions / 252
John Jay on the "Silent Majority," 1786 / 256
John Adams's Dread of Popular Control / 258
Jefferson's Misgivings on the Constitution, 1787 / 259
The Science of Liberty / 268

EPILOGUE: THE THRESHOLD OF NATIONALITY   273

INDEX   279

MAPS

Indian Tribes in Colonial America, 1600-1700 / 40
Colonial Settlement, 1660 / 69
Colonial Settlement, 1700 / 102
Colonial Economy and Trade Routes / 112
Victorious British Empire after 1763 / 134
Colonial Settlement, 1760 / 145
Siege of Boston, 1775 / 182
Revolutionary Troop Movements / 204
Siege of Yorktown, 1781 / 212
Peace of 1783 / 219

CHAPTER 1

PROLOGUE: PERVASIVE PATTERNS

I shall give them as much gold as they want... slaves as many as they shall order, and I shall find a thousand other things of value." So Christopher Columbus promised his patrons, Ferdinand and Isabella of Spain, epitomizing motives which would stir other fifteenth-century Europeans to seek overseas empire. Few, however, would reap the golden harvest forecast by Columbus.

Monarchs and explorers, gentlemen and commoners, the Church — each sought a form of wealth, whether counted in ounces of yellow metal, acres of green forest, or a pride of salvaged souls. For most, gold glinted brightest. Hernando Cortes, conqueror of Mexico, once reflected: "We Spaniards suffer from a disease that only gold can cure." Countless adventurers sought that cure, leaving the comforts of a known, traditional

European merchants in the Levant, fifteenth century. New tastes and appetites whetted by the Crusades led to increasing trade between Europe and the Orient, with the Eastern Mediterranean becoming the marketplace for the exchange of goods. Such trade marked Europe's first important contact in modern times with the outside world. (Historical Pictures Service, Chicago)

situation to head for a vast, terrifying unknown. Ferdinand Columbus, Christopher's son, reported that crews dreaded "the fire in lightning flashes, the air for its fury, the water for its waves, and the earth for its reefs and rocks." Yet, they pressed on.

Finding a cure for Cortes's "Spanish disease" was but one reason why Europeans embarked on the "bloody ocean, seething like a pot on a hot fire." A burst of energy, stimulated by a variety of factors, stirred Europe to expand outward and altered its life-style. The Crusades had created new markets and introduced new commodities, the collapse of feudalism and the disruption of the medieval church had created nation-states and national churches, and the Renaissance had rediscovered classical learning and exposed the traditional order to the challenge of science and rationalism. New vistas opened; old moods shattered.

As the Crusades opened Europe to the world, initial attention focused on the Near East, entrepot for Asia's exotic goods. Venice's rise as commercial intermediary between Europe and the Levant, between Christian and Moslem, came about because of Europe's increasing lust for spices, silks, sugar, and finery. However, Venice's monopoly aroused the jealousy of western Europeans, and those nations fronting on the Atlantic began exploratory efforts to find more direct routes to the source of oriental wealth.

Portugal and Spain, on Europe's western fringe, began the outward expansion. Portugal, which broke the Venetian monopoly by circling South Africa, soon suffered from its own avarice. When it closed the Lisbon market to Dutch and English merchants in 1594, those nations began their own exploratory ventures toward Asia. Europeans exploited civilizations far older and more sophisticated than their own and sought to exchange their crude products for the Orient's rare and exotic goods.

The Christian Heritage

As the Europeans ventured abroad, they carried Christianity with them. By the seventeenth century that term represented a common religious attitude and outlook, even though theology, ritual, and organization varied widely from country to country. For all Europeans — and especially for the overwhelming peasant majority — religion and superstition had much in common. God threatened, demons hovered, and fear ruled.

The variety in theology, ritual, and organization stemmed from new ideas and new institutions unleashed by Martin Luther and other reformers. The medieval Roman Catholic Church would lose its hegemony over western Europe because of challenges to the ever-widening gap between the Church's ideals and its practices. Spiritual reformers argued for individual and mystical piety and faith; others urged institutional reform through ecumenical councils; and still others insisted upon humanism, a

Martin Luther (1483-1546), the monk who, beginning in 1517, challenged medieval Catholicism and made possible the Reformation. (Historical Pictures Service, Chicago)

worship of knowledge, in the belief that education would lead to a higher ethical standard which would cleanse the world.

From these diverse approaches emerged the Reformation. Martin Luther posted his famous Ninety-Five Theses on the door of the Wittenberg Church in 1517 and proposed to debate them. Within a few months, Luther's condemnation of Church practices (especially the selling of indulgences to the gullible) spread across Europe and challenged the Church's hierarchy and its hegemony. By 1520 in *An Appeal to the Ruling Clergy* Luther declared that the Church could not or would not reform itself and that the secular state must undertake the task.

Luther appealed to German princes by emphasizing secular control and inadvertently to the people by using the vernacular. By touching two responsive chords, he destroyed the harmony of medieval Catholicism. Reformed churches sprang up in Central Europe as local rulers seized the

*John Calvin
(1509-1564), austere
founder in Geneva
of a major branch of
Protestantism. His
emphasis on discipline
and rigor, on an
absolute, awesome,
and dreadful God is
reflected in his visage.
(Historical Pictures
Service, Chicago)*

chance to bring religion under their control, thereby strengthening their political authority. John Calvin, a Frenchman who favored discipline and rigor in religion, sought refuge in Switzerland, wrote the first full exposition of reformism, and founded an austere theocratic state in Geneva. John Knox, who led a reform movement in Scotland that owed much to Calvin's ideas, aimed his faith at an agricultural society while Calvin had developed his for an urban elite.

Religious reformation destroyed the last remnant of institutional unity in Europe. Northern Germany and Prussia adopted Lutheranism, as did Sweden and Denmark. The Netherlands turned Calvinist, while Scotland adopted Knox's Presbyterianism, and England strove to establish its own national church. The bastions of Roman Catholicism remained South Germany, France, Italy, the Iberian Peninsula, and much of Eastern Europe. Just as Europe divided religiously by nation-states, so individual nations found sharp divisions among their populations. The manner of worshipping God became increasingly either a matter of political expediency or of individual conscience.

THE NATION-STATE

Religion had lost its control over politics, but politicians had captured the churches. Civil authorities found religion a useful tool for arousing the martial spirit of a people whose attitude toward religion remained simple and primitive. Church and state, regardless of which church or which state, became two sides of the same coin. This served effectively to gain popular support for nationalistic crusades in the seventeenth and eighteenth centuries. Religion served the same function at that time as political ideology has served in our own time.

As the hegemony of the Roman Catholic Church crumbled, the new institution of the nation-state replaced it as the locus of authority, particularly on the western edge of Europe. Portugal, Spain, The Netherlands, France, and England organized themselves into nation-states. Each gradually developed within itself a centralized unity that over-arched traditional feudal relationships and transferred privately-owned, hereditary rights of law enforcement, taxation, and administration to a monarch who utilized these prerogatives in the name of the state. The rest of Europe, however, continued as weak petty feudalities, as heterogeneous empires under constant internal stress, or as small states subject to constant depredations from their neighbors.

Europe's western fringe produced the first nation-states because of unique geographical features and peculiar local situations. Portugal, hemmed in by the Atlantic on one side and by Spaniards and Moors on the other, organized itself to strike at Moorish power in Africa. Spain, divided into petty kingdoms, acquired national identity through its religious crusade against the Moors whom it finally defeated in 1492 at Toledo. The Netherlands, long under alien political and religious domination, unified to overthrow its distant Spanish rulers.

Of all the nation-states, England had the most favorable situation because of its insular position. If its kings had not wasted their energies in the fourteenth and fifteenth centuries trying to seize France's throne and territories, English national unity might have emerged even earlier than it did. Once expelled from the Continent after the Hundred Years War (1337-1453), English kings were thrown on the island-kingdom's resources. A unity, patriotism, and new sense of destiny emerged. The English language, widely used in the kingdom, even replaced "court French" in official circles.

The Hundred Years War unsettled English politics and led to the bloody dynastic Wars of the Roses. Lancastrian and Yorkist claimants to the throne slaughtered one another until, by 1485, only shrewd Henry Tudor remained to seize the Crown. As Henry VII, he took advantage of the destruction of the old aristocracy during the wars and created his own dependent nobility, thus reversing feudal decentralization and domination of the monarch by the aristocracy.

The next Tudor, Henry VIII, cleverly refined his father's expansion of royal authority. One power still challenged the English monarch's supremacy — the Roman Church. Not only did it claim absolute hegemony over man's relations with God; it also exercised significant secular power. Henry VIII broke with Rome, ostensibly over his marital problems, in order to obtain for England what other rulers had already won for their kingdoms — a national Catholic Church with only nominal control by Rome. He intended no alteration of dogma, theology, or ritual, but he acted when others, such as Luther and Calvin, challenged Rome for different purposes. Thus he, too, unleashed forces for change.

For the next two decades Englishmen debated church reform, finally achieving an equilibrium under Queen Elizabeth in the 1560s. The Church of England, as shaped by Elizabeth, was a shrewd compromise which retained much of medieval Catholic ritual, introduced Calvinist theology, and made the monarch its supreme head. This Elizabethan Settlement set at rest those concerned primarily with tradition and liturgy, appeased the middle-class and intellectuals who advocated Calvinism, and satisfied the Queen's need for control over ecclesiastical affairs.

Elizabeth, resourceful and dauntless, completed the organization of the English nation-state. Its first test came in 1588 when the Spanish Armada sailed up the English Channel. England was pitted against the power of international Catholicism as represented by the sprawling Hapsburg Empire — Spain, the Spanish Netherlands, Naples, Sicily, Milan, Austria, and Spanish America with its great wealth. This array of power, embodied in the Armada, came to naught as the mighty fleet foundered in a storm on Scotland's bleak coast after being rebuffed by English ships. Hapsburg power had peaked. Soon, The Netherlands broke from Spanish Catholic dominance and won its independence. Both England and The

DESCRIPTION OF ELIZABETH, 1558-1603

SHE WAS IN STATURE indifferent tall, slender and straight, fair of Complexion, her hair inclining to pale yellow, her fore-head large and fair, her eyes lively and sweet, but short sighted; her nose somewhat rising in the midst; the whole compasse of her countenance somewhat long, yet of admirable beauty, but the beauty of her minde was far more admirable: She had been a subject, which taught her to rule; she had been in misery, which taughte her to be mercifull; and indeed, never Prince ruled with more Justice, and with her Justice mingled more mercy. She had more Valour in her then was fit for a woman, but that she was a Ruler over men; and more Humility in her then was fit for a Prince, but that she meant to be a President to women. She delighted in nothing so much, as in the love of her People, which she procured by ordaining good Magistrates, and forbearing Impositions. Her way not to need them was frugality; and her way to have them when she needed them, was liberality. She made Honour in her time the more honourable, by not making it common; and indeed, knowing it to be

☆☆☆☆☆☆☆☆☆☆☆☆☆☆☆☆☆☆☆☆☆☆☆☆☆

Netherlands, it should be noted, achieved their victories against Spain by interrupting its communications with its overseas empire.

The year 1588 also marked the beginning of England's rise to power. In the process, it faced a new series of rivals in the next few centuries. First came The Netherlands, which finally succumbed during the Anglo-Dutch wars of the mid-seventeenth century, leaving England dominant on the high seas. Next came France, which proved a more formidable foe. Its power was continental, not maritime, and England did not finally triumph over France until the defeat of Napoleon in 1815. The story of England's overseas expansion is largely a reflection of its European rivalries.

England's Baroque Political System

England's victories, even as late as 1815, were accomplished by a political and administrative system that retained much of medievalism. The English, as traditionalists, rarely discarded offices or titles; rather, they changed the function of the office, or they let it wither. Sixteenth-century England

an influence from her self, she kept it, as her self, a Virgin, and would not prostitute it to unworthy persons. She declined being a mother of children, to the end she might be a mother of her Countrey; and indeed, no mother ever loved her children more, then she did her people; and therefore never children loved a mother more, then her people did her. She coveted not so much to be an owner of riches, as of rich Subjects; for she thought money did as well in their Coffers, as in her own: and indeed, she never wanted it, when they had it; and they always had it, when she needed it. Never Prince had a wiser Counsell than she, yet never Prince needed it lesse; for she was her self a Counsellor to her Counsell. In sum, whatsoever may in flattery be said of a wise, just, mercifull, religious, and learned Prince, may truely be said of her; in all which, if ever she had an equall, yet she never certainly had a superiour. In playing her game of Fortune, she loved not an after-game; for she liked Preventions, better than Remedies. . . . (Richard Baker, Chronicle of the Kings of England *[London, 1641], pp. 118-119)*

☆☆☆☆☆☆☆☆☆☆☆☆☆☆☆☆☆☆☆☆☆☆☆☆☆

was thus a political amalgam of feudal traditions being quietly reshaped by the Tudors. All national life focused on the Crown, the fountain of honors and offices, source of justice, Supreme Head of the Church, and originator of public policy. Theoretically all-powerful, the monarch's real strength lay in keeping England's varied interests happy. The Tudors had this political genius; the Stuarts, their successors, did not. Therein lies the key to much of England's political history in the sixteenth and seventeenth centuries.

The Crown possessed extensive power on paper, but it depended on a concert of key ministers, the Privy Council, men who had easy access to the monarch. They handled all business in the King's name, but upon them centered all responsibility and, if their policies failed, all blame. The Council's agenda included a variety of problems — ranging from foreign affairs, great trading companies, textile manufacturing, mining, and shipping to alehouses and taverns — in short, all the varied threads of English life. This diversity of responsibilities led the Privy Council to establish committees for specific problems. By the end of the seventeenth

PARLIAMENT IN ACTION, 1583

IN LIKE MANNER in the lower house the speaker sitting in a seate or chaire for that purpose somewhat higher, that he may see and be seene of them all, hath before him in a lower seate his Clarke, who readeth such bils as be first propounded in the lower house, or be sent down from the Lords. For in that point ech house hath equal authoritie, to propounde what they think meete, either for the abrogating of some law made before, or for making of a newe. All bils be thrise in three diverse dayes read and disputed upon, before they come to the question. In the disputing is a marvelous good order used in the lower house. He that standeth uppe bareheaded is understanded that he will speake to the bill.... He that once hath spoken in a bill though he be confuted straight, that day may not replie, no though he would chaunge his opinion. So that to one bill in one day one may not in that house speake twise, for else one or two with altercation would spende all the time. The next day he may, but then also but once.

No reviling or nipping wordes must be used.... At the afternoone

☆☆☆☆☆☆☆☆☆☆☆☆☆☆☆☆☆☆☆☆☆☆☆☆☆☆

century, the Lords of Trade had gained increasing prominence and authority in colonial matters. By 1696, after several reorganizations, it had become the Board of Trade; it dominated Anglo-colonial relations in the eighteenth century.

Parliament, legislative arm of the English government, increased in importance during the seventeenth century. The House of Commons by that time represented rural gentry, urban merchants, and lawyers, and it gradually assumed control over the appropriation of funds for implementation of royal policy. So powerful did it become in the seventeenth century that it ordered one monarch's execution, another's abdication, and finally the succession to the throne. Its coordinate branch, the House of Lords, represented the kingdom's spiritual and temporal nobility. Although powerful in the sixteenth century, subservience to the monarch gradually weakened the Lords, for the King retained the feudal right to elevate his friends and allies to the nobility and thereby pack that House in his favor.

Despite the power invested in these institutions, they dealt with only

PROLOGUE: PERVASIVE PATTERNS

they keepe no parliament. The speaker hath no voice in the house, nor they will not suffer him to speake in any bill to moove or diswade it. If the commons doe assent to such billes as be sent to them first agreed upon from the Lords thus subscribed, Les commons ont assentus, *so if the Lords doe agree to such billes as be first agreed uppon by the Commons, they sende them down to the speaker thus subscribed,* Les Seigneurs ont assentus. *If they cannot agree, the two houses (for everie bill from whence soever it doth come is thrise reade in each of the houses) if it be understoode that there is any sticking, sometimes the Lordes to the Commons, sometimes the Commons to the Lords doe require that a certaine of each house may meete together, and so each part to be enformed of others meaning, and this is alwaies graunted. After which meeting for the most part not alwaies either parte agrees to other billes. . . . (Sir Thomas Smith,* De Republica Anglorum *[Cambridge: The University Press, 1906], pp. 54-55)*

☆☆☆☆☆☆☆☆☆☆☆☆☆☆☆☆☆☆☆☆☆☆☆☆☆☆

a small fraction of the business of running the nation and they had but little impact upon the ordinary Englishman. Local institutions of government exerted a far greater influence upon the King's subjects than did either Parliament or the monarch himself. England was predominantly rural and it was largely decentralized. Thus sheriffs and justices of the peace did more than Crown, Lords, and Commons combined to make most Englishmen aware of governmental power.

The King annually selected sheriffs from lists for each shire prepared by leading judges and the Privy Council. The office of sheriff carried heavy burdens, and men did not seek this post, but central government depended upon local magnates whose power base remained in their home counties. Sheriffs collected money due the Crown and handled the pomp and circumstance attending a state occasion such as the King's visit or a Court of Assizes session. Frequently the sheriff paid these expenses from his own pocket. He also had an important function in criminal cases, for he served as agent for the justices of the peace and for courts of Quarter Sessions and Assizes.

The King also selected justices of the peace from lists prepared by the Privy Council, again utilizing local magnates who dominated their counties. These positions were eagerly sought by country gentry who relished the responsibility of keeping the peace, supervising the county's day-to-day administration, and presiding over minor civil and criminal proceedings. Indeed, on Quarter Sessions day, when all the shire came to watch the trial of cases, the justices sitting *en banc* were truly made aware of their importance. Justices and sheriffs constituted the backbone of English government. Upon them depended the vitality and validity of broad policies enunciated in London.

England's Social Structure

Underneath the prestigious national and county governments lay the primary unit of English society — the family. This term meant something different in the seventeenth century than it does today, because it incorporated three societies in one: the man and his wife, the parents and their children, and the master and his servants. The seventeenth century believed the family to be an ancient institution, eternal and unchanging. By making life highly personalized and thoroughly structured, it set the tone of English society from the highest levels to the lowest.

The family's importance emerged from the role of marriage in providing social status and in signifying economic independence. As a self-contained economic unit, a family could not be begun unless there was some guarantee of a home and a livelihood. Until a son first achieved that kind of economic independence, he remained within his parents' household or in someone else's in the status of a servant. Oftentimes, families sent their children as servants to other families, replacing them with the children of others. This may have reflected the unwillingness of parents to subject their own offspring to the rigors of work and discipline.

Work was essential within the family, because it provided economic security for all of its participants. As a self-contained and sharply circumscribed social grouping, it carried on its economic activity and its daily life at one and the same place. Insecurity threatened whenever the head of the household died, for the family's economic viability ended with him. If a son took over, if a daughter married a capable apprentice, or if the widow continued the enterprise, the family could continue. However, the succession of a son or son-in-law often meant the displacement of the widow and siblings, sometimes abandoning them to pauperism and beggary, because the heir needed the family enterprise to establish and provide for his own family.

Indeed, families tended to be two-generational, especially among the poor. Married children did not live with parents, largely because the economic enterprise (whether agricultural, craftsmanship, or trade) was too limited to support an expanded multi-generational living group. Since a child had first to become economically independent, marriages occurred late in life, with men averaging twenty-eight years of age and women twenty-four at the time of wedding. Given the general brevity of life in the seventeenth century (only a little less than 30 percent of the population was over forty at the end of the century), marriages rarely lasted long, the early death of parents combined with the low fertility of wives limited the number of children, and infant mortality constantly took its awesome toll.

This created two situations totally different from our own day. There was little conversation across the generations, because grandparents rarely lived long enough to know their grandchildren. The short life span also created a society that was perpetually young. It is estimated that in the seventeenth century 45 per cent of the population was under twenty years of age, 27 per cent was between twenty and forty, and the balance of 28 per cent was over forty. English villages swarmed with young people (the proportion of children was higher in villages than in London), and their very presence in such numbers demanded discipline. Otherwise, they seriously threatened the established way of life, the traditional order which was the only known means for survival. Thus youngsters were treated as little adults and given no chance to enjoy childhood as a world separate from adulthood. The separate world of the child was a Victorian concept alien to the seventeenth century.

Discipline and authority underlay English society. Submission maintained stability and order and prevented anarchy and chaos which constantly threatened to overwhelm a society continuously on the edge of a subsistence crisis. Accustomed as most people were from time immemorial to poverty or near-poverty and to the limits of their own geographical and social milieu, they had no opportunity to develop aspirations which they could not fulfill. They accepted their lot in life, the traditional order, and resented efforts to overturn it. Religion buttressed this attitude, especially through the catechism which interpreted and reinforced the Fifth Commandment.

Only two institutions in seventeenth century England extended beyond the limited horizons of the family unit and the village — the aristocracy and the church. Both gave English society its continuity and its permanence. The church connected the illiterate masses to the educated handful who governed England. This handful of leaders, often based in the villages (about 80 per cent of which had resident members of the gentry or nobility), interacted with one another across local boundaries. They composed a separate class marked off from the rest of society by simple distinctions — the gentry and nobility possessed leisure and never worked with their hands — and they defined for the lower classes the world in which they lived. The bottom two-thirds of England was an oral society; its members had no past other than what the clergyman might remember for them and no outside world other than what the local magnate might describe to them.

The Old Life-Style: English Agriculture

Population densities increased markedly as England and Wales went from 3 million people in 1500 to about 5.5 million in 1700. However, agriculture still dominated, based on the medieval manorial system with its closed and barely self-sufficient economy, on human muscles and primitive tools, and on the preconception of a fixed supply of goods and amount of labor for an increasing population.

The organization of agriculture varied in England. In the southeastern area, lands had been enclosed for some time; in other regions, land was farmed in a communal pattern, with enclosure movements beginning to change the economic and social patterns of agricultural life. Land was usually owned by manor lords who leased tracts to tenant-cultivators, often under complex long-term arrangements. These tenants ranged from "dirt-farmers" to landed entrepreneurs employing others as day laborers.

Tenant farmers in seventeenth-century England faced constant rent increases as landlords sought to maximize profits. In those areas still engaged in communal farming, landlords used enclosure as a means of converting tenant rights to common pastures and wastelands into controlled grazing areas for the landlord's flocks of sheep. Enclosures reflected the growing importance of the wool trade and put increasing pressure upon farmers of small tracts by forcing more efficient, consolidated farms.

Efficiency was not the hallmark of seventeenth-century English agriculture. In a society without enough work to go around, the practice had

Woman and Child. (c. 1600). The artist's similarity of treatment of mother and child typified the attitude toward childhood at this time. The child is a small adult, and the symbolic presence of death hovered near both young and old. Adrien van Cronenburg, (Museo Nacional del Prado, Madrid)

emerged of spreading work among as many people as possible. Sixteenth- and seventeenth-century statutes prescribed minimum hours and maximum wages for laborers, artisans and apprentices, but workers rarely performed at peak efficiency or for wages commensurate with the needs of their families. Productivity was probably impaired by malnutrition and chronic diseases. Thus low wages produced minimum productivity which, in turn, justified low wages. Rarely could an industrious individual take on an additional job without receiving severe criticism and even legal penalties for depriving another of his livelihood. The sixteenth and seventeenth centuries looked upon social stability, upon the spreading of labor among as many hands as possible in the face of rapid population expansion, as the desideratum of public policy.

THE IMPACT OF THE ENCLOSURE MOVEMENT

FORSOOTH, . . . your sheep, that were wont to be so meek and tame and so small eaters, now, as I hear say, be become so great devourers and so wild that they eat up and swallow down the very men themselves. They consume, destroy and devour whole fields, houses and cities. For look in what parts of the realm doth grow the finest and therefore dearest wool, there noblemen and gentlemen — yea, and certain abbots, holy men, no doubt — not contenting themselves with the yearly revenues and profits that were wont to grow to their forefathers and predecessors of their lands, nor being content that they live in rest and pleasure, nothing profiting, yea much annoying the weal public, leave no ground for tillage; they enclose all in pastures; they throw down houses; they pluck down towns, and leave nothing standing but only the church, to make of it a sheephouse. And, as though you lost no small quantity of ground by forests, chases, lawns and parks, those good holy men turn all dwelling places and all glebe land into desolation and wilderness.

Therefore, that one covetous and insatiable cormorant and very plague of his native country may compass about and enclose many

☆☆☆☆☆☆☆☆☆☆☆☆☆☆☆☆☆☆☆☆☆☆☆☆☆

THE NEW LIFE-STYLE: ENGLISH COMMERCE

Since English society focused on agriculture as its primary support, and since stability and continuity marked that way of life, Englishmen stubbornly opposed innovation. Yet change was in the wind, particularly in the great metropolis of London with its half million inhabitants. This urban cluster, which contained one-tenth of England's population, played a role out of proportion to its size as it led the country's transformation from an agricultural to a commercial economy. As England's only large city — Bristol, York, Norwich, and Southampton each averaged twenty-five to thirty thousand at the end of the seventeenth century — London dominated commerce and was largely responsible for making England Europe's foremost power.

Until the mid-sixteenth century English trade rested largely in foreign hands, particularly those of the Hanseatic League of North German cities and of the Venetians. Hanse merchants controlled the Baltic trade, while the Venetians monopolized the oriental trade, sending annual fleets to

thousand acres of ground together within one pale or hedge, the husbandmen be thrust out of their own; or else either by covin deceit or fraud, or by violent oppression, they be put besides it, ousted, or by wrongs and injuries they be so wearied that they be compelled to sell all. By one means therefore or by other, either by hook or crook, they must needs depart away, poor, silly, wretched souls — men, women, husbands, wives, fatherless children, widows, woeful mothers with their young babes, and their whole household, small in substance and much in number, as husbandry requireth many hands. Away they trudge, I say, out of their known and accustomed houses, finding no place to rest in. All their household stuff, which is very little worth . . . they be constrained to sell it for a thing of nought. And when they have, wandering about, soon spent that, what can they else do but steal, and then . . . be hanged, or else go about a-begging? And yet then also they be cast in prison as vagabonds, because they go about and work not. . . . (From J. H. Lupton, ed., The Utopia of Sir Thomas More *[Oxford: Clarendon Press, 1895], pp. 51-54)*

☆☆☆☆☆☆☆☆☆☆☆☆☆☆☆☆☆☆☆☆☆☆☆☆☆☆☆☆☆

Southampton until 1553. While others exploited England as a market, its merchants remained passive and supplied raw materials such as tin, lead, alum, and raw wool, receiving more expensive manufactured goods and spices in return.

As wool become more important in the increasingly wealthy European markets, subtle but significant changes occurred in England's foreign trade. The expanding exports of raw wool brought England more gold and silver. English landlords began enclosing lands for sheep grazing, increasing the wool supply. The missing ingredient — knowledge of the "mysterie" of weaving — came with the Flemings, who fled the consequences of the Hundred Years War and sought refuge in southeastern England.

Flemish weaving techniques opened new and different markets to English merchants. Previously, they could export raw wool to a few continental towns where skilled artisans practiced weaving and dying. Now, as England began to weave its own cloth, all of Europe opened as a market. In 1350, England exported 30,000 sacks of raw wool and 5,000 pieces of woolen cloth; in 1500, it exported 5,000 sacks of raw wool and 60,000 pieces of textiles. Public policy played a part in this transformation, for Henry VII recognized the importance of the cloth trade and encouraged it while he simultaneously placed heavy taxes on exports of raw wool. Indeed, so important was wool to England that the Chancellor of the Exchequer sat in Parliament on a woolsack to remind him constantly that England's strength depended on that commodity.

As a consequence of the increased weaving of woolens, changes also occurred in the structure of England's foreign commerce. The Hanse and Venetian traders had controlled about 65 per cent of the wool trade, with the balance in the hands of the Merchants of the Staple organized in the thirteenth century. Essentially a medieval guild, this group protected its members from competition by regulating and limiting trade, setting up a mart in Amsterdam, and guarding the interests of its members trading in Flanders.

The Merchants of the Staple concerned themselves with trade restriction, perfectly understandable in the context of medieval society which viewed productive capacity as rigidly limited and expected underemployment as a normal situation. However, as trade expansion became possible with the change in exports from raw wool to finished textiles, a new organization replaced the old guildlike one. The Merchant Adventurers, as the name denoted, aggressively sought out new trade opportunities. Each participant risked his own capital in private ventures under the aegis of the Company. Soon the Merchant Adventurers found itself incapable of coping with the expanding trade, and specialized joint-stock companies emerged, beginning with the Russian (or Muscovy) Company in 1553 and the African Company in the following year.

Joint-stock companies differed from the earlier trading groups in that they pooled the resources of a number of merchant-investors for a series of ventures in the company's name, thus utilizing only a small part of each merchant's capital in any one voyage. These groups could hire managerial talent, attempt more speculative ventures because they spread the risk, and consequently maximize profits. Such companies usually enjoyed monopoly rights granted by the English Crown.

Emergence of Urban Values

As trade moved into new channels and utilized new devices such as the joint-stock company, more and more attention began to focus on the metropolis of London. Those who sought preferment in politics, law, or church — the traditional sanctuaries of the younger sons of the gentry and nobility — found their best opportunities in the capital city. So, too, did those seeking economic opportunity or anonymity. London's society was changing rapidly, and standards and mores were frequently ill-maintained. Civil servants, for example, from highest to lowest ranks, received modest salaries and customarily supplemented them with expected gratuities for performing official duties, whether affixing a royal seal or opening a door. Such demands were accounted a normal cost of doing business in official London, and these gratuities gave officeholders a decent livelihood without draining the royal exchequer.

Not only did London grow as the center of official life, but it rapidly became a middle-class city as merchants and artisans flocked to it. These shrewd, enterprising people, selfishly interested in their own profit, lent a new air to the town. Shops filled with exotic goods, docks crammed with ships from far corners of the earth, and the ever-present possibility of great profit at every turn were the contributions of London's middle class to English life.

London's excitement and greatness heightened the contrast between rich and poor far beyond what had ever existed in the countryside. At one end of the spectrum stood prominent government officials, wealthy merchants, and prosperous artisans. At the other end lay the mass of urban poor who found in the city a different and more debilitating poverty than existed in the average village. Perhaps the most striking factor in urban poverty was its anonymity, which contrasted with the tight, highly personalized community structure of rural England. London's poor experienced something new — a feeling of relative deprivation — as they viewed the wealth around them. They formed the London mob, an ever-present factor in English politics.

England's Intellectual Life

London, focus of England's political, social, and commercial alterations, also became the center of its intellectual activity. The city contained most of the country's printing presses, which helped to explain its impact on the world of ideas. While Cambridge and Oxford retained titular leadership in education, they had in reality been supplanted, and great leaders of thought joined the migration to London.

Perhaps one reason for the decline in importance of Oxford and

Seventeenth-century London. The crowded conditions of urban life reflected medieval times when merchants and others kept within city walls for protection. So valuable was urban land that even London Bridge became the location of multistory buildings. (Historical Pictures Service, Chicago)

Cambridge at this time lay in the heavy hand of medievalism and scholasticism that dominated their curricula. Universities were privileged, self-governing corporations or guilds of teachers with students as apprentices. Conservative by nature, universities failed to keep abreast of newer ideas and interests. Most European universities were small, with the largest rarely exceeding a thousand students, and they existed to transmit a fixed body of knowledge, to preserve tradition and order, and to prepare students for careers in law, medicine, or theology.

English universities were associated with the religious orthodoxy of the Church of England. Those who dissented from the religious establishment found themselves excluded from the universities and the grammar schools. In the seventeenth century these dissenters set up their own academies, primarily to educate their own ministry. However, since they did not prepare students for entrance into the universities, dissenting academies were more innovative in curricula matters than the tradition-bound institutions.

Education of the poor seemed to be purposefully neglected in the seventeenth century. Not until 1698 did the Society for Promoting Christian Knowledge begin its charity schools, and even then it met opposition because it created a set of rising expectations on the part of the poor, because it took workers away from day labor and made them unfit for manual tasks. Education of the poor had to await a changed set of values on the part of the ruling classes — the realization that the total available quantity of goods was not finite but could be increased, and with it entrepreneurial profits. Then a citizenry that could read, write, and do numbers, a people with rising expectations, could benefit an expanding industrial society.

Education for the elite remained the rule in sixteenth- and seventeenth-century England, but it brought that country the first fruits of the Renaissance. Such poets as Edmund Spenser, Christopher Marlowe, William Shakespeare, up to and including John Milton, represented the true glory of the English Renaissance. They rediscovered classical literature which had a pragmatic value for Elizabethan society. Thucydides, Tacitus, and Livy not only delighted sixteenth-century readers, but presented them with didactic political lessons which seemed applicable to their own day.

The Purpose and Shape of Adventure

By mid-sixteenth century, England looked out on a New World which offered the prospect of adventure. Englishmen participated vicariously in Spanish and Portuguese explorations by reading translated reports of the voyages. Peter Martyr, the Hakluyts, and others had translated and edited these documents in order to stir their countrymen to break with the traditional order and seize their share of the profits and the glory of adventure.

Europeans conquered strange lands to secure trade, territory, and souls. The Portuguese had circled Africa in search of a route to Cathay's wealth; the Spaniards, stimulated by Portuguese success, stumbled upon the American continents. Exploitative trade was their primary motive, but settlement soon became equally important as land-hungry Europeans gazed upon sparsely populated and attractive territory. A third motive — missionary efforts to convert the natives — coexisted with the other two. With Europe's growing religious diversity, each country shared the obsession to win the indigenous people to the "true faith."

When Europeans faced native populations, especially in America, they triumphed and accomplished their purposes because they had superior fighting techniques, organization, and motivation. In every instance the indigenous peoples far outnumbered their conquerors, but numerical odds gave way to technological superiority in weapons, unity born out of desperation, and belief in a divinely-ordained cause.

Portugal and Spain, first to create overseas empires, set up exploitative colonies in which a handful of Europeans controlled a large indigenous population and shaped it to their wishes. Their small stations, or "fac-

Dutch embassy to the Tokugawa Shogun, 1657. Initial penetration of Japan in the mid-sixteenth century by Spaniards, Portuguese, and English merchants ended by 1640. By 1641 only the Dutch retained a post on an island in Nagasaki Harbor and were subjected to various indignities. In the year of this print, a fire destroyed most of the area depicted here — the Edo or capitol at Tokyo. (Historical Pictures Service, Chicago)

tories," in such tropical areas as Latin America, the Philippines, Guinea Coast, and India were usually all-male establishments. Intermarriage frequently took place between European men and local women, leading to so-called half-caste civilizations.

This set the pattern for initial English settlement in North America. However, Englishmen quickly abandoned that idea in favor of the migration of entire families who sought to recreate their original way of life in the new colony. In North America, almost all English settlement was by family units, which helps explain why Englishmen frowned upon intermarriage with the natives and why the offspring of such unions were often looked upon as outcasts.

As England's population expanded in the seventeenth century, government leaders responded to the threat posed to the traditional order, and to their inability to increase production of basic foodstuffs and to provide work for an increasing number of people, by using overseas empire as an outlet for unwanted people. Stability of numbers so ruled English thought, as it had that of the Greek city-states thousands of years earlier, that it determined public policy. Moreover, overseas empire offered the advantage of solidifying England's control of a valuable trade area.

These, then, were England's motives for creating an empire. Trade, settlement, and conversion of natives provided the rationale for its colonial system in the seventeenth century. Its settlements and claims often overlapped those of other European powers, and this led to conflicts among the imperial rivals. On the North American continent, France occupied the St. Lawrence River valley, an important path into the interior; the Dutch settled the Hudson River valley and collaborated with the natives in exploiting rich fur resources; Spain pushed upwards from Mexico into the Gulf Coast area of the Southeast; and England nestled its settlements along the coastal plain between the Atlantic and the Appalachian range. This set the stage for the drama of America's initial development.

Selected Bibliography

To understand the attitudes and ideas of Europeans at the opening of colonization, several excellent studies should be consulted. Carl Bridenbaugh has imaginatively captured the spirit of England's poorer classes in his *Vexed and Troubled Englishmen* (1968). The upper strata of society is dealt with in Wallace Notestein's *The English People on the Eve of Colonization* (1954). Peter Laslett's *The World We Have Lost*

(1967) and Lawrence Stone's *Crisis of the Aristocracy, 1558-1641* (1965) set the stage of Elizabethan England more fully.

Europe's religious outlook is well described in Harold J. Grimm's *The Reformation Era, 1500-1650* (1954) and E. H. Harbison's *The Age of Reformation* (1955). Roland Bainton's *Here I Stand* (1950) is lucid and definitive on Martin Luther. François Wendel's *Calvin: The Origins and Development of His Religious Thought* (1963) is important and worth consulting. All should be familiar with R. H. Tawney's readable *Religion and the Rise of Capitalism* (1926). William Haller's *Rise of Puritanism* (1938) and Perry Miller's *Errand into the Wilderness* (1956) are both significant for the American extension of religious reformation. Darrett B. Rutman's *American Puritanism* (1970) offers an interesting and important definition of the meaning of the Puritan experience.

Herbert Heaton's *Economic History of Europe* (1936) deals with the economic aspects of European development. More detailed treatments of special topics are found in Laurence B. Packard's *The Commercial Revolution, 1501-1650* (1927) and in John U. Nef's *Industry and Government in France and England, 1540-1640* (1940).

Three standard works which may prove helpful for the period before and during exploration and colonization are G. N. Clark's *The Seventeenth Century* (1950), George M. Trevelyan's *England Under the Stuarts* (1946), and A. L. Rowse's *The England of Elizabeth* (1951).

CHAPTER 2

THE EMPIRES FOUNDED, 1603-1640

Tradition-bound Europeans stood in awe and fear of the New World. Its distance, its immensity, and their total unfamiliarity with even its Atlantic fringes threatened them. Yet, these very qualities also fired their imaginations. Initially an obstacle in the route to Oriental wealth, the New World quickly became an object of desire in its own right. Europeans seeking power and profit either in this life or the afterlife quickly learned that the Americas could offer both. The New World had an abundance of land claimed by no one. It had virgin forests, fur-bearing animals, and mineral wealth; it offered a refuge in which those seeking escape could lose themselves; and its inhabitants were heathens who had never heard the Gospel.

The New World became all things to all men. European nation-states began the parade across the Atlantic to establish their claims. Some created empires under state control, while others relied for leadership on private entrepreneurs. From these endeavours there emerged by mid-seventeenth century a series of New World dependencies which struggled to serve the needs of their European founders. Some colonies satisfied those needs more readily and easily than others, but unless it did so within a reasonable time, a settlement had no viability and would probably be abandoned.

Spain's Crusade for Empire

Spain embarked upon its empire with certain advantages. It took the first step toward nationhood in 1469 with the union of Aragon and Castile through the marriage of Ferdinand and Isabella; the intense crusade which expelled the Moors from Granada in 1492 created a consolidated nation. That crusade molded the Spaniards into a proud and religiously fanatic people who viewed overseas exploration as still another crusade to save souls.

Concurrently with the expulsion of the Moors, Spain's monarchs invested in Christopher Columbus's attempt to find a new route to Japan and China. Instead, he stumbled upon the Caribbean islands. By the early sixteenth century Spaniards had traced the Gulf of Mexico's contours from Yucatan to Florida and had identified the islands of Cuba, Puerto Rico, Jamaica, and Haiti. By 1513 Balboa had marched across the Isthmus of Panama to the Pacific Ocean, thereby proving the correctness of Columbus's basic theory — by going West one could eventually reach the Far East.

Spain's interest in the Orient was deflected by discoveries of the gold and silver of the Aztecs, Incas, and Chibchas. Reports of other bullion sources drew greedy Spaniards deeply into the interior of the American Southwest, Peru, the Amazon, Venezuela, and the Rio de la Plata. Only in Mexico, Peru, and Colombia did they find treasure, but elsewhere they found native laborers to exploit and rich lands to cultivate. From these they created a vast empire in which subjugated natives greatly outnumbered their conquerors.

This posed dilemmas for Spanish authorities — how to convert the heathen, adapt them to Spanish ways, and govern the vast territory. Contradictory approaches developed. Some Spaniards concentrated on plunder and immediate wealth, regardless of the effects upon the natives,

Christopher Columbus (1451-1506), son of a Genoese weaver. His discovery of the Bahamas, Cuba, and Santo Domingo caused great excitement in Europe. (By Ridolpho Ghirlandaio, c. 1525, courtesy of Museo Navale, Genova, Italy)

while others, most notably Franciscan and Dominican friars, took a humanitarian approach. Thus some recklessly destroyed Indian civilizations, while others vainly sought to preserve them.

Spain's colonies formed part of the king's domain and thus fell under his control. Not only did this eliminate the Cortes, or Parliament, from any voice in imperial administration, but it subverted that institution by giving the monarch an independent source of wealth and lessening his dependence on the legislature. Spain's New World empire would leave its clear mark upon the development of the mother country's domestic political institutions as well as its economy.

America's gold, silver, and raw materials supported Spain far beyond even Columbus's fertile imagination. The sudden infusion of wealth distracted Spaniards from the harder, more pedestrian occupations of trade and manufacturing, leaving the country in the unique position of retaining a feudal system that it could afford. Spain's economic development lagged behind that of other European nations which were less fortunate in the race for empire.

France's Hesitant Adventure

Spain's success led to envy and then to imitation, but its rivals did not possess the same advantages. Spanish unity fostered by the Moorish Crusade, its isolation guarded by the Pyrenees, and its luck in tapping those New World areas possessing bullion were unique characteristics that could not be duplicated.

France, for example, had little tranquility because of its central geographical location and its easily crossed borders. Its internal political and religious dissensions frequently became international crises during the upheavals of the Reformation and Counter-Reformation, sapping its energies and distracting it from overseas exploration. Not until 1598, with the issuance of the Edict of Nantes which offered toleration to Calvinists or Huguenots, did France acquire internal tranquility and begin to think seriously of overseas ventures. Earlier, spasmodic efforts had led to investigations by Giovanni de Verrazano and Jacques Cartier of the region from Newfoundland to New York, but these had never been followed up.

Samuel de Champlain began serious French efforts at colonization in 1603 when he arrived at the St. Lawrence River. The establishment of Quebec in 1608 gave France a foothold on the continent and an entrance into the great interior valleys of North America. Champlain soon made contact with the major Indian confederacies, and a French alliance with the Algonquins against the Iroquois set the pattern for French-Indian relations for the next century and a half. Although Champlain explored as far west as Lake Huron, he never achieved his primary goal of finding gold and silver mines.

Instead of bullion, Champlain found furs, but trapping animals and trading for peltry did not lure settlers, and many years elapsed before the struggling St. Lawrence Valley settlements developed and prospered. Meanwhile, the impetus for colonization passed to the Jesuit Order. The history of its missionary effort includes many stories of courage, determination, adventure, and martyrdom, but splashing baptismal water on Indians, young and old, neither populated nor conquered the wilderness.

New France did not develop as a colony until the mid-seventeenth century. Jean Baptiste Colbert, chief minister of Louis XIV, encouraged migration, but more men than women voyaged to the colony. The Crown hampered New France's growth by permitting only French Roman

Champlain aids the Algonquins against the Iroquois. The introduction of firearms made the Indians dependent allies of the Europeans who were the sole supply of lead, gunpowder, weapons, and repairs. Superior tools gave a small group of Europeans, such as Champlain's force, a major technological advantage over tribes still living in the Stone Age. (Champlain, S., Les Voyages..., Rare Book Division, The New York Public Library, Astor, Lenox and Tilden Foundations)

Catholics to enter, thereby eliminating the most likely immigrants — the Huguenots, who added a notable ingredient to the English Empire after the revocation of the Edict of Nantes in 1685.

Having settled along a natural pathway to the interior, the French readily took to exploration. By 1673, Marquette had descended the Mississippi River. Shortly thereafter La Salle took possession of the entire valley in Louis XIV's name; he ambitiously conceived of an empire from the St. Lawrence to the Gulf of Mexico. Part of La Salle's dream materialized with the establishment of New Orleans in 1718, but that outpost and Quebec were never effectively linked. In the 1740s the French ventured to the Black Hills of the Dakotas, and a few years later they reached the Rocky Mountains. In the process they crossed over great gold and silver deposits; ironically, they never knew it. Geography played a cruel trick on the French by making available more opportunities than they could exploit.

Louis XIV, King of France (1643-1715). By 1661, he had established himself as absolute monarch. Louis's aim was to expand French control eastward to include the Spanish Netherlands (modern Belgium), Holland, and the Rhineland principalities. This policy brought into being an alliance against France headed by William of Orange, who later gained the English throne and brought England into that alliance. (Museo Nacional del Prado, Madrid)

The Dutch Search for Profit

If the French failed to take advantage of their New World opportunities, they were not alone. The Dutch embarked on a colonization scheme which never produced the results they anticipated. Having developed a national consciousness, a common language, and a remarkable degree of commercial prosperity, the Dutch by the early seventeenth century had repelled the Inquisition and their Spanish overlords, founded their Calvinistic faith, and conquered the sea. Dutch independence, won by 1612, was finally grudgingly conceded by Spain in 1648.

Spain gave The Netherlands its incentive for overseas ventures by closing the port of Lisbon in the late sixteenth century, thereby cutting Dutch merchants out of an extensive trade in oriental goods between Portugal and the Baltic ports. These merchants then sought their own route to the Orient, and in 1609 the Dutch East India Company hired the intrepid Englishman Henry Hudson. Although employed to find a route across the north of Europe, Hudson chose instead to go West, where he found the river that bears his name. Other Dutch explorers, bypassing Hudson's discovery, followed Portuguese fleets to the East, some going around the Cape of Good Hope and others through the Straits of Magellan. The Dutch East India Company monopolized Dutch trade in the Indian and Pacific oceans, thereby founding a new empire.

Enticed by Far Eastern wealth, most Dutchmen ignored North America's potential until Spain threatened a new war in 1621. The Dutch West India Company, formed at the expiration of the twelve-year truce between The Netherlands and Spain, was to provide bases for the harassment of Spanish treasure fleets, secure the New World's fur trade, and convert the heathen Indians before the zealous Jesuits got to them.

Even then, Dutch interests centered on Brazil, where they hoped to corner the profitable slave trade and to cultivate sugar. Within a few years, they controlled the coastal area from the Amazon to Recife, as well as the islands of St. Eustatius and Curaçao. A Portuguese offensive, however, easily ousted the Dutch, who next moved to the Cape of Good Hope and established themselves athwart the major route to the Orient. Capetown became an important base for Dutch fleets going to and from the East Indies.

Dutch efforts on the Hudson River, which began in 1626, were far less impressive. The famous purchase of Manhattan Island established the colony in an ideal location for defense, but it matured slowly. The fur trade became the major occupation, and the Dutch used the Indians to gather furs for exchange at their trading posts. The Iroquois, who by the mid-seventeenth century became middlemen for the Dutch and later the English, expanded into the Ohio Valley in their search for furs, thereby coming into conflict with the Algonquin tribes and their French allies.

Control of New Netherland, as the Dutch called their Hudson River colony, rested in the Dutch West India Company, a group of wealthy merchants of The Netherlands, and the directors-general or governors it sent to the settlement. The colony suffered from the indecisiveness of the Company, for its leaders could not decide how to use New Netherland most profitably. The fur trade suggested that it become an outpost; the granting of large tracts of land as patroonships or manors indicated a desire to create a permanent settlement.

This indecisiveness was reflected in the population pattern. New Netherland had the most polyglot population of all New World colonies, for Dutchmen seemed reluctant to leave their prosperous and tolerant homeland, and the Dutch West India Company welcomed all newcomers as its employees. Walloons (or French-speaking Belgians), Swedes, Englishmen, Frenchmen, and Dutchmen comprised the colony's settlers, and from very early times Negroes provided a labor force. Dutch interest in the slave trade led to a steady flow of black laborers from Angola and Brazil into New Netherland. Since the Dutch occupied themselves with trade rather than commercial agriculture and had a reputation for an easygoing pattern of life, most black slaves worked on Hudson Valley farms or received training as craftsmen and were probably treated humanely.

New Netherland was a holding operation, and tenuous Dutch control, when challenged, crumbled easily. The Dutch possessed a major route to the interior through the Hudson and Mohawk valleys. By mid-seventeenth century English settlements to the Northeast and French intrusions from the North pressed the Dutch. The more aggressive English realized the location's importance and by 1664, under the Duke of York's guidance, seized the Dutch colony, thereby closing a gap in England's control of the North American coast.

England's Brave Experiment

In 1606, James I chartered two new companies — the Virginia Company of London and the Virginia Company of Plymouth — thereby marking England's first serious contention for empire. Earlier efforts had been tentative gestures, beginning with John Cabot's voyage five years after Columbus's initial crossing of the Atlantic. Financed by a group of Bristol merchants, Cabot sailed under a patent from Henry VII, sighted America, and returned to England to receive a royal welcome and a gift of £10. Cabot and his son Sebastian made other voyages to seek the elusive Orient, but these efforts ended in 1509 when Henry VIII, who did not share his father's interest, however frugal, in exploration, succeeded to the throne.

During Henry VIII's reign, private individuals carried on England's overseas exploration. An expedition organized in 1553 to find a passage to China around Europe's northern coast led to the chartering of a new

THE EMPIRES FOUNDED 33

Elizabeth I, Queen of England (1558-1603). She created the compromise Church of England and developed a foreign policy which proved effective in dealing with Spain, with an Irish rebellion, and with the Scots under Mary Stuart. She consolidated the English as a nation and began its outward expansion. (By M. Gheeaerts the Younger, National Portrait Gallery, London)

trading group, the Muscovy Company, which was soon followed by the establishment of the Eastland Company, the Levant Company, and finally the East India Company (1600). These adventurous merchants met with success, some more than others, and established a pattern of private corporate initiative for the creation of England's overseas empire.

These private ventures during Elizabeth's reign added to England's increasing rivalry with Spain over a variety of other issues. The two nations were ostensibly at peace, but rivalry led to antagonism and finally to undeclared war. Spain's far-flung empire, with its great wealth, tempted assault, but Elizabeth could not risk open warfare. She relied instead on unauthorized attacks on Spanish treasure fleets by buccaneers such as Sir Francis Drake.

By the late 1580s, Philip II of Spain had determined to end English interference with the flow of American bullion to his coffers. The Spanish navy assembled in 1588 for a massive invasion of England. The Armada sailed, was attacked in the English Channel, and was driven into the North Sea where half the ships foundered on the coasts of Scotland and Ireland. Philip's invasion attempt had failed. By 1604 England and Spain concluded their war, and the English could now direct their energies toward the New World in a more constructive fashion.

Virginia: Foothold of Empire

As early as 1555 Englishmen read Peter Martyr's translated *De Orbe Novo*, an account of Spain's successful endeavors in the New World. It stirred the imaginations of adventurers such as Sir Humphrey Gilbert and his half-brother Sir Walter Raleigh. Gilbert took the leadership in English efforts to duplicate Spain's triumphs and profits, and he projected a voyage to find a northern route around America which would lead to China. Soon, he became enamored of the idea of creating a colony in the New World. In 1578 Elizabeth granted him a charter to create a settlement, giving him almost absolute power over the lands he claimed.

Gilbert's interest in colonization had been whetted by Richard Hakluyt the elder, who set forth a program for the development of the New World which guided Englishmen throughout the seventeenth century. The elder Hakluyt's cousin, also named Richard, carried on the same theme through an extensive propaganda campaign, making documentary evidence on America available to his compatriots and further stirring their interest in settlement.

In 1578 Gilbert and Raleigh left England with a fleet of ships and several hundred men to begin the first effort at serious colonization, but storms forced them back. Five years later, once new funds had been secured, Gilbert sailed again, and this time he reached Newfoundland, which he claimed in the name of Elizabeth. Again, storms destroyed the venture, and this time Gilbert lost his life.

His dream was picked up by Sir Walter Raleigh and a group of land-hungry English gentry whose imaginations converted the New World's virgin wilderness into tranquil English farms and meadows. In 1584 Raleigh received a charter from Elizabeth and sent out a reconnoitering group that finally came to Albemarle Sound and the island of Roanoke. He named his territory for the Virgin Queen, presented her with a statement of strong arguments in favor of colonization as compiled by Richard

Sir Walter Raleigh (1552-1618), explorer and colonizer who first named the area of Virginia. Raleigh created the ill-fated Roanoke settlement. His involvement in domestic political intrigues under the early Stuarts and his anti-Spanish attitude led to his execution after he attacked Spanish towns on the Orinoco River. (National Gallery of Ireland)

Hakluyt the younger, and hoped for financial aid from the Crown. Elizabeth's interest lay elsewhere, particularly in the pending war with Spain, and thus she offered no other aid than royal sanction. Private sources would have to finance any settlement, not the Crown.

Raleigh raised sufficient private funds for his expedition and set sail in 1585. Following Hakluyt's advice, he sent along a variety of "experts" on minerology and agriculture, as well as craftsmen, an artist (John White), and a mathematician-historian (Thomas Hariot). Richard Grenville headed the expedition, which landed its party at Roanoke in June. The settlers arrived too late to plant, found hostile natives, and suffered from severe winter storms. By the following summer, the men were ready to return home.

From this exploratory voyage, Raleigh and his supporters gained much knowledge of the territory. Thomas Hariot published his *Brief and True Report*, which he illustrated with John White's paintings. This propaganda enticed more than one hundred settlers to join the next voyage to Virginia.

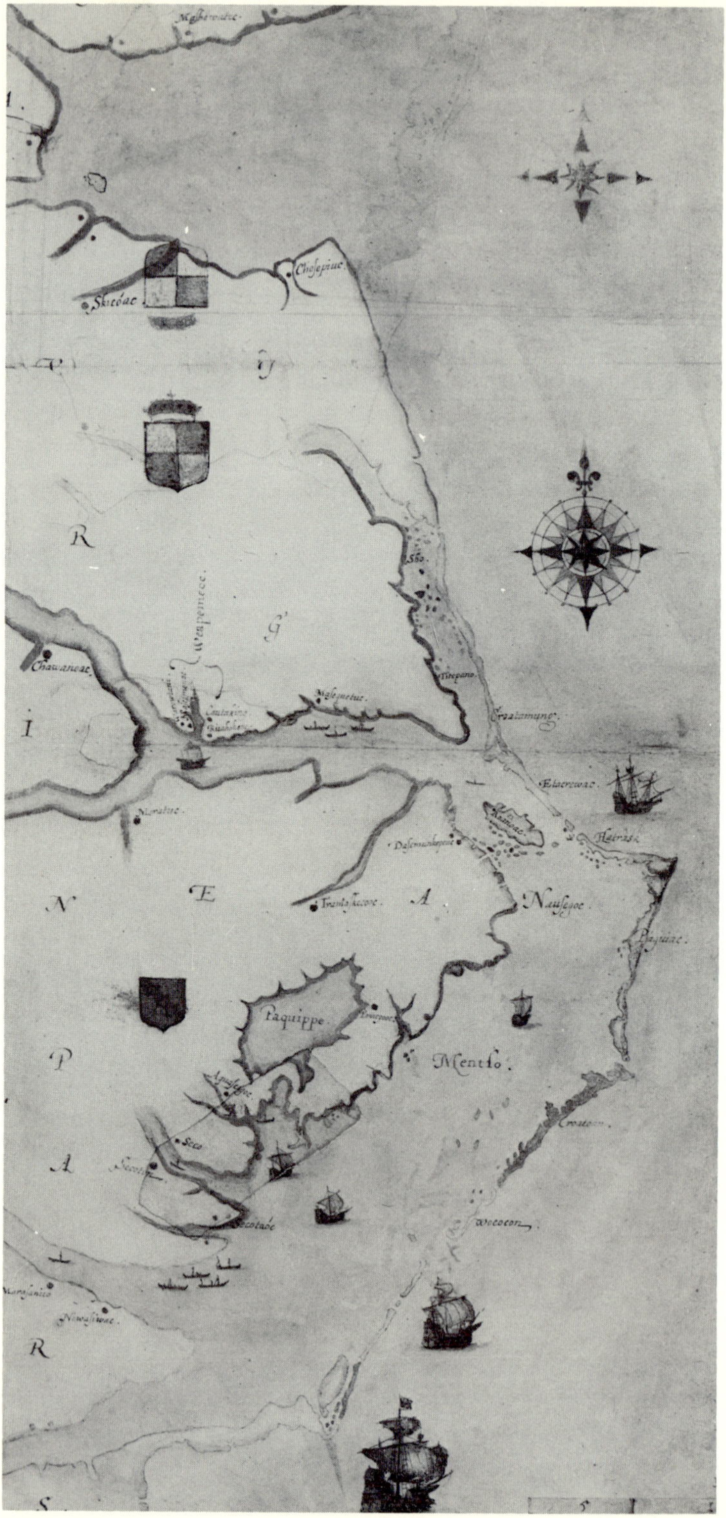
Chesepiuc
Skicoac
Chawaneac
Weapemeoc
Moratuc
Dasemunkepeuc
Roanoac
Hatrask
Nausegoc
Paquiac
Trantaskecoc
Paquippe
Mentso
Secota
Croatoan
Wococon
Newasiwac

White was appointed governor, and the party landed in July 1587 at Roanoke, although they had been ordered to go to Chesapeake Bay. White returned to England for additional supplies, leaving his daughter and granddaughter, Virginia Dare, the first English child born in America, and the other settlers behind. England, preoccupied with the Armada, found little time for Roanoke, and not until 1591 could White return to the colony. When he did, he found the settlement in ruins, presumably destroyed by the Indians.

Once England had settled its differences with Spain, it could direct its energies, talent, and wealth into the settlement of America. Overseas expansion had captured the imagination of England's merchant community, and it took up the cause where Raleigh and Gilbert had left it. The chartering of the two great Virginia companies in 1606 marked this renewal of effort and presaged the beginning of England's first permanent colony in North America.

By chartering the Virginia companies, the English Crown gave away little of immediate value. It had only tenuous claims to the land involved: the area between the Cape Fear River and present-day Bangor, Maine. The London Company would occupy the southern section, while the Plymouth Company would have the more northerly section, with a hundred-mile buffer zone between their settlements. The Crown promised to protect the companies from the intrusion of any other Englishmen.

Under the charters granted to the companies, they would each appoint a resident council to govern their settlements, while the King would set up a royal council in England to supervise them. Prospective colonists were guaranteed the "liberties, franchises and immunities" of Englishmen, a vague provision which would later be elaborated upon and made meaningful. The companies held title to these new lands, part of the king's domain, in the same way that a feudal lord held his lands from the Crown. Although the charters mentioned religion and proselytizing Indians as motives for colonization, the true purposes were to find bullion, a passage to the South Seas, products necessary and desirable for the English economy, and profits for the companies' stockholders.

(Opposite page) John White's map of the Chesapeake Coast. White, an English painter, led the fourth expedition to Roanoke Island, and his grandchild Virginia Dare was the first English child born in the present United States. White's paintings of Indian life became the standard depictions of the aborigines. (British Museum, London)

The Virginia Company of London, most active of the two corporations, sent out three vessels with 144 settlers in December 1606 under Captain Christopher Newport's command. They entered Chesapeake Bay in April 1607, found the James River, and decided upon Jamestown peninsula for their settlement because it could be easily defended. The 105 survivors who landed at Jamestown came to the New World weighted down with preconceptions based upon English society and Spanish triumphs. They sought gold, plunder, and easy wealth; none envisioned the hard work necessary to establish a prosperous colony, none were willing to abandon their customs, privileges, and specializations in order to do the work at hand. By January 1608, as a consequence of bickering, exhaustion of supplies, and ineffective leadership, the colonists decided to abandon Jamestown and return to England. Only the arrival of a supply ship from the mother country on January 4 prevented that calamity.

Virginia obviously needed a strong hand, and Captain John Smith provided it. As Council President from fall 1608 to summer 1609, he forced recalcitrant settlers to work. By this time, too, the company in London understood the need to get "wife, children and servants to take fast hold and root in that land" and make the colony a success. They had to replace gentlemen and drones, goldhunters and troublemakers, by those who intended to make Virginia their permanent home and to duplicate English society there. The Company's leaders, after their initial experience, were also convinced of the mistake of limiting membership in the company itself. Virginia required a constant infusion of funds, which meant more stockholders. A second charter, issued in May 1609, permitted the Company to sell stock to all potential purchasers at £12. 10s. 0d. per share. This open joint-stock company would be controlled by a treasurer, or chief administrative officer, and a general court elected by shareholders. Thus the Company broadened both its membership base and financial support, while a small group retained control.

The 1609 charter also changed the governmental structure in Virginia. Power was centralized in a Lord Governor and Captain General, rather than the council, which had spent most of its time bickering. In June 1609 a flotilla of nine vessels with 800 settlers departed from England under command of Sir Thomas Gates. The first of the fleet arrived during the "starving time" in Virginia, and the unfortunate choice of Jamestown as their destination became evident as malaria and dysentery took their toll of the weakened colonists. The first seven vessels with 400 settlers found no provision had been made for them. By May 1610, Gates's own ship finally arrived, bringing another 175 people and no supplies. Enough food for only sixteen days remained and the colonists abandoned hope and the settlement, sailing downriver for England. En route, they encountered a relief fleet under Lord de la Warr and returned to reestablish Virginia.

This incident taught the Company several more lessons. Gates had been shipwrecked on the Bermuda Islands. The Company now saw an opportunity to develop sugar cultivation on those islands if it could gain control of them; this might give it a ready cash crop to sustain its efforts on the mainland. More immediately, however, the Company now appreciated its own inability to provide the continuing infusion of funds and settlers because its stock would not sell without a prospect of immediate profits. A new charter, the third, issued in 1612, applied these lessons. It included the Bermudas within the Company's territory, converted the general court from a representative body into the entire stockholder group (thus making the stock more saleable), and authorized lotteries to raise funds for the colony. Lotteries became "the real and substantial food by which Virginia hath been nourished."

Virginia's inhabitants represented a cross section of English society, motivated not by basic dissatisfactions with conditions at home, but by possibilities of quick wealth. They brought with them the restrictive attitudes of their villages toward labor, and they seemed unable to grasp the fundamental transformation of ideas demanded by the New World. Indeed, frequent complaints about the early settlers suggest that gentry and sons of gentry rather than hard-working laborers had arrived in Virginia. Also included in the first migrations were troublesome elements — the criminal, the destitute, the poverty-stricken — whom the miracle of Virginia would hopefully redeem. This explains some of the colony's difficulties and the need for Captain John Smith's use of simple and direct force.

Finding a basic crop for the English market proved even more difficult than dealing with settlers unwilling to work at the tasks at hand. While hunting gold and silver, settlers thought of cultivating cotton, oranges, and melons as suggested by the Company. Gold-fever, instead of dissipating quickly, increased in intensity and compounded Virginia's problems. And agriculture conducted on a communal basis in the traditional English pattern, with individuals working Company lands and drawing supplies from Company stores, offered minimal incentives in the New World as

INDIAN TRIBES IN COLONIAL AMERICA 1600–1700

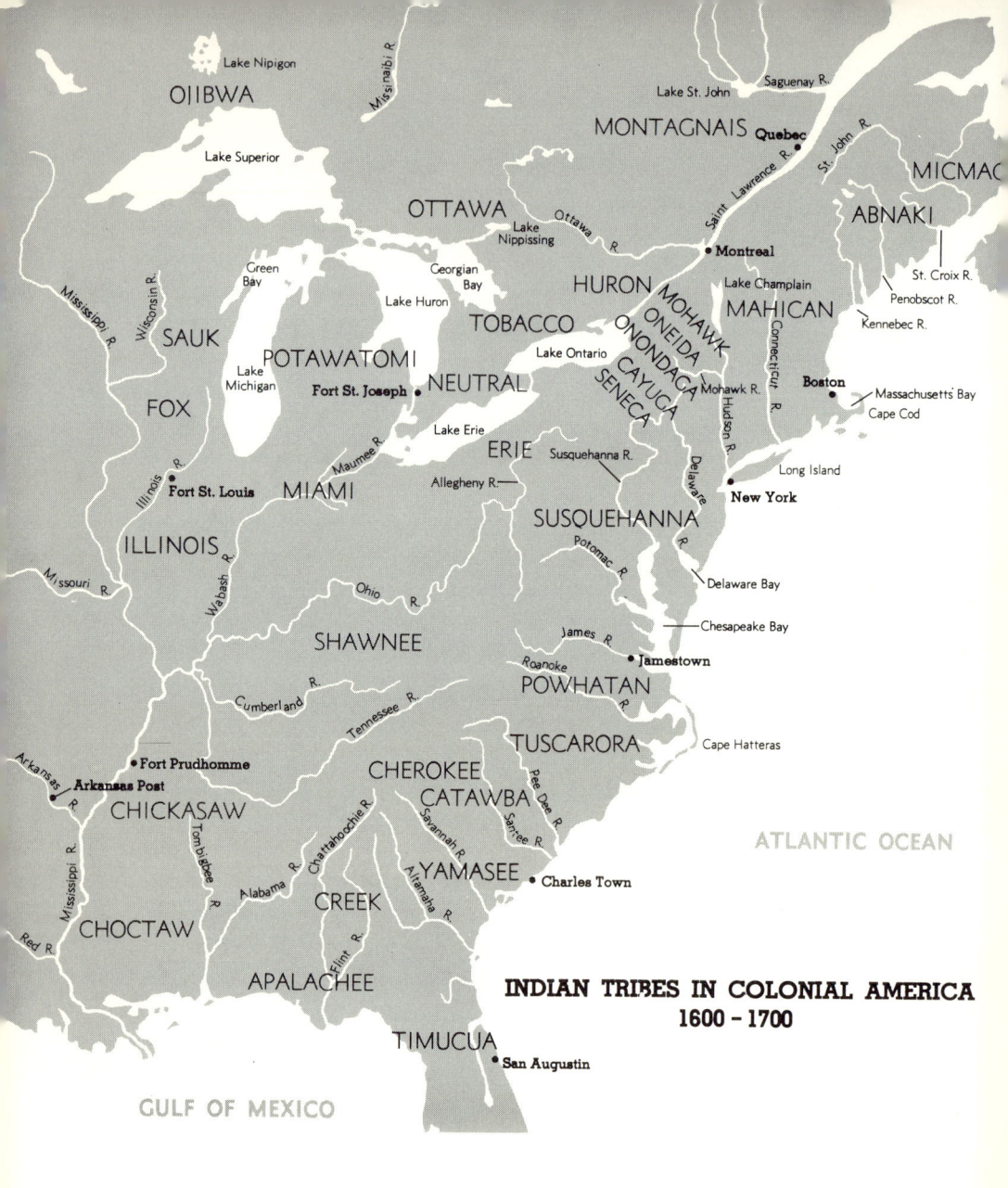

it did in the Old. Sir Thomas Dale changed this by allocating three acres to each settler for his own farm. In 1618 each subscriber to company stock (and each settler was accounted a subscriber) received a headright of fifty acres per share.

Before the granting of headrights, John Rolfe in 1612 experimented with an Indian crop—tobacco—and hit upon Virginia's staple commodity.

Within two years he produced enough to make his first shipment to London. Englishmen had long been addicted to tobacco-smoking, a habit picked up from Spaniards but one which created a serious economic problem. The drain of bullion from England to Spain caused James I to issue a pamphlet denouncing tobacco as the source of all evils. Now, with Virginia supplying the weed and the Crown deriving a revenue from each pound imported into England, James played down his moral aversion and emphasized instead his potential tax revenue. Virginia had found its place within England's mercantilistic empire.

Discovery of a cash crop did not resolve all of Virginia's troubles. Englishmen hesitated to venture overseas, and the Company desperately needed colonists. To encourage private groups to come to Virginia, the Company agreed to give them lands and power over their own settlements. (One such agreement was made in 1619 with the Separatists residing in Leyden, The Netherlands.) Despite these efforts, the colony's population dwindled. By 1621 there were a little more than 800 settlers, although over a thousand had entered Virginia in the two previous years. Adjusting to the climate and fighting the diseases endemic in Jamestown took a heavy toll of newcomers weakened by lengthy ocean voyages. Virginia gained an ugly reputation from its high death rate. Convicts reportedly chose the quick death of execution rather than the lingering death of banishment to the colony.

The Virginia Company of London was in desperate straits by the early 1620s. A reform faction under Sir Edwin Sandys had taken control and proposed a bold and vigorous expansion program for the colony. The Company was deeply in debt, its exemption from customs duties ended in 1619, and tobacco as a cash crop was endangered by threats of heavy taxation. Sandys proposed to diversify the colony's output, and the Company sent experts in iron manufacturing, logging, glassblowing, and saltmaking. They worked on an experimental estate designed to test new products and to encourage their development by the settlers. Others experimented with silkworms, sugar cane, cotton, and tropical fruits.

As Sandys's diversification program got underway, the King banned lotteries in 1621 because they stimulated a gambling fever in London, thereby depriving the Company of an important source of funds for the experimental program. Moreover, in the following year an Indian attack wiped out 400 seasoned settlers and forced the remainder to barricade themselves behind stockades; 500 more died that year. Plans for a rapid

THE SUCCESSFUL PLANTATION, 1625

PLANTING OF COUNTRIES is like planting of woods; for you must make account to lose almost twenty years' profit, and expect your recompense in the end: for the principal thing that hath been the destruction of most plantations hath been the base and hasty drawing of profit in the first years. It is true, speedy profit is not to be neglected as far as may stand with the good of the plantation, but no further. It is a shameful and unblessed thing to take the scum of people and wicked condemned men to be the people with whom you plant; and not only so, but it spoileth the plantation; for they will ever live like rogues, and not fall to work, but be lazy, and do mischief, and spend victuals, and be quickly weary, and then certify over to their country to the discredit of the plantation. The people wherewith you plant ought to be gardeners, ploughmen, labourers, smiths, carpenters, joiners, fishermen, fowlers, with some few apothecaries, surgeons, cooks, and bakers. (From S. H. Reynolds, ed., The Essays . . . of Francis Bacon [Oxford: Clarendon Press, 1890], pp. 237-38)

☆☆☆☆☆☆☆☆☆☆☆☆☆☆☆☆☆☆☆☆☆☆☆☆☆☆☆☆☆

expansion of Virginia and a diversification of its economy collapsed. The Company was bankrupt, and the Crown issued a writ of *quo warranto* (i.e., by what right) alleging violations of the Charter of 1612, and the court ordered the charter forfeited in May 1624. Virginia became a Crown possession, and the Virginia Company shareholders lost all chances to regain their investments.

Although the London Company had failed, it left behind a colony and lessons for future colonizers. After the Virginia failure, Englishmen better understood the investment necessary in a New World colony before any returns could be expected. The East India Company pattern — extracting exorbitant profits from a well-populated country with an advanced civilization — would not work in America. The experience in Virginia also taught something about planning, organizing, and timing. Success depended upon proper equipment and supplies, authoritarian control in the early years, and establishing a colony in the right season to permit clearing ground and planting foodstuffs so that it became partially self-sufficient. Perhaps the most traumatic lesson, however, was the need to change the value standards common to all Europe. The amount of work to be done was infinite, not finite; the potential productivity of labor and capital was limitless, not limited. This overturn of established thought patterns was necessary because the assumptions on which they were based no longer held true. Land, scarce and precious in the Old World, existed in abundance in the New; population, surplus in Europe, was America's scarcest commodity. Hoarding land in the colonies made little sense when it could attract potential settlers for whom there were an abundance of productive tasks.

Virginia prospered despite the Company's failure. One institution introduced by the Company before its collapse was a representative assembly — the House of Burgesses. Started as an experiment to answer criticisms in London and Virginia about the harsh and authoritarian government in the colony, the Burgesses were patterned after the Company's General Court in London, except that each geographical area was allotted representatives on the basis of its population. Its first meeting in Jamestown in 1619 led to the adoption of various laws, petitions to the Company, and a tax of one pound of tobacco per adult male to pay its expenses.

In 1623, with the Company's collapse anticipated, the Burgesses sought to save what they could for themselves. They petitioned the Privy Council to restrain future governors by insisting upon retention of a legislature. Then the House declared that no taxes could be raised without its consent. While royal governors ruled the colony between 1623 and 1639 the House of Burgesses met periodically, but no royal authorization existed for such meetings until 1639. The repercussions of this self-government, perhaps the Virginia Company of London's most significant legacy, would be felt for centuries.

Maryland: Feudalism Revisited

To the north another colony developed which mirrored Virginia in some ways, but not in others. Maryland began as a feudal proprietary owned exclusively by the Calverts, the Lords Baltimore, rather than as an offspring of a corporation. Beginning in 1632, a quarter century after Virginia, the colony profited from many of its neighbor's mistakes. Settlers' motives, population composition, and religious patterns also differed. Both Virginia and Maryland, however, depended solely upon tobacco as an export crop, and this imposed a general pattern of life common to both.

Sir George Calvert, who had earlier attempted unsuccessfully to colonize

BISHOP OF DURHAM CLAUSE

IV. ALSO WE DO GRANT and likewise Confirm unto the said Baron of Baltimore, his Heirs, and Assigns . . . with all, and singular such, and as ample Rights, Jurisdictions, Privileges, Prerogatives, Royalties, Liberties, Immunities, and royal Rights, and temporal Franchises whatsoever, as well by Sea as by Land, within the Region, Islands, Islets, and Limits aforesaid, to be had, exercised, used, and enjoyed, as any Bishop of Durham, within the Bishoprick or County Palatine of Durham, in our Kingdom of England, ever heretofore hath had, held, used, or enjoyed, or of right could, or ought to have, hold, use, or enjoy. (From Charter of Charles I to George Calvert, June 20, 1632, in Francis N. Thorpe, ed., The Federal and State Constitutions . . ., 7 vols. [Government Printing Office, Washington, D.C.], III, 1669-86)

☆☆☆☆☆☆☆☆☆☆☆☆☆☆☆☆☆☆☆☆☆☆☆☆☆☆☆☆

Newfoundland, had important family connections and was involved in the Council for New England, successor to the Virginia Company of Plymouth. His connections proved more important than his Catholicism, ordinarily a handicap in Protestant England, and won him Charles I's support for establishment of a Chesapeake Bay colony as a Catholic refuge. He applied for a charter in February 1632 and, though he died before its issuance, his son Cecilius received the grant from the Crown.

The Maryland Charter of 1632 gave the proprietor absolute power, employing the "Bishop of Durham" clause. Like the County Palatine or Bishopric of Durham, Maryland was a frontier outpost, and in consideration of the ruling lord's obligation to protect the kingdom, the Crown granted him as much authority within his territory as the king had outside it. All legal writs ran in the proprietor's name, appeals could be made only to him, and settlers held their lands from him and owed him fealty. Finally, the charter stipulated that all interpretations would favor proprietary authority.

Maryland, a proposed Catholic refuge, began with strong religious influence. The Jesuit order sponsored the first sailing, handled publicity, and opened a London office to register prospective migrants. Although all colonists took an oath denying papal authority, two Catholic priests were aboard the *Ark* and the *Dove* when they sailed in 1634. Seventeen gentlemen and nearly two hundred laborers and servants, the majority of whom were Protestants, made up the first migration.

Cecilius Calvert, Lord Baltimore, compromised the colony's religious purpose in order to secure settlers. Few Catholics in England were under any pressure to leave. Well-to-do members of that faith saw no reason to migrate, and they in turn provided protection for their friends, relatives, and servants. Calvert therefore accepted good workers regardless of religious affiliation because his only asset as proprietor was land, and that was worthless unless peopled. However, he took every precaution to avoid religious controversy in Maryland, for in the seventeenth century such disputes readily led to bloodshed, as England soon learned when the Civil War erupted in 1642.

Maryland's economy rapidly became a carbon copy of its southern neighbor's, with tobacco as the cash crop. Baltimore also sought to duplicate the ideals of English society by reestablishing the manorial system in the colony, and to this end he granted lands in large tracts to friends and relatives, while yeomen farmers secured smaller grants of from a hundred to a thousand acres. All landholders paid a quitrent (fixed rent fee) to the proprietor, which gave him an immediate but small income. As settlement progressed, the proprietor's real profit would come from the increased value of lands he retained.

Southern Society

The social structures of Maryland and Virginia, despite Baltimore's efforts to impose feudalism on his colony, resembled one another. Both had an exclusively agrarian base and both contained a dominant small planter class. (The legendary great planters developed in the eighteenth century once society became more stratified.) A native aristocracy emerged, based upon talent rather than birth, which imitated the English country gentry as best it could, took seriously its responsibilities, and worked hard at its tasks. The rude wilderness provided little opportunity for formal education, but planters acquired rudimentary libraries and employed tutors, since this natural aristocracy understood the need to prepare its sons for leadership.

More important numerically in early seventeenth-century Virginia and Maryland than these natural aristocrats were the yeoman farmers, whose economic and political strength reached a peak by mid-century. Their

AN INDENTURED SERVANT'S COMPLAINT, 1620's

I HAVE NOTHING to Comfort me, nor ther is nothing to be gotten here but sicknes, and death, except that one had money to lay out in some thinges for profit; But I have nothing at all, no not a shirt to my backe, but two Ragges nor no Clothes, but one poore suite, nor but one paire of shooes, but one paire of stockins, but one Capp, but two bands, my Cloke is stollen by one of my owne fellowes, and to his dying hower would not tell mee what he did with it but some of my fellows saw him have butter and beife out of a ship, which my Cloke I doubt paid for, so that I have not a penny, nor a penny Worth to helpe me to either spice, or sugar, or strong Waters, without the which one cannot lyve here, for as strong beare in England doth fatten and strengthen them so water here doth wash and weaken theis here, onelie keepe life and soule togeather. but I am not halfe a quarter so strong as I was in England, and all is for want of victualls, for I doe protest unto you, that I have eaten more in day at home than I have allowed me here for a

☆☆☆☆☆☆☆☆☆☆☆☆☆☆☆☆☆☆☆☆☆☆☆☆☆☆

position declined because of a sharp drop in tobacco prices after England's adoption of the Navigation Acts in 1660-63 and its enumeration of tobacco as a commodity which could only be shipped in vessels English owned and manned to England, Ireland, Wales, or Berwick-on-Tweed. The Navigation Acts eliminated Dutch competition, beneficial to the colonists, for Chesapeake tobacco, and enumeration glutted the London tobacco market and depressed prices for Virginians and Marylanders. This, combined with increasing competition from large-scale planters employing Negroes, suggested the end of yeoman farmer dominance in the near future.

The first black servants entered Virginia in 1619, a year before the Pilgrims set foot on Plymouth Rock. These involuntary migrants, first brought by Dutch trading ships, initially received the same treatment as white indentured servants. They were bound to labor for from five to seven years to pay for their transportation, and colonists in need of workers then bought their contracts. Upon expiration of the indentures, the blacks probably received their freedom just as did white laborers. For the next forty years blacks and whites alike became indentured servants for a specific number of years, and free blacks appeared in the Virginia records

Weeke.... Goodman Jackson pityed me ... and he much marvailed that you would send me a servaunt to the Companie, he saith I had beene better knocked on the head, and Indeede so I fynd it now to my greate greife and miserie, and saith, that if you love me you will redeeme me suddenlie, for wch I doe Intreate and begg....
O that you did see may daylie and hourelie sighes, grones, and teares, and thumpes that I afford mine owne brest, and rue and Curse the time of my birth with holy Job. I thought no head had beene able to hold so much water as hath and doth dailie flow from mine eyes, But this is Certaine I never felt the want of ffather and mother till now, but now dear ffrends full well I knowe and rue it although it were too late before I knew it.... (From: S. M. Kingsbury, ed., The Records of the Virginia Company of London, *4 vols. [Washington, D.C.: Government Printing Office, 1906-35]. IV, 59-62)*

☆☆☆☆☆☆☆☆☆☆☆☆☆☆☆☆☆☆☆☆☆☆☆☆☆☆☆☆

as landholders and artisans. Not until 1661 did a legal distinction between white and black servants develop in Virginia statutes. The House of Burgesses then referred to "servants indentured for life" and prescribed for them different penalties for misdeeds because they could not satisfy their masters by adding time to their indentures. In 1662 another Virginia law determined that the child acquired its status from its mother, thus eliminating questions of paternity in cases of children born of black women. Finally, in 1670, Virginia clearly established slavery by a law that "all servants not Christians imported into this colony by shipping [i.e., Negroes] shall be slaves for their lives; but what shall come by land [i.e., Indians] shall serve until thirty years of age." Maryland had done the same seven years before.

Slavery thus emerged in response to constant and pressing demands for more docile manpower, for laborers who did not have the poor work habits of Englishmen. As farms increased in size and the cash-crop of tobacco dominated the economy, the price of tobacco gradually declined, putting an emphasis upon maximum productivity from laborers unconcerned with rights and privileges. Preconceived prejudices of Englishmen concerning the black man's status formed the foundation of slavery. In the colonies, with the need for a large, steady labor force, black slavery offered a peculiar advantage over enslavement of either Indians or whites: blacks, uprooted from their African homeland and cast into an alien society, had no place to which they could run and their color readily identified them; Indian slaves could melt into the hospitable forest and rejoin their tribes, and whites could blend into neighboring English communities. Black slavery's main advantage for the colonists lay in the relatively permanent labor force it provided and in the greater tractability of the blacks, together with the fact that slaves reproduced themselves. By the time of the English Civil War, Virginia had some three hundred blacks, including freemen. After the Restoration, increased English participation in the slave trade and increased emphasis on tobacco culture led to greater importations of blacks. By 1700, more than a thousand were entering Virginia each year.

Chesapeake Bay geography aided in imposing a new labor system; it also precluded development of trading centers and thus of commercial classes. With about 150 navigable rivers and streams running deep into the interior, planters followed waterways as they expanded tobacco culture. For several generations, easy water transportation was readily available, and vessels arriving from England could visit most plantations by moving up the James, York, Rappahannock, and other rivers. No need existed for a central depot for tobacco storage or distribution of European manufactures, and each planter served as his own agent, dealing directly with ship captains.

Economics and geography thus combined to create in the Chesapeake Bay area a widely dispersed population with no merchant class (though many planters doubled as merchants), no urban centers, and no manufacturing concentrations. Jamestown, capital of Virginia, remained a little hamlet that came to life only during court days, for it served no significant economic function. The urban center for Virginia and Maryland was London, some three thousand miles away, and settlers in the Chesapeake region frequently had closer contact with London than they did with other nearby colonies.

Escape to Plymouth

The Reformation in England, made possible by Henry VIII's break with Rome, had led eventually to the fragile compromise of the Elizabethan

PERSECUTION OF PURITANS, 1591

THERE IS MUCH DISCONTENT at this time amongst those that favour the Puritan principles: for the labouring and striving to bring in a uniformity cause, and seems likely to cause, nothing but desolation. The best and faithfullest preachers, say they, are cast into prison, sometimes being closely shut up from the speech and company of their dearest friends, degraded and deprived of their livings, some even having six or seven children, who are sent begging, for all the pillars of the church would do for them. Mr. Cartwright has lain in the Fleet since September; Mr. Fenne of Coventry with many more is in the Clink; Udall, a profitable preacher of Kingston-on-Thames, lies sentenced to be hanged for a book called Demonstrations of Discipline; *and having been condemned before as its author, they now try to make him acknowledge it as his doing. His life is spared hitherto by the intercession of Sir Walter Ralegh. All these things seems but a way to bring in popery, for atheism is here already, and soon will overflow the land. It is rumoured that a general demand is proposed not only of the ministry but of all who bear public office throughout the land to subscribe that the authority of the bishops is lawful by God's Word. When the Lord Treasurer was asked to subscribe to it, he answered, "It is lawfully the positive law; but to say it is lawful by the Word of God, that is another matter." There the matter stayed for the time. (G. B. Harrison, ed.,* An Elizabethan Journal *[New York: Cosmopolitan Book Corporation, 1929], pp. 14-15)*

☆☆☆☆☆☆☆☆☆☆☆☆☆☆☆☆☆☆☆☆☆☆☆☆☆☆☆

Church of England. This brought together Catholic country dwellers, Protestant townspeople, and powerful Protestant leaders who dominated the House of Commons. The Church's official status found definition in the Act of Supremacy, the Book of Common Prayer, and finally the Thirty-Nine Articles adopted in 1563. Its doctrinal base became Protestant, but its organization and ritual remained Catholic except for the position of the papacy. The Crown, through the Archbishop of Canterbury, headed the Church of England.

However, by the early seventeenth century the compromise of the Elizabethan Church disintegrated. Some argued that Calvinist thought had too much influence; others insisted that medieval Catholicism still played too dominant a role. Among the latter critics, one group concluded that the

Church could not reform itself and must therefore be abandoned lest its adherents imperil their souls. These Separatists, later known as the Pilgrims of Plymouth Colony, objected to both the church's hierarchy and to its inclusion of those who had not experienced saving grace. Their insistence upon the congregation's purity carried Protestant reformism to an extreme; they insisted that early Christianity's true faith could be retrieved only by an entirely new establishment composed exclusively of Saints.

English Protestant reformers shared not only a basic dissatisfaction with the Church of England but also a belief in the importance of the conversion experience. This marked off the individual elected by God for salvation. It began with the person's rapt attention to God's Word, moved to his intellectual awareness of sin, continued with his sense of repentance based upon his fear of sin's consequences, entered a higher plane with his faith and his desire to believe, plunged into his doubt and despair of ever receiving salvation, received reinforcement from his sense of God's mercy and his realization that sin itself (not its consequences) was evil, and reached its culmination with his attainment of the Grace to obey God's Commands. The preface to this internal process within the individual was his election by God for eternal salvation; the conclusion of the process was his soul's salvation and eternal life. Over both preface and conclusion the individual had no control.

Conversion was the rebirth of man — a vivid, personal experience in which the soul encountered the love of God. Although a church might prepare a man for this experience, it could not give it to him. Once saved, or elected, or chosen, the saint was obligated to search out and abide by divine law. Thus discipline was essential to the life of the saint, as was self-examination, continual self-trial. These duties were facilitated by the joining together of the elect in a visible church, by which means they could both test themselves and make others aware of the corruptions of the society in which they lived.

Thus the Protestant reformers posed a threat to any establishment other than their own. Their own awareness of evil and their insistence upon making others cognizant of its existence challenged the status quo. When James I ascended the English throne in 1603, he rebuffed all who challenged the Elizabethan Settlement because they also threatened his position as monarch. Separatists who abandoned the Church, Puritans who wished to cleanse it of Catholicism, and Catholics who sought to restore papal authority found a common response from the new monarch. Raised as

DESCRIPTION OF JAMES I, 1603-1625

HE WAS OF MIDDLE STATURE, more corpulent through his clothes than in his body, yet fat enough; his clothes ever being made large and easy, the doublets quilted for stiletto proof; his breeches in plaits and full stuffed: he was naturally of a timorous disposition, which was the reason of his quilted doublets: his eyes large, ever rolling after any stranger came in his presence; insomuch as many for shame have left the room, as being out of countenance: his beard was very thin; his tongue too large for his mouth, and made him drink very uncomely, as if eating his drink, which came out into the cup of each side his mouth; his skin was as soft as taffeta sarsenet; which felt so because he never washed his hands, only rubbed his fingers' ends slightly with the wet end of a napkin. His legs were very weak; having, as some thought, some foul play in his youth; or, rather, before he was born, that he was not able to stand at seven years of age; that weakness made him ever leaning on other men's shoulders; his walk was ever circular. (Lucy Aikin, Memoirs of the Court of James the First [London: Londgman, Hurst, Reese, Orme, Brown, and Green, 1822], 1, 97-98)

☆☆☆☆☆☆☆☆☆☆☆☆☆☆☆☆☆☆☆☆☆☆☆☆☆☆☆

King of Scotland under the Calvinistic tutelage of John Knox's disciples, James resented the Presbyterian's Church's domination of the Scottish monarchy and envied the English monarch's position as established by Elizabeth. When selected by Elizabeth to succeed her, James saw an opportunity to become a true king unhindered by preachers, whether Calvinist or Catholic. England seemed to offer him the chance to become Supreme Head of the Church and monarch by divine right, and he intended to permit no challenge to his authority over either Church or state.

James promised dissenters they would suffer harrassment until they either conformed to his Church or left the land. In 1608 a congregation of Separatists fled to Amsterdam and then to Leyden in The Netherlands, the most tolerant country in all Europe in the early seventeenth century. The English Separatists drew much of their theology from John Calvin. They believed the true church was "a company or congregatione of the faythfulle called and gathered out of the worlde by the preachinge of the Gospell, who followinge and embracinge true religione, do in one unitie of Spirite strengthen and comforte one another, daylie growinge and increasinge in true faythe, framinge their lyves, governmente, orders and ceremonies accordinge to the worde of God." For them, the need for the independence of each congregation explained their hostility to the Church of England's episcopal organization.

The English Separatists in Leyden remained in their new home for about a decade, but as the twelve-year truce (1609-1621) between Spain and The Netherlands came to an end, they reexamined their position. Changes taking place among their own members disturbed them. Their original unity, fostered by persecution in England, broke down under Leyden's tolerant atmosphere. Their own children became more Dutch than English and drifted away from the true faith. Moreover, Spain and Catholicism posed imminent and real dangers.

Virginia's recent settlement and propaganda of the Virginia Company of London appeared to offer a solution to the Separatists. Their interest was particularly aroused by efforts to entice groups of settlers by offering them large tracts of land and full control over their own affairs. But the Separatists still required money and supplies, and, as artisans, they had little of either. Nonetheless they reached an agreement with the Virginia Company of London in 1620 whereby these Separatists organized themselves, received a grant of land, and cast about for financial support for their venture.

The Pilgrims' financial dilemma seemed resolved when an English merchant, Thomas Weston, offered to supply them if they agreed to form a joint-stock company for a seven-year period. Each investor would buy shares at £10 apiece and each settler would be credited with one share for migrating. Everything would belong to a joint stock for seven years, after which all shareholders would divide the capital equally. A Treasurer and Company in England would control the colony's finances, while a Governor and Council in the colony would deal with civil government. The Pilgrims received land and political self-control, the Weston group gained trade benefits, and the London Company spurred the process of settlement, thereby increasing the attractiveness and value of its other lands.

The Pilgrims in Leyden purchased the *Speedwell*, whose name belied its nature, and Weston hired the *Mayflower*. In 1620 the handful of migrants, about thirty-five Pilgrims and sixty-five employees of Weston, set sail for Virginia. Through a navigational error they reached Cape Cod in November and decided to settle there. Though the reason for their decision not to press on to Virginia remains clouded, they probably appreciated the fishing opportunities at Cape Cod and they probably realized that they would have greater religious freedom in an area untouched by the Church of England. Both considerations seemed weighty to these humble folk, these farmers and artisans.

From the moment the Pilgrims chose New England rather than Virginia, they faced a serious problem — they had no legal right to soil or government. They had settled in territory belonging to the Council for New England, successor to the old Virginia Company of Plymouth. To remedy their status as interlopers, they applied to the Council for a land patent which they received in 1621, but this granted title to the soil and not power of government. Before debarking from the *Mayflower* they had agreed among themselves (omitting the Weston employees) to a government patterned upon their church organization. Under this Mayflower Compact they created secular government by common consent and elected a governor and assistants to whom they gave full power. William Bradford served as governor for thirty terms from 1621 to 1656, a reflection of the colony's unity of purpose. This remained the basic frame of government during the colony's entire history.

Plymouth's economy, tied to the Weston partnership, centered upon farming and fishing. One of the settlers' first ventures was construction of a small fishing vessel, the *Little James*, which foundered on its trial run. By 1624 the English merchants, deploring the colonists' devotion to religion rather than profit, decided to make no further advances. In 1627 the Pilgrims bought out the English shareholders, divided all assets among themselves, and placed trade in a combine responsible for repayment of the colony's debt. Shortly thereafter Plymouth's economic future was secured by the demand for wheat and cattle created by a heavy and sudden migration into Massachusetts Bay.

Massachusetts Bay: The New Jerusalem

Massachusetts Bay had always been considered a prime location for the fishery industry, and throughout the 1620s efforts were made to start fishing settlements there, including one at Cape Anne in 1625. Among those who saw even greater possibilities was the Reverend John White, who interested a group in establishing a New England Company to develop the straggling fishing settlement into a religious colony. They approached the Earl of Warwick for a grant from lands he had received from the Council for New England. Matthew Craddock, Sir Richard Saltonstall, Isaac Johnson, Hugh Peter, and their associates received a tract running from three miles north of the Merrimac River to three miles south of the Charles River and from the Atlantic to the Pacific oceans.

This New England Company immediately sent out a small expedition in the *Abigail*, but a flaw in their land title temporarily prevented them from following up this venture. In 1629 the original incorporators went to the Crown, source of all land titles, for a direct grant to the area they desired. This would have the further advantage of giving them the right to govern their settlements, a power that the Earl of Warwick could not convey.

The new charter from Charles I provided for a trading corporation, the Massachusetts Bay Company, to be controlled by a governor, deputy governor, and eighteen assistants elected by the generality of freemen, meaning shareowners, who would themselves meet four times a year to legislate for the company. Many original shareowners, though not all, were nonconformists or Puritans who disagreed with the Church of England because it had not completely reformed itself. They took as their mission purification of the Anglican Church. The colony they sought to establish would demonstrate the perfection of their religious beliefs.

The Massachusetts Bay Company charter provided for the usual type of commercial corporation, but either by oversight or studied neglect, no mention was made of the Company's headquarters. English officials undoubtedly assumed that the Company would remain in England and govern its colony from there, but this omission provided an opportunity for the nonconformists to move the Company to America, thereby freeing it from immediate royal control or supervision and protecting its special religious purpose from episcopal interference.

When the Company's General Court met in the summer of 1629, they decided to remove the company to America. Only twenty-seven of the 125 members participated, and they made every effort to keep the decision secret. John Winthrop was chosen governor, and shareowners who intended to remain in England were bought out. In March 1630, a fleet of eleven ships with 700 passengers left for Massachusetts, carrying with them their precious charter. Thus began the great migration. The Puritans learned effectively from others' mistakes. The expedition left at the proper time, carried the correct equipment and supplies, and was organized effectively. Its leadership was largely middle class and strongly dominated by religious motives. From 1630 to 1643 some 20,000 people migrated to the Bay Colony at a cost of over £200,000 — the largest colonizing exodus in English history to that time.

A CHURCH COVENANT, 1630

IN THE NAME OF Our Lord Jesus Christ, and in Obedience to His holy will, and Divine Ordinaunce
Wee whose names are hereunder written, being by His most wise, and good Providence brought together into this part of America in the Bay of Masachusetts, and desirous to unite our selves into one Congregation, or Church, under the Lord Jesus Christ our Head, in such sort as becometh all whom He hath Redeemed, and Sanctifyed to Himselfe, doe hereby solemnly, and religiously (as in His most holy Proesence) Promisse, and bind our selves, to walke in all our wayes according to the Rule of the Gospell, and in all sincere Conformity to His holy Ordinaunces, and in mutuall love, and respect each to other, so neere as God shall give us grace. (Charlestown Church, July 30, 1630, from First Church of Boston Records, 1630-87 *[Massachusetts Historical Society])*

Once settlements began, the new government started to function. The Company's General Court held its first meeting in Charlestown in October 1630, with only eight freemen present. With the sole purpose of creating a purified community as an example to the Church of England, John Winthrop and his associates began converting a trading company charter into the government of a state. They did not believe in popular government, but felt that there were those "called" by God to serve in public office, just as there were those "called" by Him for special service in the ministry. However, Puritan leaders faced a dilemma. The charter placed all power in the hands of freemen, meaning shareowners, and only a few of these had come to the New World. Moreover, those who did not hold Puritan beliefs might purchase stock and thus gain a voice in government. To prevent this, Winthrop altered the definition of freemanship from shareowning to religious affiliation. He invited all who wished to become freemen to submit their names, and about a hundred new freemen were admitted in 1631. The newly enlarged General Court then directed that "no man shall be admitted to the freedom of this body politic, but such as are members of the [Congregational] churches within the limits of the same."

This began the conversion of a trading company charter into a govern-

PLANTING A TOWN: WOBURN, MASS., 1640

BUT TO BEGIN, this Town, as all others, had its bounds fixed by the General Court, to the contenese [contents] of four miles square, (beginning at the end of Charles Town bounds). The grant is to seven men of good and honest report, upon condition, that within two year they erect houses for habitation thereon, and so go on to make a Town thereof, upon the Act of Court; these seven men have power to give and grant out lands unto any persons who are willing to take up their dwellings within the said precinct, and to be admitted to al common priviledges of the said Town, giving them such an ample portion, both of Medow and Upland, as their present and future stock of cattel and hands were like to improve, with eye had to others that might after come to populate the said Town;' this they did without any respect of persons, yet such as were exorbitant, and of a turbulent spirit, unfit for a civil society, they would reject, till they come to mend their manners;

☆☆☆☆☆☆☆☆☆☆☆☆☆☆☆☆☆☆☆☆☆☆☆☆☆☆☆

ment for a religiously-oriented state. Freemanship, with ultimate governmental authority, had been changed from simple ownership of shares, or property rights, into adherence to certain religious beliefs. Further alterations quickly molded the charter to the community's needs. A change in the electoral system provided that freemen elected the assistants who then chose the governor and deputy governor, thereby depriving freemen of an important power. It was further stipulated that the governor, deputy governor and assistants, rather than freemen in General Court, possessed exclusive power to make laws.

Such alterations in the colony's charter soon met with objections. In 1632 Watertown refused to pay a tax levied by the assistants for palisading Cambridge, denying the assistants' authority to levy taxes without popular consent. Winthrop quickly backed away from his extreme authoritarianism and now agreed that freemen in General Court could consider any matter they wished and that all officers would be chosen by the General Court, stipulating only that the governor must himself be a freeman.

A second major protest, led by Thomas Dudley in 1634, denounced Winthrop's conduct of government as too liberal and demanded to see the charter. This would unmask the illegal conversion of a commercial

such came not to enjoy any freehold. These seven men ordered and disposed of the streets of the Town, as might be best for improvement of the Land, and yet civil and religious society maintained; to which end those that had land neerest the place for Sabbath Assembly, had a lesser quantity at home, and more farther off to improve for corn, of all kinds; they refused not men for their poverty, but according to their ability were helpful to the poorest sort, in building their houses, and distributed to them land accordingly; the poorest had six or seven acres of Medow, and twenty five of Upland, or thereabouts. Thus was this Town populated, to the number of sixty families, or thereabout, and after this manner are the Towns of New England peopled. (From J. F Jameson, ed., Johnson's Wonder-Working Providence *[New York: C Scribner's Sons, 1910], pp. 213-4)*

☆☆☆☆☆☆☆☆☆☆☆☆☆☆☆☆☆☆☆☆☆☆☆☆☆

company into a government with heavy religious overtones. Winthrop finally agreed that only the General Court could levy taxes, dispose of lands, and confirm land titles, thereby stripping executive officers of these powers. He also decided, because of the colony's rapid expansion, to institute a representative system. Each town would send deputies to three of the four General Courts to sit together with the Governor and assistants, while the general election of representatives and officers replaced the fourth Court.

The 1634 General Court had completed the Bible Commonwealth. Massachusetts became a Puritan state with the clergy playing a vital role; yet it was not a theocracy. The clergy functioned as teachers expounding on the Bible, and their election sermons shaped governmental policy, but secular officials executed that policy. No clergyman held government office, but no government officer acted without clerical advice. In return for advice and guidance, the state "nursed" the Puritan Church. Thus religious and secular power were sharply separated, but nonetheless subtly overlapped.

Massachusetts became a colony whose *raison d'être* was religion. The Bible contained God's positive command to man, this life prepared man

JOHN WINTHROP'S DEFINITION OF LIBERTY, 1645

... THERE IS A TWOFOLD liberty, natural (I mean as our nature is now corrupt) and civil or federal. The first is common to man with beasts and other creatures. By this, man as he stands in relation to man, simply, has liberty to do what he lists; it is a liberty to evil as well as to good. This liberty is incompatible and inconsistent with authority, and cannot endure the least restraint of the most just authority. The exercise and maintaining of this liberty makes men grow more evil, and in time to be, worse than brute beasts.... The other kind of liberty I call civil or federal; it may also be termed moral, in reference to the covenant between God and man in the moral law.... This liberty is the proper end and object of authority and cannot subsist without it.... This liberty you are to stand for, with the hazard not only of your goods, but of your lives, if need be.... This liberty is maintained and exercised in a way of subjection to authority.... The woman's own choice makes such a man her husband; yet being so chosen, he is her lord and she is subject to him, yet in a way of liberty, not of bondage, and a true wife accounts her subjection her honour and freedom.... (From J. K. Hosmer, ed., John Winthrop's Journal, History of New England, 2 vols. [New York: C. Scribner's Sons, 1908], II, 233-9.

☆☆☆☆☆☆☆☆☆☆☆☆☆☆☆☆☆☆☆☆☆☆☆☆☆☆☆☆☆☆

for the next world, and man owed loving acceptance and obedience to God's inscrutable will. In theory, Puritans remained within the Anglican Church, though they stripped it of all authority. They were not Separatists who vested authority in independent congregations, nor were they Presbyterians who gave full power to church elders and synods. Puritanism struck a delicate balance between the two, as difficult to describe as to preserve. Indeed, that very difficulty plagued the Commonwealth with heretics and dissenters. In 1647 a law required the banishment of Anabaptists, rigid Separatists, Jesuits, and other undesirables. This statute suggested that deviants existed in significant numbers in the community.

Early in its history, two religious crises shattered the tranquility of Massachusetts. First came Roger Williams's denial of secular authority over men's consciences. The civil magistrates' role was essential to Puritanism. As nursing fathers of the Church, magistrates rooted out heresy and violations of God's commandments as defined by the clergy. Williams, a rigid Puritan, hastily and indiscreetly avowed his own strong convictions, rejected magisterial power over anything dealing with men's religious beliefs, and denounced Bay Colony clergy for refusing to break completely and openly with the defiled Church of England. He also questioned the colony's land title, alleging that only the Indians could transfer such rights to colonists. Faced with a clear-cut challenge to the whole foundation of their society, the magistrates ordered Williams banished in October 1635. Warned of his fate, he fled south toward the Narragansett River.

Anne Hutchinson, who also carried Puritanism to extremes, espoused another heresy at about the same time. A woman of dominant personality and sharp intellect, she decried the alleged emphasis of the churches upon outward conformity to society's standards, on "good works," as a method of determining whether or not God had predestined an individual for salvation. Salvation of the soul, Anne Hutchinson insisted, depended upon individual awareness and acceptance of the inward dwelling of the Holy Spirit which gave direct communion with God — on grace. God's presence within each person far outweighed all other considerations. These views threatened to jar the political and social structure of Puritanism. Clergymen had little value. The individual obeyed God's direct, personal commands, and responsibility shifted from the individual to God himself. Anne Hutchinson won several influential converts to her views, including Governor Harry Vane, soon defeated for reelection, and several prominent ministers. Tried for heresy and convicted and banished in 1638, she, too, settled in the Narragansett region.

Protestantism bred dissension, and the Puritan experience epitomized this. Protestantism's birth as a dissent from Catholicism precluded its enforcement of a new orthodoxy which denied others the right to different religious views. Similarly, when Puritanism challenged the Church of England, it opened itself to challenge. This, indeed, was the Reformation lesson, for opening the doors to one new idea opened them to all new ideas. Moreover, Puritanism's establishment in the New World compounded this. Though the Bay Colony formed compact town settlements, each existed on the edge of a never-ending wilderness with all of its psychological implications. As a faith born in Old England, in a fully established and settled society which knew the familiar parameters of life, it accepted a new and subtle challenge upon transplantation, for men's personal experiences and environment markedly affected their contemplation of God. Yet, Puritans did not understand this. Jeremiads

ROGER WILLIAMS ON LIBERTY AND RESTRAINT, 1655

THAT EVER I should speak or write a tittle that tends to such an infinite liberty of conscience, is a mistake, and which I have ever disclaimed and abhorred. To prevent such mistakes, I shall at present only propose this case: There goes many a ship to sea, with many hundred souls in one ship, whose weal and woe is common, and is a true picture of a commonwealth, or a human combination or society. It hath fallen out sometimes, that both papists and protestants, Jews and Turks, may be embarked in one ship; upon which supposal I affirm that all the liberty of conscience that ever I pleaded for, turns upon these two hinges — that none of the papists, protestants, Jews, or Turks be forced to come to the ship's prayers or worship, nor compelled from their own particular prayers or worship, if they practice any. I further add, that I never denied that, notwithstanding this liberty, the commander of this ship ought to command the ship's course, yea, and also command that justice, peace, and sobriety be kept and practiced, both among the

---

increasingly bewailed the failure of Bay Colony settlers to maintain standards in the later seventeenth century, increasingly bemoaned the children's rejection of their parents' rigorous faith. The Bible Commonwealth understood little of what the New World demanded of it.

The Overflow of Grace

Rhode Island and Connecticut developed as an overflow of grace from the Massachusetts Bay Colony, with the first receiving exiles banished for criticizing the Puritan Commonwealth as too restrictive and conservative, while the second received an exodus of those who sought greater economic opportunity than the rocky soil of Massachusetts could provide. Settlers of both Rhode Island and Connecticut reflected the problems encountered by transplanting a utopian concept into an inhospitable and unyielding soil. A sense of discontent with conditions in Massachusetts, however varied, provided incentive for settlement of both Rhode Island and Connecticut.

Rhode Island began when Roger Williams, banished from the Massachusetts Bay Colony in 1635, fled with some friends to the Narragansett

seamen and all the passengers. If any of the seamen refuse to perform their services, or passengers to pay their freight; if any refuse to help, in person or purse, towards the common charges or defence; if any refuse to obey the common laws and orders of the ship, concerning their common peace or preservation; if any shall mutiny and rise up against their commanders and officers; if any should preach or write that there ought to be no commanders or officers, because all are equal in Christ, therefore no masters nor officers, no laws nor orders, nor corrections nor punishments; — I say, I never denied but in such cases, whatever is pretended, the commander or commanders may judge, resist, compel, and punish such transgressors, according to their deserts and merits. This if seriously and honestly minded, may, if it so please the Father of lights, let in some light to such as willingly shut not their eyes. (From: J. R. Bartlett, ed., The Letters of Roger Williams [Providence: The Narragansett Club, 1874], pp. 278-279)

☆☆☆☆☆☆☆☆☆☆☆☆☆☆☆☆☆☆☆☆☆☆☆☆☆☆

area. He found refuge with Indians and bought land from them. Warned away by the governor of Plymouth from an area claimed by the Pilgrims, Williams moved on to the Great Salt River, called the area Providence, and began a settlement that straggled along the river front. The town he laid out differed from the orderly Massachusetts settlements because it focused on the river, not the village green and meeting-house. Williams also differed by insisting upon purchasing lands from Indian owners at a fair price. His community prospered as other exiles joined him, and an economy based upon corn, tobacco, cattle, and sheep soon developed.

Rhode Island, of course, faced the same problem as Plymouth — no legal authority for government. Its settlers fell back upon the same English village heritage of common consent, and heads of families met every fortnight to consult. Soon the inhabitants signed a social compact, drafted by Williams, in which each person joined freely in obedience to the majority of householders. Williams later amended it to read obedience "only in civil matters."

Among others who flocked to Rhode Island from Massachusetts Bay Colony were groups led by William Coddington and Anne Hutchinson.

These two joined forces and founded Portsmouth, where they attempted to create a land-owning democracy in which no one was to be attacked for religious doctrine. Such toleration was too much for the seventeenth century, however, and Coddington finally moved in 1639 to Newport. Another malcontent, Samuel Gorton, moved from Portsmouth to found Warwick in 1640. By the early 1640s, Rhode Island consisted of four separate communities, each of which had Indian title to its lands, and each of which lacked any legal authority for government.

Roger Williams, more than any other person, stamped his social philosophy on these communities. His writings dealt with the necessity for a complete separation of Church and state, not because of libertarian views, but because he felt that the state had no voice in religious matters. Each church was a civil corporation to be protected, as any other corporation, by the state, but not to be favored one above the other. To avoid anarchy, Williams also emphasized that freedom was a privilege acquired by membership in a social group and that such membership also imposed duties.

Rhode Island, lacking both legal governmental authority and English sanction, quickly faced challenges from its neighbors. The other New England colonies formed a federation in 1643 for a variety of reasons, but they purposely omitted inviting Rhode Island. Massachusetts and Plymouth both pressed claims to its territory, a serious threat compounded by divisiveness within the colony. Only Roger Williams's dominant will kept the collection of strong personalities together. To protect Rhode Island, Williams went to England to secure a patent from the Parliamentary Commission headed by the Earl of Warwick. In 1647 he received a grant which confirmed the Indian title to the lands and gave the colony authority to govern itself. More important, the Warwick Patent had the sanction of Parliamentary forces identified with the Church of England's overthrow, and this helped protect Rhode Island from its rapacious neighbors.

To the east of Rhode Island lay Connecticut, whose history of development differed markedly. Interest in this area emerged from a trade rivalry between Massachusetts and New Netherland over control of its fur resources. The lengthy Connecticut River, penetrating into New England's interior, tapped a hinterland rich in fur-bearing animals. The Dutch set up a trading post at Hartford in 1633, and within a year New England traders also entered the area. Soon the Connecticut Valley's rich lands attracted settlers from Dorchester, Newtown, and Watertown in Massachusetts.

As settlers established towns in the Connecticut Valley and along Long Island Sound, the absence of governmental authority posed a problem. They found a temporary solution when Massachusetts took the fledgling settlements under its wing for a year. In 1637 the Connecticut towns formed their own General Court patterned after that of the Bay Colony. A more permanent arrangement followed in 1639 with adoption of the Fundamental Orders, the first written constitution to create a government. This established a commonwealth with an elective governor, magistrates, and representatives, and remained in effect until 1662. Connecticut represented no disagreement with Puritanism or the Bay Colony, only a lust for land.

Its homogeneous population gave New England a sense of unity. The Calvinist heritage, despite sectarian differences, unified English settlers more than it divided them. Perhaps the only truly discordant note came from black slavery, since these involuntary migrants possessed a strong cultural heritage totally different from that of the dominant English population. By 1638 blacks entered Massachusetts, and they became an increasingly important supply of labor once the English Civil War halted English migration.

As in Virginia, blacks probably had the status in early years of indentured servants. The same motive of securing a permanent labor force soon transformed such servitude into slavery. The 1641 Body of Liberties prohibited slavery except for lawful wartime captives, voluntary self-enslavement of "strangers," or sale of "strangers." Legal acceptance of slavery developed in the late seventeenth century, but much earlier the social and economic system adopted the institution as a means of increasing the labor force.

By the 1640s Anglo-America had become a reality. England's toehold on the continent included settlements in the Boston area, the Narragansett River, the Connecticut River Valley, and the Maryland and Virginia tidewater regions. No one yet knew either the potential or the future patterns of their development. Imperial policy, such as it was, had not been defined much beyond the ideas of the Hakluyts, and the governmental role had not changed significantly since the days of Elizabeth. Inevitably these things would change, but the catalyst would be an upheaval at home. The English Civil War, the Cromwellian interregnum, and the Restoration era would precipitate several sharp shifts both in imperial policy and in colonial reactions.

SELECTED BIBLIOGRAPHY

The early years of colonial settlement are conveniently depicted in two highly interpretive and very readable studies which have commanded a good deal of attention: Clarence Ver Steeg's *The Formative Years, 1609-1763* (1964) and Daniel J. Boorstin's *The Americans: The Colonial Experience* (1958). A brief volume, with a good bibliography, is Carl Ubbelohde's *The American Colonies and the British Empire, 1607-1763* (1968).

The Indian civilization, which antedated European settlement, is dealt with in *The Americas on the Eve of Discovery*, edited by Harold E. Driver (1964). Another group, very much neglected until recently, is treated by Lerone Bennett, Jr. in *Before the Mayflower* (1968). A more traditional emphasis in migration history is given by Marcus Lee Hansen's *The Atlantic Migration* (1940).

Charles E. Nowell's *The Great Discoveries and the First Colonial Empires* (1954) provides a convenient comparison of the competitive systems as does *Three American Empires* (1967), edited by John J. TePaske. Louis B. Wright's *The Atlantic Frontier: Colonial American Civilization* (1947) details European reactions to the colonial milieu. Howard Mumford Jones's *O Strange New World: American Culture, The Formative Years* (1967) presents a masterful study of Anglo-American culture.

New England history has been detailed many times. Among important works are Samuel Eliot Morison's *Builders of Bay Colony* (1964) which treats the major personalities who founded Massachusetts, Sumner Chilton Powell's *Puritan Village: The Formation of a New England Town* (1965) which used Sudbury as a case study, Edmund S. Morgan's provocative *The Puritan Dilemma: The Story of John Winthrop* (1958) and his equally interesting *Roger Williams* (1957).

Among important works on Puritanism are Darrett B. Rutman's *American Puritanism* (1970) which essays a new interpretation of Puritanism, Samuel Eliot Morison's *The Intellectual Life of Colonial New England* (1963), and Edmund S. Morgan's *Visible Saints: The History of a Puritan Idea* (1965).

The southern colonies are fully treated in Wesley Frank Craven's *The

Southern Colonies in the Sevnteenth Century (1949). Virginia's founding is described fully by Philip L. Barbour in *The Three Worlds of Captain John Smith* (1964), and by David B. Quinn's *Raleigh and the British Empire* (1949). Elizabeth Baer's *Seventeenth Century Maryland* (1949) is the most recent detailed study.

Two basic studies of colonial labor are: Abbot E. Smith's *Colonists in Bondage: White Servitude and Convict Labor in America 1607-1776* (1947), and Marcus W. Jernegan's *Laboring and Dependent Classes on Colonial America 1607-1783* (1931).

Finally, two standard works which must always be included in any list are Charles McLean Andrews' four-volume *The Colonial Period of American History* (1934-38) and Herbert Levi Osgood's *The American Colonies in the Seventeenth Century* (1904-07).

CHAPTER 3

UNSETTLED HUMORS, 1640-1705

The years from 1603 to 1705, from the accession of James I to the throne to the determination by Parliament of the Hanoverian succession, were dominated by sharp contests for power between monarch and legislature. These battles had both direct and indirect effects upon the development of England's New World empire. In the early years they so preoccupied the nation that its colonies received little attention. Even when the empire's expansion by mid-seventeenth century made necessary some form of control by the mother country, internal problems distracted England from any effective efforts. Thus American settlements grew without close supervision and took forms perhaps unintended by those few who seriously thought about the nature of empire. By the time England settled its domestic difficulties, rivalry with France emerged as a new problem which precluded serious consideration of imperial relationships or effective efforts to control the destiny of a New World empire which contained the promise of limitless expansion.

ENGLAND'S TURMOIL

From James I's accession to the throne in 1603 until 1639 the monarch and his Parliament fought bitterly about the Crown's authority over finances, refashioning the Anglican Church, and common law as opposed to prerogative rule. All of these blended into one another, and opposition to any aspect of the policy of the early Stuarts became identified with Parliament, Puritanism, and common law. In 1640 the opposition took control of the so-called Long Parliament, and the situation rapidly deteriorated until in 1642 Charles I finally issued a call to arms and civil war erupted. Four years later parliamentary forces made the king a prisoner. Things remained in flux for another three years until Roundhead extremists in Parliament insisted upon a permanent solution — execution of the monarch.

The 1650s, the Interregnum, found England controlled by a military dictatorship under Oliver Cromwell as Lord Protector. Upon his death in 1658, his son Richard tried unsuccessfully to carry on, but a reaction set in against Calvinist extremism, and General Monk, later Duke of Albemarle, led the move to invite the legitimate heir, Charles II, to return to England in 1660. This restoration was not a full return to the situation of 1639. The monarch's powers were trimmed, but the Restoration Parliament enthusiastically supported the Crown.

COLONIAL REACTIONS

While these events, so briefly summarized, occurred in England, the process of colonization continued in America. Each settlement felt the consequences of events in England, but each reacted differently. The English Civil War halted the migration to the New World of men and money in large quantities. The Civil War, coming so soon after the planting of colonies, forced upon them a certain self-reliance that shaped their development.

Virginia, for example, remained loyal to Charles I in his hour of trial. Settled before any serious controversies in England, Virginia developed with little involvement in the mother country's problems. Economic motives, rather than political or religious ones, guided the colony's establishment. The colonists identified the old Virginia Company of London

COLONIAL SETTLEMENT, 1660

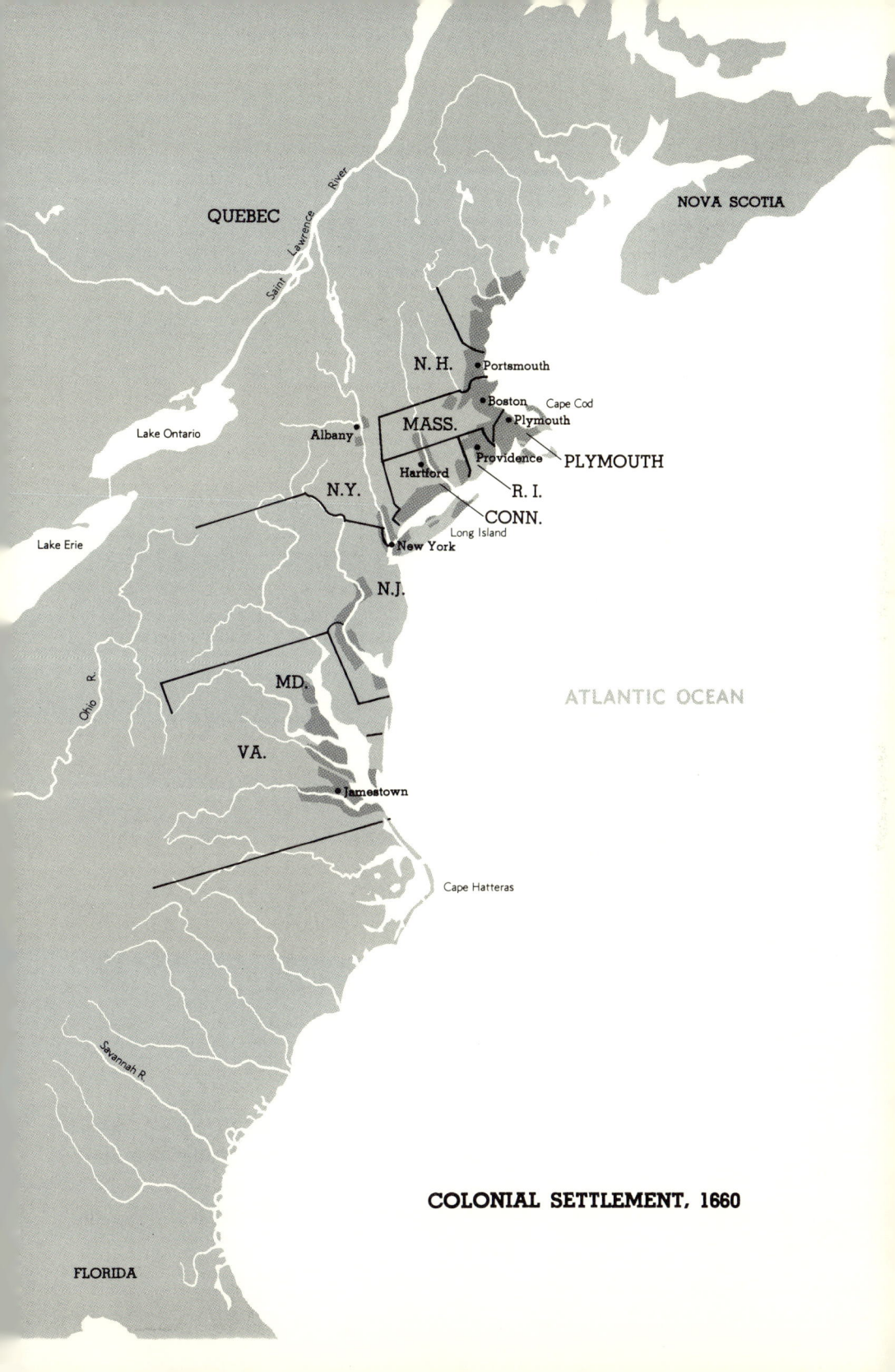

with the parliamentary forces contesting with Charles I. Above all, Virginians did not want the old company restored, since this might threaten the rights granted them by the Crown. In 1641, when the King appointed Sir William Berkeley as Governor and assured him that the company was a dead issue, the loyalty of Virginians to the Crown seemed certain.

Virginia also reacted in a hostile manner toward Puritanism. In 1643, following the outbreak of civil war in the mother country, the colony strengthened its laws in behalf of the Anglican Church and ordered nonconformists to depart. Puritans were harassed at Norfolk and elsewhere and Quakers were persecuted for questioning public authority. Challenges to the foundations of civil government in Virginia could not be permitted at a time when those same foundations were collapsing in England.

Virginia's loyalty to Charles I caused severe economic complications. Dependent upon its cash crop of tobacco, the colony used London as its entrepôt, but that city was in parliamentary hands from the very outbreak of hostilities. The House of Burgesses proclaimed a policy of free trade with all Englishmen and, as a safety measure, also invited the Dutch to trade with them. Most parliamentary shipping would not enter Virginia for fear of capture by royal forces, while royalist ships stayed away in fear of parliamentary seizure. Thus most of Virginia's trade passed into Dutch hands.

Dutch trade saved Virginia, but also created problems because The Netherlands could not supply the colony with the necessary manpower and funds which traditionally came from England. The Dutch attempted to substitute for English laborers by importing black slaves, whose numbers increased from three hundred in 1650 to two thousand by the end of the Civil War. But they could not provide investment funds, and their attempts to substitute liquor brought protests from the Burgesses and led to regulatory laws.

Disruption of trade also bothered Cromwell who, once he established the Protectorate throughout the British Isles, moved to regain control of the tobacco trade. In 1650 and 1651 Parliament passed the first Navigation Acts designed to monopolize colonial trade for England's benefit. In 1652, as a direct consequence, the first Anglo-Dutch War occurred and began a conflict between the rival mercantile powers that continued for two decades.

Cromwell also sent a three-man commission to bring Virginia under submission. Governor Berkeley talked of resistance, but only for the record, and the people submitted when Berkeley went into retirement. Virginia established an interim government with the governor and Council selected by the Burgesses, but little really changed since the same local group continued in control. Instead of undergoing a political upheaval, Virginia developed a remarkable continuity of leadership, not only on the provincial level, but most importantly on the local, county level at the expense of gubernatorial authority.

The number of counties in Virginia had doubled during the Interregnum, particularly after 1647 when the Indian menace had been suppressed. Wasteful agricultural methods and open-handed land distribution, plus availability of easy water transportation, spread the population thinly. This led to demands for greater authority in county courts as a convenience now that many settlements were distant from Jamestown. During the Interregnum, a number of functions — issuing marriage licenses, probating wills, recording land titles, levying local taxes — were turned over to local magistrates. These may seem insignificant, but they constituted the major functions of government insofar as it touched the daily lives of the people.

The House of Burgesses acquiesced in the transfer of these powers. The legislators were actually transferring power from their right hand to their left, for county court magistrates, recipients of greater power, controlled the Burgesses. These magistrates viewed sitting in the Burgesses as an obligation to be undertaken by each in his turn. Virginia society operated under the concept of *noblesse oblige*. These changes, therefore, merely juggled responsibilities among community leaders chosen for talent rather than birth. Charles II's restoration in 1660 and Sir William Berkeley's return to power as royal governor did not modify these changes. Indeed, Berkeley went to England to secure royal confirmation of the innovations.

These shifts in governmental structure brought about a subtle alteration in Virginia's politics. Magistrates, not the royal governor, became the focus of power. Indeed, gubernatorial authority from this time forward rested not on royal commissions or instructions, but on that officeholder's ability as a political leader. Virginians became skillful at conducting their own affairs. Governors who could manipulate local politicians adeptly had great authority, those who could not became frustrated and isolated.

Just to the north, in Maryland, a similar pattern emerged, but the proprietary powers of the Baltimores warped it somewhat. During the Civil War the proprietor's Roman Catholicism made him suspect, and he expended much effort in England to preserve his authority over Maryland. In the colony much energy went into maintaining religious tranquility. The violence of a religious war in England had obvious repercussions for Maryland, where Protestants and Catholics had struck an uneasy compromise. Since toleration at this time was foreign to Englishmen, upheavals followed.

Almost immediately upon receipt of news of the Civil War, a group identifying itself with Parliament assumed control in Maryland, even driving Leonard Calvert, the proprietary governor, to seek refuge in Virginia in 1644. Lord Baltimore sought to appease Maryland's Protestants by inviting to the colony Puritans suffering persecution in Virginia. He also sought to calm Maryland by issuing "An Act Concerning Religion" which prohibited the use of reviling terms and demanded maintenance of religious harmony. But Baltimore's demands could not subdue the natural impulses of Englishmen, which wracked the colony with periodic upheavals until the Restoration in 1660.

During these years efforts were made in Maryland, as in Virginia, to expand the role of local government, but Baltimore staunchly opposed any diminishing of his authority. The Restoration played into the proprietor's hands as Marylanders momentarily lost their appetite for religious and political disorders. The 1660s, therefore, saw proprietary control strengthened and consequently central control of the colony. Yet expansion of county courts in Maryland paralleled that in Virginia, as did growth of a local governing class. The consequence would be a series of collisions between colonists and proprietor, between local and central power, which would reach their peak in the 1680s.

Somewhat ironically, the Puritan Revolution in England offered few opportunities to New England. With Puritanism victorious in Old England, New Englanders thought their religious beliefs were vindicated. They were not associated with royal officials or proprietary power and quickly acknowledged the Cromwellian government, thus suffering no direct interference from England. They complained, however, that the Civil War not only cut off new immigration, but began a reverse migration as Puritan leaders returned home to participate in the Revolution and to forward the reform of the Church of England.

Massachusetts, only a decade old, still needed a continuous flow of capital and manpower from the mother country. Since it produced no staple commodity for England as did the southern colonies, the Bay Colony had to find its own way economically during the Cromwellian period. New England turned to trade, particularly with the sugar-producing West Indies, which became its prime market for agricultural products, fish, and lumber. Since shipping could not be secured from the mother country, these colonies used their natural resources and constructed their own vessels. This became New England's economic pattern throughout the colonial period, confirming its marginal relationship to English mercantilism, and reinforcing the original settlers' independent attitude.

Increasing conflicts between Parliament and the Crown in England and the eventual outbreak of the Civil War also forced New England to settle its own problems with the Indians, its non-English neighbors, and its own dissenters, thereby hardening its self-reliance. The Indian menace had never been serious because a great plague had decimated the Indian population just prior to English settlement. Nonetheless, rapid English expansion in the 1630s led to collision with the natives, particularly the Pequot and Narragansett Indians. The Pequot War of 1637, which wiped out that tribe, made possible rapid settlement of the Massachusetts and Connecticut backcountry.

More pressing than the Indian conflict, however, was the Anglo-Dutch rivalry for control of the Connecticut River, the Delaware River, and even the Hudson. To oust the Dutch, the fragmentation of authority and even purpose in New England first had to be overcome. Connecticut was a series of small communities with no effective central control, Rhode Island was even more decentralized, and other settlements were developing in Plymouth, New Hampshire, and Maine. The latter two areas fell under the control of Massachusetts, but the independent colonies presented the basic problem of divided authority.

By 1640, New England had about eighteen thousand settlers, with nearly fourteen thousand in Massachusetts alone. In the next twenty years, the Bay Colony's population grew nearly 60 per cent, but the others expanded by 400 per cent. Obviously, though Massachusetts dominated, its ability to control the area was lessening. Moreover, the possibility of substituting English Puritan leadership seemed slight since Cromwell emphasized those areas most economically beneficial to England, such as the southern colonies and the West Indies. New England had to fend for itself, and Massachusetts, as the most populous and powerful colony, had to lead. Unity of New England under Massachusetts was perfectly logical, but so too were the fears of the Bay Colony's neighbors.

In 1643 the New England Confederation was formed as a compromise between the need for unity and fear of dominance by Massachusetts. Massachusetts, Plymouth, Connecticut, and New Haven (then a separate colony of extreme Puritans) joined together, purposely excluding the New Hampshire and Maine settlements, over which the Bay Colony exerted control, and Rhode Island, which they all viewed as an aberration because it abounded in heretics. They signed a "firm and perpetual league of friendship and amity for offense and defense, mutual advice and consent."

The Confederation set up a board of two commissioners from each colony, with each having an equal vote. A majority of six of the eight commissioners must approve any action; if the commissioners disagreed, the matter went to the colonies themselves. The compromise was effective because, while Massachusetts loomed large, the Confederation preserved the other colonies' independence. Rarely would smaller colonies venture any action without Bay Colony support, and Massachusetts could never take action without approval of at least two others.

The Confederation intended to oust the Dutch from the Delaware and Connecticut rivers. Neither Dutch nor English had clear land titles, but the English outnumbered the Dutch twenty to one and the land was rich. Disputes continued over the years until Governor Kieft of New Netherland wearily complained: "When we hear the inhabitants of Hartford complaining of us, we seem to hear Aesop's wolf complaining of the lamb." In 1650, Governor Peter Stuyvesant and the Connecticut authorities signed the Treaty of Hartford and drew boundary lines. They divided Long Island at Oyster Bay, and the Dutch retained the area ten miles east of the Hudson River. Although The Netherlands accepted this treaty, Cromwell repudiated it because it would validate Dutch claims to the Hudson Valley. Two years later, the first Anglo-Dutch war broke out. New England attacked Dutch shipping, but the unwillingness of Massachusetts to declare war prevented formal and full-scale hostilities between the colonies. Cessation of the conflict between England and The Netherlands left unresolved the problem of their rivalry in America.

New England's need to find its own solutions during the Civil War and Interregnum extended to religious dissent as well. The Protectorate had moved toward religious toleration of all Protestant sects, for the fratricidal warfare which had been waged in God's name, especially over details of dogma or structure, had threatened to decimate England and expose it to its enemies. But New England and particularly the Bay Colony, isolated from the winds of change, rigidly adhered to Congregationalism and violently struck out at all dissenters.

In 1646 the Massachusetts ministers petitioned for a synod of ministers and elders to "agree upon one form of government and discipline" for the church. The synod completed its labors in 1648, accepting Parliament's Westminster Confession, but flatly rejecting toleration: "Idolatry, blasphemy, heresy, venting corrupt and pernicious opinions are to be restrained and punished by civil authority. If any church one or more shall grow schismatical, rending itself from the communion of other churches, or shall walk incorrigibly or obstinately in any corrupt way of their own, contrary to the rule of the Word; in such case, the magistrate is to put forth his coercive power as the matter shall require." After bitter debate and strong opposition from local congregations, the General Court finally adopted this as law in 1651. Puritanism had reached its zenith.

Boston's first town house (1657-1711), a monument to the town's increasingly important merchant class. At the time of its construction, it was the most imposing building in Boston. Its first story housed market stalls; its upper stories had rooms for courts, church elders, and the "Ancient and Honorable Artillery Company." (Bostonian Society, Old State House)

This statute represented less a fulfillment of ministerial power than a fear of its loss. Bay Colony Puritanism had become self-conscious and defensive, as though its leaders understood the inadequacy of their responses to problems, but had no others. They saw England's liberal tendencies, the colony's increasing secularism, and the younger generation's lack of religious enthusiasm, and the Devil's successes bothered and bewildered them.

Given this attitude, the Massachusetts authorities magnified heretical dangers out of all proportion to their importance. When three Baptists arrived from Rhode Island and violated the 1644 statute regarding baptism, they were arrested, convicted, and sentenced to stiff fines or whipping. The law provided only for banishment, but the Reverend John Cotton defended the magistrates' actions: "There is a vast difference between men's inventions and God's institutions," he announced. "We fled from men's inventions, to which else we should have been compelled; we compel none to men's inventions."

Cotton's simple analogy, pregnant with meaning, summed up the ministerial mind in Massachusetts. The Congregational Church was God's institution, while all other religious forms were men's inventions. More important, Cotton succinctly stated the colony's policy of rejecting all outside influence or interference. None could challenge the New England Way; none could question the peculiar relationship between religious and secular institutions in Massachusetts.

The determination of others, however, prevented Massachusetts from having or enjoying its isolation. The Quakers (or Friends), looking upon New England as fertile ground, presented the same serious challenge as had Anne Hutchinson's earlier heresy. They, too, emphasized the Inner Light of God within each man and a continuing revelation from Him, while Puritans took the Bible as His final word subject to interpretation only by ministers specially trained for the task. Thus, Quakerism demoted the ministers and elevated the importance of the individual, destroying a vital element of the New England Way.

The Quaker invasion in the late 1650s evoked a series of violent repressive measures, beginning with banishment, continuing with whippings, and ending with hangings. The English looked with horror on such repression committed in the name of God, but Cromwell did not interfere. However, Charles II, after the Restoration, ordered a halt to all religious persecution in Massachusetts. This reaction by Bay Colony authorities to a challenge reflected their growing fear of losing control. The greater the challenge, the more irrational and violent the response. Puritanism in America was undergoing traumatic changes which the older generation simply would not accept. They answered by persecuting dissenters. This did not halt change because it attacked the symptoms, rather than the causes.

The Civil War and Interregnum affected all of England's fledgling settlements across the Atlantic. In the southern colonies as in New England, a spirit of self-reliance and autonomy prevailed. The English limited their interference to enforcement of trade restrictions, but once Virginia and Maryland agreed to abide by the Navigation Acts, Cromwell paid little attention to these colonies. The New England settlements, largely ignored, sought their own solutions to domestic and international problems. England's most difficult task after 1660 would be to try to align these self-contained units economically and politically with the new imperial system.

Stuart Imperialism

England's imperial policy before 1660 had little coherence and even less central direction. Individual entrepreneurs, commercial companies, and landed proprietors determined the shape of England's empire for their own purposes. Imperial warfare, however, demanded a coherent colonial policy in order to protect and expand England's increasingly valuable acquisitions. The later Stuarts and the politicians surrounding the throne understood the strategic and economic importance of England's American possessions and therefore encouraged an aggressive, expansive, and coherent attitude.

The Stuarts' imperial policy, in a sense, had been heralded by Oliver Cromwell, but he never developed it fully. Parliament reenacted his trade and navigation laws in the early 1660s with only minor modifications. The Duke of York, as Lord High Admiral, continued Cromwell's original naval policy. And a Privy Council committee, known as the Lords of Trade, replaced the old parliamentary commission to supervise the colonies.

This agency, formalized by 1675, gathered information and recommended policy to other executive officials. A secretariat, the Plantation Office, handled its work and became increasingly powerful because of its intimate knowledge of colonial affairs, a knowledge acquired from a

PROBLEMS OF PRIVATE COLONIES, 1701

HAVING FORMERLY ... humbly represented ... the state of the Government under Proprietors and Charters in America; and perceiving the irregularities of these Governments dayly to increase, to the prejudice of Trade ... as well as of your Majesties Revenue arising from the Customes here, we ... humbly ... represent to your Majesty;

That those Colonies ... have not conformed themselves to the severall acts of Parliament for regulating Trade and Navigation, to which they ought to pay the same obedience ... as the other Plantations....

That they have assumed to themselves a power to make Laws contrary and repugnant to the Laws of England, and directly prejudicial to Trade, some of them having refused to send hither such Laws as they had enacted, and others having sent them but very imperfectly.

That diverse of them have denied appeals to your Majesty in Councill, by which not only the Inhabitants of those Colonies but others your Majesties subjects are deprived of that benefit, enjoyed in the Plantations, under your Majesties immediate Government, and the Parties agrieved are left without remedy from the arbitrary and Illegal proceedings of their Courts.

That these Colonies continue to be the refuge and retreat of Pirates & Illegal Traders, and the receptacle of Goods imported thither from foreign parts contrary to Law....

That by raising and lowering their coin from time to time, to their particular advantage, and to the prejudice of other Colonies, by exempting their Inhabitants from Duties and Customes to which the other

variety of sources. The orientation of the Lords of Trade was heavily political rather than economic and English rather than colonial, for it had no direct representation of merchants trading to America or of colonists. Interested primarily in creating a uniform trade policy, the Lords of Trade tried to overthrow chartered rights of companies, proprietors, and colonists alike. During the reigns of Charles II and James II it consistently urged establishment of standard royal governments in each colony, and just as consistently, though not as successfully, opposed issuance of new charters.

Of all colonies, Massachusetts presented the most difficult challenge

Colonies are subject, and by Harbouring of Servants and fugitives, these Governments tend greatly to the undermining the Trade and Welfare of the other Plantations, and seduce and draw away the People thereof....

That these Independent Colonies do turn the Course of Trade to the Promoting and propagating woolen and other Manufactures proper to England, instead of applying their thoughts and Endeavours to the production of such commodities as are fit to be encouraged in these parts according to the true design and intention of such settlements....

That this chiefly arises from the ill use they make of the powers entrusted to them by their Charters, and the Independency which they pretend to, and that each Government is obliged only to defend itself without any consideration had of their Neighbours, or of the general preservation of the whole....

We humbly conceive it may be expedient that the Charters of the severall Proprietors and others intitling them to absolute Government be reassumed to the Crown and these Colonies put into the same State and dependency as those of your Majesties other Plantations, without prejudice to any man's particular property and freehold ... by the Legislative power of this Kingdome.... (From: Report of the Board of Trade, March 26, 1701, in William L. Saunders, ed., The Colonial Records of North Carolina, 10 vols. [Raleigh, N.C.: P. M. Hale, State Printer, 1886-90], I, 535-37)

☆☆☆☆☆☆☆☆☆☆☆☆☆☆☆☆☆☆☆☆☆☆☆☆☆☆☆☆☆

to the Lords of Trade, although Rhode Island and Connecticut proved troublesome also. The latter two had been established without royal sanction, but in the confusion of the Restoration they secured charters as self-governing commonwealths, a decision imperial officials later regretted. The Bay Colony became the *bête noire* of the Plantation Office. Not only did the colony's Puritanism offend and irritate English officials, but Massachusetts flagrantly disobeyed the Navigation Acts. In challenging the Bay Colony, however, the Lords of Trade had to observe exact legal procedures, as a charter was a property right and could not be lightly attacked.

By the end of Charles II's reign the Lords' policies began to yield results. In 1684 Bermuda lost its charter and became a royal colony. A year later, with Charles II's death and the Duke of York's accession as James II, New York, which had become English in 1664, automatically became a Crown possession. The Lords of Trade purchased the land title to New Hampshire and took over its government on behalf of the King. Massachusetts finally lost its charter by legal proceedings. The Crown's active interest in colonies led to creation under James II of a consolidated government, the Dominion of New England, over Massachusetts, New Hampshire, Connecticut, Rhode Island, New York, and New Jersey. The Lords of Trade envisaged either extending the Dominion to include all other colonies or establishing a similar southern dominion to embrace the remainder. The Dominion sought to unify the colonies under a governor-general, lieutenant governor, and council, and to eliminate legislative assemblies which constantly interfered with royal policy. This would permit easier enforcement of trade laws, establish a unified defense posture against the French and Indians, and simplify the administrative system.

During this period of imperial reorganization, colonists regarded themselves as Englishmen and identified with the English world. In responding to the growth of "Whiggism" in England, they drew parallels between their situation and events in the mother country. The contest in the 1680s between Crown and Parliament — the Civil War and Restoration had merely been a long chapter — seemed remarkably similar to contemporary controversies between colonial legislatures and representatives of Crown or proprietary authority. As English administrators tightened controls over the colonies, the colonists themselves, identifying as Englishmen, sought to preserve English liberties as they understood them.

The English and New Netherland

Anglo-Dutch rivalry, which began during Cromwell's Protectorate, reached its climax in Charles II's reign. This contest over trade, although worldwide in scope, had immediate consequences for New Netherland. The Dutch enclave irritated Englishmen for several reasons. Geographically, it broke the chain of English colonies and controlled the important Hudson River-Mohawk River route to the interior. Economically, it dominated a valuable fur trade, while English fur resources had dwindled

Peter Stuyvesant (1592-1672), Commissioner in Brazil, Governor of Curaçao, and Director-General of New Netherland from 1647 to 1664. Stuyvesant reluctantly surrendered the colony to the English in the second Anglo-Dutch War. (New York Historical Society)

greatly, and it supplied English colonies with European goods in violation of the Navigation Acts.

New England had its own grievances against the Dutch, especially over the Connecticut River Valley and the fur trade. However, little would have come of this had not the Duke of York, brother of the King, taken an intense interest in furthering English trade. As Lord High Admiral the Duke was aware of the merchant marine's importance as a nursery of sailors. In addition, he was involved in the Royal African Company, which sought to control the slave trade against stiff Dutch competition. Finally, he saw the possibility of personal profit in the acquisition of New Netherland, a settled area with an already developed trade.

When the Anglo-Dutch War erupted in 1664, events moved quickly for New Netherland. The Duke secured a charter, establishing New York as a proprietary colony, which received full approval in a record four days. The Crown entrusted him with greater power than any other proprietor, largely because he was heir apparent to the throne and his colony would eventually become royal when he succeeded as king. He thus posed no threat to imperial policy then developing. The grant extended from modern New York to the Delaware River, embracing Martha's Vineyard, Nantucket, and Maine (then claimed and controlled by Massachusetts).

In the fall of 1664, Richard Nicolls, commanding the Duke's forces, captured New Amsterdam (renamed New York City), Fort Orange (renamed Albany), and the Delaware River settlements. Conquest was easy because the Dutch were unprepared and unwilling to fight. Peter Stuyvesant, Director-General of New Netherland, stomped on his wooden leg around the ramparts of New Amsterdam's fort and talked stoutly of defense, but the town's merchants convinced him to surrender.

England, for the first time, controlled a colony with a large alien and cosmopolitan population. The Dutch had welcomed settlers from their own country and from Belgium, France, Ireland, Germany, and even England. The Duke, interested in profit from taxes and land sales, understood that inhabitants, a scarce commodity, made the colony valuable. To encourage those already settled there to remain, he instructed Nicolls to treat them "with all humanity and gentleness that can consist with the honor and safety of the government."

The Duke's hoped-for profits from New York never materialized, and instead the colony became a drain on his private purse. Bordering New France and containing an easy route to Canada through the Mohawk Valley, New York competed with the French for Indian support and furs. This required large outlays for Indian gifts and defense, but the colonists reluctantly complied with the Duke's financial requests and consistently opposed taxation without a representative legislature's approval. The Duke hesitated to give in, but finally authorized an assembly which met in 1683, held several sessions, and became extinct in 1686 when James became king. New York had become a Crown possession, and James II's imperial plans involved elimination of representative institutions and consolidation of New York into the Dominion of New England.

The Confusion of New Jersey

Within a few months after receiving his own charter in 1664, the Duke of York gave New Jersey to two close friends, Sir George Carteret and Lord John Berkeley, both involved in imperial expansion after 1660 into the Carolinas. Interested exclusively in profits from land speculation, they

William Penn (1614-1718), son of Admiral Sir William Penn and founder of Pennsylvania. Penn sought an absolute proprietary colony which would also be an experiment in the application of the Quaker ideal. An excellent publicist, he attracted immigrants from Wales, Ireland, Germany, and Holland. (By Sylvanus Bevan, Historical Society of Pennsylvania)

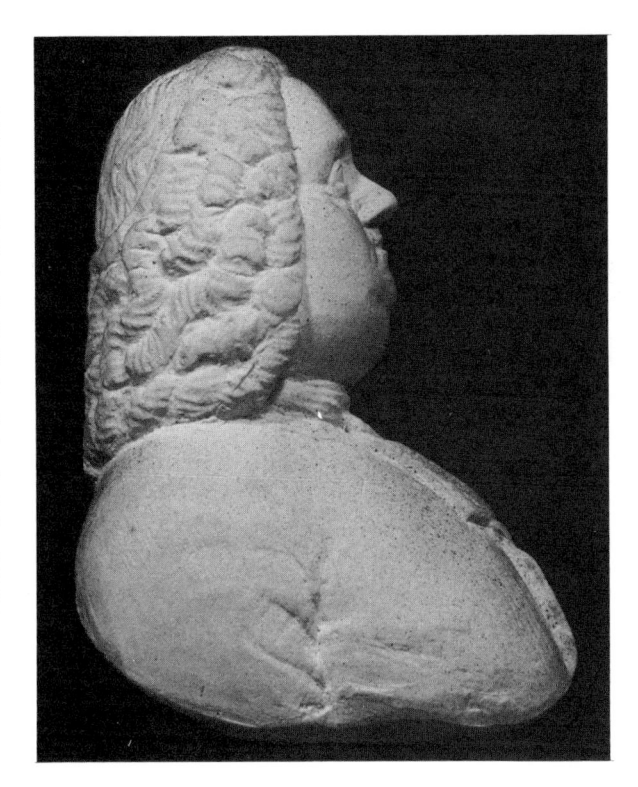

issued liberal terms to those already in New Jersey and encouraged newcomers. However, the Duke's governor in New York, unaware of the Berkeley-Carteret grant, simultaneously issued land patents in New Jersey, which resulted in conflicting land claims. Further confusion ensued when Berkeley and Carteret, finally realizing that the colony would not return immediate profits, sold their rights. Berkeley transferred his half-interest in 1674 to two Quakers whose share by 1692 was held by forty-eight men. Carteret died in 1680, and his share eventually went to twenty-four owners. New Jersey land titles consequently became a nightmare of complexity.

The colony's geographic location hampered its economic growth. New York City dominated East Jersey's trade, while Philadelphia controlled West Jersey's. The proprietors tried to develop Perth Amboy as a free port, but this encountered hostility from New York. Consequently, New Jersey remained an economic backwater during the colonial period. The

Philadelphia in 1702, showing the rapid growth of the "City of Brotherly Love," which had been but a dream of William Penn twenty years earlier. Note the Delaware River in foreground and the Schuylkill River perpendicular to it in the left center of the engraving. ("Portrait of Philadelphia in 1702," lithograph by F. J. Wade, courtesy of The Library of Congress)

colony's politics were just as confused. Berkeley and Carteret assumed, when the Duke granted them the land in 1664, that governmental power went with it. The Duke's failure to confirm or deny this led to continuing controversies with New York's governors. In 1702 the proprietors finally agreed among themselves long enough to resign political control to the Crown, and New York's governor became New Jersey's as well, thus ending one aspect of the colony's tribulations.

Penn's Holy Experiment

Although imperial authorities determined to end proprietary grants, they frequently ran afoul of influential courtiers, including William Penn, who sought such patents from the Crown. Penn had proved a great disappointment to his father, Admiral Sir William Penn, when he espoused Quakerism, but his father's career introduced the young man to powerful politicians, including the Duke of York. This, plus his own status in English society, gave young Penn, despite his religious peculiarity, sufficient influence to win a patent for Pennsylvania as an experimental religious colony.

Penn's charter made its way through the Lords of Trade and the Privy Council in 1680 with great difficulty. As Charles II's friend, Penn's request could not be denied, but it was sharply circumscribed. Imperial authorities placed strict limits on his powers: he could pass laws only with the freemen's consent in an assembly, he had to observe the Navigation Acts and keep an agent in London to answer violations, all laws must be either affirmed or disallowed by the Privy Council, the Crown retained an appellate jurisdiction over Pennsylvania courts, and Penn could not prevent establishment of the Church of England.

These restrictions reflected England's concern over control of the growing empire, but they did not interfere with Penn's plans. He immediately began planning his colony and sent surveyors to lay out a townsite at the junction of the Delaware and Schuylkill rivers, naming it Philadelphia, City of Brotherly Love. Penn sought the friendship of neighboring governors, Indians in his territory, and those Europeans already settled there. He made his major contribution, however, as a colonial promoter, and he published several tracts describing the colony's advantages, circulated them in Britain, and translated them for distribution in Germany. His ideas had great appeal among German pietist sects, and they migrated in great numbers to Pennsylvania, where they became known as the Pennsylvania Dutch.

Penn's basic interest, of course, was the Holy Experiment of Quakerism. He intended his colony not as a refuge, but as an opportunity to permit the application of Quakerism and its ideas — liberty of conscience, pacifism, and man's direct relationship with God — without restraint by an already organized society. His approach, utopian in one sense, paralleled Puritan efforts in New England, but differed in the nature of its ideas and the structure of its society. Another of Penn's interests was the vast profit potential of his estate, for he, like other proprietors, speculated in land on a grand scale. He expected an income from quitrents and fees, but his real profit would come from retained lands whose value would rise as population increased. However, Penn was a bad businessman, and his colony cost him far more than he received in revenues — over £24,000 by 1703.

Penn found it difficult to govern his colony. His powers as proprietor, however circumscribed, were still great and did not jibe with ideas developing in England. He had great difficulty retaining his proprietary authority and found himself defending the grant in London rather than supervising the colony in America. His governors constantly gave in to assembly pressures, especially when bludgeoned by threats to tax proprietary lands, which would have imposed an impossible financial obligation on Penn. By 1701, the assembly won the war, for even the governor's council lost its legislative and judicial functions, becoming only an advisory body. One of Penn's governors, a Puritan named John Blackwell, commented upon leaving office that a Philadelphia Quaker "prays for his neighbor on First Days and then preys upon him for the other six."

Spillover Into the Carolinas

Just as England extended its northern colonies, so it pushed southward from Virginia. Beginning in the 1650s, an unorganized but continuing spillover of population from Virginia began the settlement of the Carolinas. Frequently these people kept one step ahead of the sheriff, a fact Virginia recognized in 1656 when it passed a law to prevent men from heading south and leaving their debts behind.

The Carolinas interested those men already experienced in colonial affairs. Governor Sir William Berkeley understood its strategic importance as a buffer to protect Virginia. John Colleton, an influential Barbados planter, saw an opportunity for Barbadians dispossessed as the island's economy shifted from small tobacco farms to large-scale sugar plantations. Anthony Cooper, Earl of Shaftsbury, realized the speculative possibility of a rich land already partly populated and an available group of prospective seasoned colonists. To guarantee receipt of a proprietary grant, they added to their group some important leaders of English political and social life: the Duke of Albemarle, the Earl of Clarendon, Lord John Berkeley, Sir George Carteret, Lord William Craven, the Duke of York, and Prince Rupert. These men dominated British politics following the Stuart restoration and easily won for themselves in 1663 a charter which included the Bishop of Durham clause, similar to the earlier Calvert grant.

The Carolina proprietors expected immediate profits from land speculation, utilizing Virginians already in the colony and Barbadians interested in settling there. They established a headright system, allowing each colonist 150 acres, and they granted full religious freedom in an effort to attract still more settlers. They also tried to recreate feudalism by establishing a landed nobility, creating titles of landgrave and cacique, and setting up a Palatine Court composed of the proprietors to govern the colony. Within Carolina, government would be in the hands of an elected assembly and an appointed grand council of landed nobles.

Carolina developed slowly at first. When control of the proprietary group passed to Shaftesbury, he began an intensive promotional campaign and effectively supplied the colony. By the 1680s there were about twelve hundred settlers. Barbadians introduced Negro slavery into the colony, and this became the basic labor force. Carolina's initial products, like those of most colonies in their beginnings, were hogs, cattle, and grain, but rice soon developed as a staple crop, and indigo was introduced in the mid-eighteenth century. In 1712, the Carolinas split into two colonies after a disastrous war with the Tuscarora Indians, and in 1729 both North and South Carolina passed into royal control.

Strains Within the Empire

The British Empire's rapid growth exposed serious internal problems. There was little sense of direction, with much expansion simply the result of individual initiative or desire. Moreover, London exerted little real control. Mercantilism defined the economic relationships of the empire, but it had never been spelled out and remained a hodgepodge of parliamentary statutes, Privy Council directives, and Lords of Trade recommendations. Moreover, no definition existed of political relationships, and not until James II's reign did a unified political approach to empire emerge. This would be the uniting in 1686 of the colonies of New England into the Dominion of New England, an ill-fated attempt at colonial reorganization.

Even before James II began his imperial experiment, Virginia illustrated both the strains of growth and England's growing awareness of empire. Social and political instability appeared first in Virginia because it was the oldest colony and had the most mature social, economic, and political system. These "growing pains" soon became part of a general pattern. The complex story of Bacon's Rebellion of 1676 involved Indian difficulties, fur trade, grievances over declining tobacco prices and rising taxes, an aging governor's obstinacy, and England's failure to take an interest in Virginia's internal development. Social tensions and economic difficulties created an incendiary situation and Indian troubles ignited it.

NATHANIEL BACON'S MANIFESTO, 1676

WE APPEAL TO THE COUNTRY itself . . . by what cabal and mystery the designs of many of those whom we call great men have been transacted and carried on; but let us trace these men in authority and favour to whose hands the dispensation of the country's wealth has been committed. Let us observe the sudden rise of their estates compared with the quality in which they first entered this country, or the reputation they have held here amongst wise and discerning men. And let us see whether their extractions and education have not been vile. . . . Let us consider their sudden advancement and let us also consider whether any public work for our safety and defence or for the advancement and propagation of trade, liberal arts, or sciences is here extant in any way adequate to our vast charge. Now let us compare these things together and see what sponges have sucked up the public treasure, and whether it has not been privately contrived away by unworthy favourites and juggling parasites whose tottering fortunes have been repaired and supported at the public charge. Now if it be so, judge what greater guilt can be than to offer to pry into these and to unriddle the mysterious wiles of a powerful cabal; let all people judge what can be of more dangerous import than to suspect the so long safe proceedings of some of our grandees, and whether people may with safety open their eyes in so nice a concern.

Another main article of our guilt is our open and manifest aversion to all, not only the foreign but the protected and darling Indians. This, we are informed, is rebellion of a deep dye for that both the governor and council are . . . bound to defend . . . the Appamatocks with their blood. Now, whereas we do declare and can prove that they have been for these many years enemies to the king and country, robbers and thieves and invaders of his Majesty's right and our interest and estates, but yet have by persons in authority been defended and protected even against his Majesty's loyal subjects. . . . Their firearms so destructful to us and by our laws prohibited, commanded to be restored them, and open declaration before witness made that they must have ammunition, although directly contrary to our law. Now what greater guilt can be than to oppose and endeavour the destruction of these honest, quiet neighbours of ours?

Another main article of our guilt is our design not only to ruin and extirpate all Indians in general, but all manner of trade and commerce with them. Judge who can be innocent that strike at this tender eye of interest: since the right honourable the governor hath been pleased by his commission to warrant this trade, who dare oppose it, or opposing it can be innocent? Although plantations be deserted, the blood of our dear brethren spilled; on all sides our complaints; continually murder upon murder renewed upon us; who may or dare think of the general subversion of all manner of trade and commerce with our enemies who can or dare impeach any of . . . traders at the heads of the rivers. . . . Who dare say that these men at the heads of the rivers buy and sell our blood, and do still, notwithstanding the late act made to the contrary, admit Indians painted and continue to commerce; although these things can be proved, yet who dare be so guilty as to do it?

Another article of our guilt is to assert all those neighbour Indians as well as others, to be outlawed, wholly unqualified for the benefit and protection of the law, for that the law does reciprocally protect and punish, and that all people offending must either in person or estate make equivalent satisfaction or restitution, according to the manner and merit of the offences, debts, or trespasses. Now since the Indians cannot, according to the tenure and form of any law to us known, be prosecuted, seized or complained against, their persons being with difficulty distinguished or known; their many nations' languages, and their subterfuges such as makes them incapable to make us restitution or satisfaction, would it not be very guilty to say they have been unjustly defended and protected these many years?

If it should be said that the very foundation of all these disasters, the grant of the beaver trade to the right honourable governor was illegal, and not grantable by any power here present as being a monopoly, were not this to deserve the name of rebel and traitor?

Judge, therefore, all wise and unprejudiced men who may or can faithfully or truly with an honest heart, attempt the country's good, their vindication, and liberty without the aspersion of traitor and rebel, since as so doing they must of necessity gall such tender and dear concerns. But to manifest sincerity and loyalty to the world, and how much we abhor those bitter names; may all the world know that we do unanimously desire to represent our sad and heavy grievances to his most sacred Majesty as our refuge and sanctuary, where we do well know that all our causes will be impartially heard and equal justice administered to all men. (From: The Virginia Magazine of History and Biography, I *[1894], pp. 55-61)*

☆☆☆☆☆☆☆☆☆☆☆☆☆☆☆☆☆☆☆☆☆☆☆☆☆☆☆☆☆☆

The colony needed a basic change of policy, but the governor remained obdurate. The frontiersmen wanted to attack, operating on the premise that the only good Indian was a dead one, while Governor Berkeley and his council, fearful of disrupting the fur trade, preferred to rely on fortifications at the heads of navigation of the rivers.

Economic considerations complicated Virginia's frontier problem. Tobacco prices declined, taxes rose, and Berkeley's fort-building program cost too much. Rumors of corruption in constructing and supplying the forts caused great discontent, especially since the basic tax was a poll, or tax per head, and the law exempted the governor's councillors from paying on the first ten polls in their households. This meant that any increase would hurt the small farmers most and leave the wealthy councillors virtually untouched.

Young Nathaniel Bacon, who headed the uprising, had been in the colony only two years. He was related to Nathaniel Bacon, Sr., eldest member of the council, to Berkeley's wife, and to the famous philosopher Sir Francis Bacon. He had been sent to Virginia by his father because his activities in England, matrimonial as well as legal, had blackened his reputation. However, upon his arrival in the colony he was well received, secured a large tract of land at the head of the James River, and obtained a seat on the Governor's Council.

Bacon and others on the James River found themselves harassed by Indians and they wanted reprisals. When Berkeley, old and irascible, refused their demand, Bacon attacked the Indians without the governor's sanction. Berkeley declared him a rebel and tried to undermine his support by calling a new assembly, but Bacon was elected a burgess. The two men finally came to terms: Bacon confessed his error and resumed his council seat; Berkeley promised him a commission against the Indians. At that point, popular acclaim went to Bacon's head. He returned home, found himself surrounded by well-wishers, and now demanded his commission. The governor acquiesced; then he declared him a rebel. Bacon gathered a military force and marched on the capital, Jamestown, thus becoming a rebel in fact, but the movement collapsed when its leader died of a fever.

However, the rebellion's real significance lay in England's sudden interest in regulating Virginia's affairs. Upon learning of the uprising, England dispatched 1,100 troops together with a commission to investigate matters and set them right. This investigatory body, and the changes

GOVERNOR BERKELEY'S APOLOGIA, 1676

NOW, MY FRIENDS, I have lived 34 yeares amongst you, as uncorrupt and diligent as ever Governor was, Bacon is a man of two years amongst you, his person and qualities unknowne to most of you and to all men else, by any vertuous action that ever I heard of, And that very action which he boasts of, was sickly and fooleishly, and as I am informed treacherously carried to the dishonour of the English Nation yett in itt, he lost more men, than I did in three years Warr, and by the grace of God will putt myselfe to the same dangers and troubles againe when I have brought Bacon to acknowledge the Laws are above him, and I doubt not but, By God's assistance, to have better success than Bacon hath had, the reason of my hopes are, that I will take Councell of wiser men than myself, but Mr. Bacon hath none about him, but the lowest of the people. (From Edward D. Neill, Virginia Carolorum *[Albany: J. Munsell's Sons, 1886], pp. 356-357)*

☆☆☆☆☆☆☆☆☆☆☆☆☆☆☆☆☆☆☆☆☆☆☆☆☆☆☆☆☆☆

it introduced, threatened Virginia's self-government and challenged its political maturity. Berkeley's recall to answer charges of having illegally oppressed rebel leaders cleared the decks of old divisions and united Virginians against the external power represented by this commission. Within the colony, a new unity emerged, forged not by Bacon, nor by Berkeley, but by the imperial authorities.

The same instability in colonial society which led to Bacon's Rebellion also gave rise to upheavals in Massachusetts, New York, and Maryland in 1689. In each colony local problems and English politics combined to create different situations, but in each the response was remarkably similar. Involved in all was James II's vigorous imperial policy which tried to tighten control of the colonies and intensified hostilities toward France and its Indian allies. James II's avowed Catholicism evoked in Englishmen and colonials fears of popery and memories of "Bloody Queen Mary," and restored a sense of English nationalism, a pride in their English identity.

Massachusetts society had lost its initial stability because it had suffered great changes. The colony had expanded into frontier areas, had developed urban centers, and had embarked on worldwide trade. No longer oriented exclusively toward God, the Bay Colony had tasted new ideas, faced new issues, and abandoned some of its old ways. Ministers still tried to rekindle the old enthusiasm. Thomas Hooker warned: "No carrion in a ditch smells more loathsomely in the nostrils of man, than a natural man's works do in the nostrils of the Almighty." And Thomas Shepherd grimly denounced the mind of natural man as "a nest of all the foul opinions and heresies that ever were invented, and his heart a foul sink of all atheism, sodomy, blasphemy, murder, whoredom, adultery, witchcraft, and buggery."

To old-time Puritans, God seemed to have abandoned His "City On a Hill," and the ministers floundered in search of the reason. But they represented the past, and their ideas seemed irrelevant to the community's new problems. Moreover, the greatest problem of all arose in 1684 when the Crown legally forfeited the colony's charter because its limits had been violated, and Massachusetts became a part of the Dominion of New England. This truly seemed to be God's wrath, for an appointed governor and council now ruled without an assembly. Although the governor was a local man, Joseph Dudley, and he sought moderation, the ministers bitterly complained that the Devil had triumphed.

The arrival in December 1686 of the new Governor-General, Sir Edmund Andros, confirmed the Bay Colony's fate, swallowed in a conglomerate Dominion of New England along with Plymouth, Rhode Island, and Connecticut. By 1688, the Crown added New York and New Jersey. The advantages of this consolidation — better quality officials, uniform laws and taxes, simplified administration, and coherent defense policies — did not outweigh its inherent difficulties. Poor communications throughout a widespread territory, obstacles presented by strong local loyalties, and hostilities created by abolition of representative government would prove serious stumbling blocks for the new government.

Sir Edmund Andros, the new Governor-General, possessed one weakness which epitomized the new government's failings. He had broad authority, including the right to dismiss any councillor, act with a small quorum of councillors, and reorganize local government, but he lacked the political astuteness that must always accompany great power. He immediately clashed with New Englanders over the delicate issue of property rights. Massachusetts, a corporation, had created new corporations, towns, and granted lands to these new towns which they in turn gave to individuals. However, one corporation could not legally create another, and this invalidated all Bay Colony land titles. Andros offered

THE NEW ENGLAND PRIMER, c. 1687

In Adam's *fall*
We sinned all.

Thy life to mend
This Book *attend.*

The Cat *doth play*
And after slay.

A Dog *will bite*
The thief at night.

An Eagle's *flight*
Is out of sight.

The idle Fool
Is whipped at school.

As runs the Glass,
Man's life doth pass.

My Book *and* Heart
Shall never part.

Job *feels the rod,*
Yet blesses GOD.

Our KING *the good,*
no man of blood.

The Lion *bold*
The Lamb *doth hold.*

The Moon *gives light*
In time of night.

Nightingales *sing*
In time of spring.

The Royal Oak *it was the tree*
That saved His Royal Majesty.

Peter *denies*
His Lord and cries.

Queen *Esther comes in royal state*
To save the JEWS from dismal fate.

Rachel *doth mourn*
For her first born.

Samuel *anoints*
Whom God appoints.

Time *cuts down all*
Both great and small.

Uriah's *beautous wife*
Made David seek his life.

Whales *in the sea*
God's voice obey.

Xerxes *the great did die,*
And so must you and I.

Youth *forward slips,*
Death soonest nips.

Zacheus *he*
Did climb the tree
His Lord to see.

(From: Paul L. Ford, ed., **The New England Primer** *[New York: Dodd Mead and Co., 1897])*

to legalize land titles for quitrents of two shillings and six pence per hundred acres, a modest amount. However, New Englanders had owned land in fee simple without quitrents, and they looked upon his offer as outright extortion. Connecticut had shrewdly avoided this legal flaw by confirming each person's land title prior to surrendering governmental power to the Crown.

Andros's other policies also stirred opposition. The king instructed him to permit, if not encourage, the Church of England. However, Puritans refused to open their church doors for such idolatrous meetings, and Andros finally forced entry into the South Meeting House, which thereafter held two services on Sundays, but under sharp protest. The king also ordered the Governor-General to levy taxes in consultation with his council, although he himself appreciated the value of a legislature. Since his royal master had so ordered, Andros and the council levied a tax in 1687. The Reverend John Wise of Ipswich opposed it as an invasion of English liberties, and he and his associates were tried, convicted, and fined for their efforts.

Expansion of the Dominion to include New York and New Jersey in 1688 compounded its problems. In addition to local matters, it now had to contend with the French and to deal with the Iroquois Indians. This required greater funds for defense and Indian presents, as well as the Governor-General's personal attention. The threads of communications were being pulled dangerously thin. As Indian raids flared along the New England border and Franco-Iroquois hostilities developed in northern New York, sensitive Protestants heard rumors of Catholic plots to subvert the English colonies, and the Dominion's whole fabric came apart. Andros's enemies used these alarms to good advantage, but their best weapon was the news, received from England in April 1689, that James II had been overthrown by the "Glorious Revolution," a bloodless coup. Armed crowds in Boston captured Andros and several other officials, took over the town, denounced Andros's government, and announced their allegiance to the new monarchs, the Protestant Stadtholder of The Netherlands, William of Orange, and his wife Mary, daughter of James II. Andros's arrest shattered the Dominion.

The Massachusetts leaders wanted restoration of their old charter with all its privileges, including election of the governor and council, reinstitution of the assembly, confirmation of land titles without quitrents, and utilization of a religious test for voting and officeholding. In the interim, they formed a council of safety, called a convention, and then resumed operations under the old charter. Simultaneously, Plymouth, Rhode Island, and Connecticut took advantage of the vacuum created by the Bay Colony and simply resumed their old governments as though the Dominion had never existed.

Massachusetts sent the Reverend Increase Mather to England to press for restoration of the old charter, but he had only partial success. The colony secured a new charter, but not a restoration of the old ways. The Crown now appointed the governor, and property qualifications replaced the religious test for voting and officeholding. In one blow the Crown destroyed both the colony's original purpose as envisaged by Winthrop and any hope of ever attaining it. The Charter of 1691 proved even more traumatic than the Dominion, for it introduced the possibility of democratization in Massachusetts on an economic basis, destroying any lingering theocratic tendencies in the colony.

New York also reacted violently to news of the Glorious Revolution in England, but for its own reasons. That colony's rapid transition from a Dutch outpost to an English proprietary colony, to a royal colony, and then to a part of the autocratic Dominion had created political tensions. Besides this pattern of uncertainty, economic discontent developed as trade declined, governmental expenses increased because of intensifying rivalry with the French, and the Duke insisted on increasing his revenues. The Dominion also caused tensions as it stabilized the social and political structure and precluded any mobility. Thus, news of James II's overthrow found fertile ground, and when those in power proved too timid to embrace the new monarchs unhesitatingly, Andros's opponents seized their opportunity. New York's discontented declared for William and Mary and destroyed the Dominion's power, completing the collapse of Stuart efforts to reorganize and unify the empire.

Jacob Leisler, a well-to-do merchant whose rise to power had been blocked by the Dominion, replaced Andros's government in New York. Within the colony, those who benefited from the Andros government now opposed Leisler, but most people supported him because they feared a French-Catholic-Indian plot against New York. Leisler took control of the fort, and a committee of safety appointed him commander-in-chief. He proposed to hold the colony for William and Mary and to frustrate their enemies, though he sometimes confused the Crown's enemies with his own.

When a letter from the Privy Council reached Leisler, he assumed, because of its address, that imperial authorities accepted him as Lieutenant Governor. He then called together a council, had an assembly elected, levied taxes, and initiated an inter-colonial expedition against Canada. Failure of the Canadian attack marked the beginning of Leisler's collapse. When the new governor arrived in 1691, Leisler's enemies wreaked their vengeance. Leisler was tried for treason and murder along with his colleagues, and he and his son-in-law were executed. This set the pattern for New York politics for the next two decades as pro- and anti-Leisler factions battled each other under a succession of incompetent governors. Only the arrival in 1710 of a capable and shrewd politician, Governor Robert Hunter, stabilized the situation.

Further south, in Maryland, the Glorious Revolution also unleashed a violent reaction. Although local circumstances differed from those in Massachusetts or New York, the pattern was similar. Maryland had previously suffered uprisings because Baltimore's charter gave the proprietor extraordinary authority which was out of step with the times. Excessive vetoes, nepotism, favoritism in granting lands and offices, partiality to the Roman Catholic minority, and the same sort of economic grievances found in Virginia and New York all aroused discontent in Maryland. Here, too, frustrated ambitions determined the nature and character of the upheaval once news arrived of William and Mary's accession to the throne.

Maryland's rebellion began with a French-Catholic-Indian scare. The proprietary government proved incapable of decisive action against the Indians and also hesitated to acknowledge the new monarchs. Discontented Marylanders, under John Coode's leadership, moved in July 1689 against the government, proclaimed the new sovereigns, and called a convention to legitimize their actions. They set up a provisional government, and Coode and an associate went to London to seek royal sanction for their actions. Coode's Rebellion received Crown approval when the English Attorney General moved against the Calvert charter. Political authority in the colony was transferred to the Crown, with the Calverts retaining possession of the land. Royal officials, a new ingredient in Maryland politics, complicated matters, particularly in the race for office, power, and money. In 1715 proprietary political authority was restored in Maryland when Charles Calvert, fifth Lord Baltimore and a Protestant convert, inherited the province.

Stability of Imperial Forms

The nature of England's eighteenth-century empire was shaped by these tremors which rocked colony after colony. England abandoned the Dominion approach and henceforth treated colonies as individual units. Occasionally two might have the same governor, or the governor of one might be given authority over a neighboring province's militia, but never again were colonies consolidated. The Glorious Revolution also idealized a standard set of governmental forms for all colonies; each should have a royally appointed governor and council and an elective assembly. The ideal was never fully applied, however, for the General Court of Massachusetts nominated councillors subject to the governor's approval, and Connecticut and Rhode Island directly elected councillors and governors. However, each colony possessed an elected assembly, and this led to the idea that representative government was a basic right of all Englishmen.

None of this signalled a change in British imperial policy or its purposes. Prerogative power in the colonies was increasing. Indeed, the Glorious Revolution undermined royal authority in England but simultaneously enhanced it in the colonies. Policy decisions fell more and more into the hands of royal governors, the Board of Trade (a royal agency created in 1696 to replace the Lords of Trade), and the Privy Council. However, the colonists increasingly identified themselves with Parliament rather than the Crown, and local legislative power expanded in much the same way and at much the same pace as had that of the House of Commons. Thus, an important dichotomy developed.

Increasing English concern over colonial affairs after 1689 did not lead to creation of new agencies for these problems. Rather, imperial administration remained an integral part of domestic English politics, and existing officials simply received added duties. This led to a confusion which was furthered by a bifurcation in the whole system: the cabinet emerged from and supplanted the Privy Council in English affairs, but the latter remained all-powerful in colonial government. The Privy Council, for example, lost its role as a court of last resort in England, but retained that function for the colonies. It lost its authority to recommend vetoes of parliamentary statutes when Queen Anne in 1707 became the last monarch to exercise that right, but continued to make such recommendations for colonies. Moreover, the Council lost its power over general administration to the cabinet (which controlled parliamentary majorities), but kept this power over the empire.

Colonial policy decisions rested in a number of officials, each with varying degrees of interest in and authority over colonial matters. The Privy Council stood at the head of the list, but also involved were the Secretary of State for the Southern Department, whose primary concern was Mediterranean foreign policy; the Board of Trade, which made recommendations to other agencies, and which became increasingly powerful through its detailed understanding of colonial affairs; the Treasury Board and its subordinate Customs Board which supervised revenues raised under British statutes; the Admiralty which protected colonial shipping in wartime and also enforced navigation and trade laws; and the War Office which dealt with the armies, their control, supply, and pay.

Beyond these formal agencies there existed something else which played an even more important role in formulating policy, something never described in any table of organization — the role of influence. The outcome of critical issues, more often than not, was determined in the eighteenth century by the political influence possessed by the parties in contention. Logic and justice did not always prevail in English decision-making, for the interest or influence of prominent personages often carried greater weight. This served to make the already complex system of the British Empire almost unfathomable, particularly to colonials some three thousand miles distant from the seat of empire.

SELECTED BIBLIOGRAPHY

The basic guide, largely political in orientation, is Wesley Frank Craven's *The Colonies in Transition, 1660-1713* (1968).

Indian relations, which played a key role in this century of warfare, can be studied in Douglas Leach's *Flintlock and Tomahawk: New England in King Philip's War* (1966), and in his *The Northern Colonial Frontier, 1607-1763* (1966). A most important study is Verner W. Crane's *The Southern Frontier, 1670-1732* (1928).

Two studies of key figures in the development of imperial policy are Michael G. Hall's *Edward Randolph* (1961), a man who became the eyes and ears of the Board of Trade, and Gertrude Ann Jacobsen's *William Blathwayt* (1932), an official who helped set Board of Trade policy. The critical point in developing imperial policy is documented in *The Glorious*

Revolution in America (1964), edited by Michael G. Hall, Lawrence H. Leder, and Michael Kammen.

The urban dimension of colonial life is discussed fully in Carl Bridenbaugh's *Cities in the Wilderness* (1954).

Biographical studies often provide an important insight into colonial development. Among the more important ones are Lawrence H. Leder's *Robert Livingston, 1654-1728, and the Politics of Colonial New York* (1961) which describes the founding of an important family. Pennsylvania's founder is treated admirably in Catherine O. Peare's *William Penn* (1957).

The nature of colonial politics can be examined from a variety of viewpoints. Wilcomb Washburn's *The Governor and the Rebel* (1957) says some important things about the nature of Virginia politics in the 1670s. Richard L. Morton's two-volume *Colonial Virginia* (1960) provides a broader perspective in time. Viola F. Barnes's *The Dominion of New England* (1923), G. M. Waller's *Samuel Vetch* (1960), and Bernard Bailyn's *The New England Merchants in the Seventeenth Century* (1955) provide different dimensions of the colonial scene.

CHAPTER 4

THE AMERICANIZATION OF THE EMPIRE, 1705-1763

England's empire in the eighteenth century bore increasingly little resemblance to the goals of those who first established it. Two significant changes occurred: quantitatively, the number of colonies expanded as did their population; qualitatively, the source of immigrants to the New World changed, and those settled in the colonies became something different than they had originally been. Transplanted Englishmen and Europeans gradually became Americans. Institutions, thought processes, lifestyles, and goals began to diverge from those of Englishmen and, although the subtlety of the process escaped many while it happened, its reality became apparent after 1763.

Physical expansion of the mainland colonies had begun earlier, with the Carolinas as a buffer between Virginia and Spanish Florida, and later,

COLONIAL SETTLEMENT, 1700

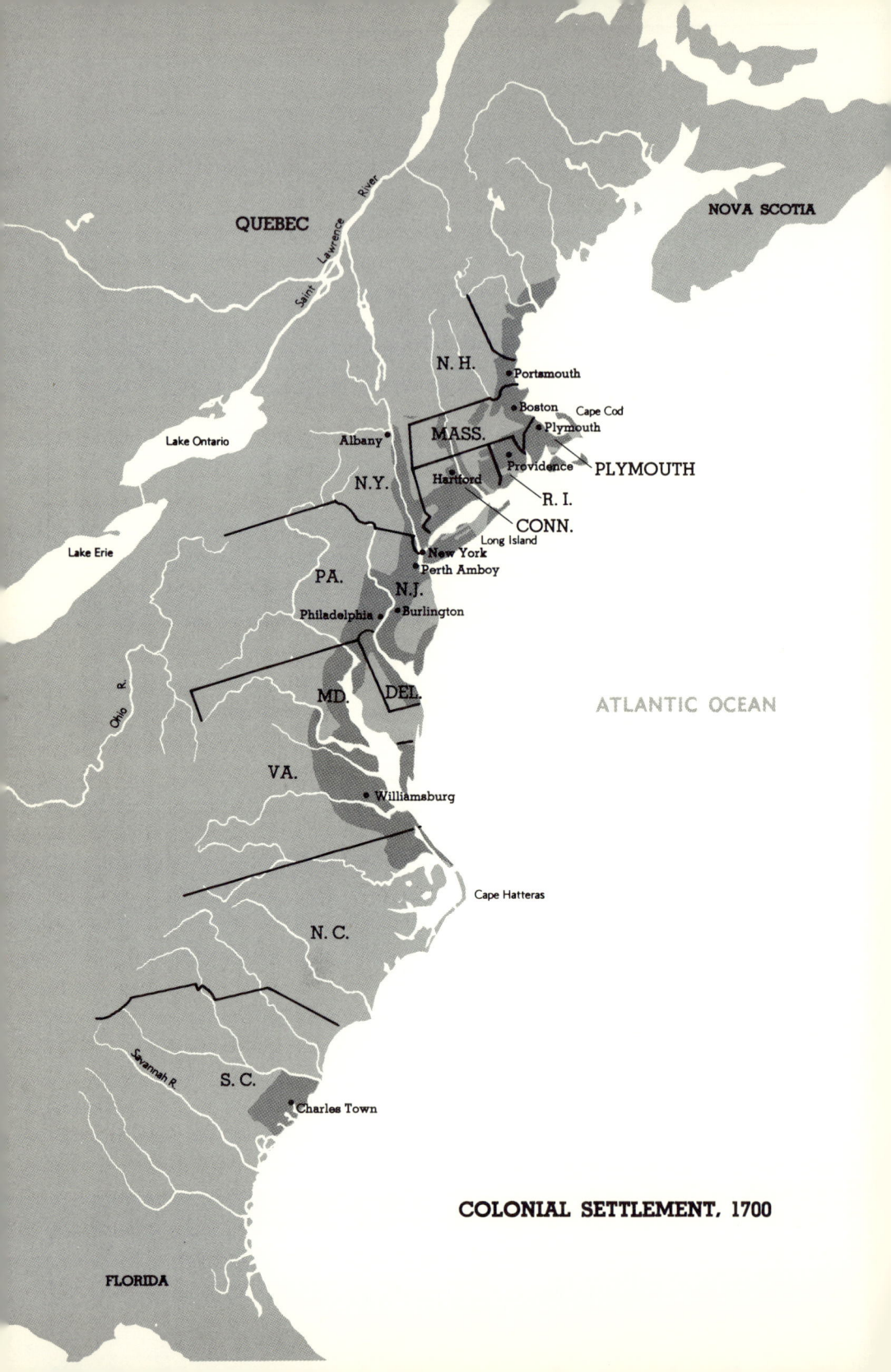

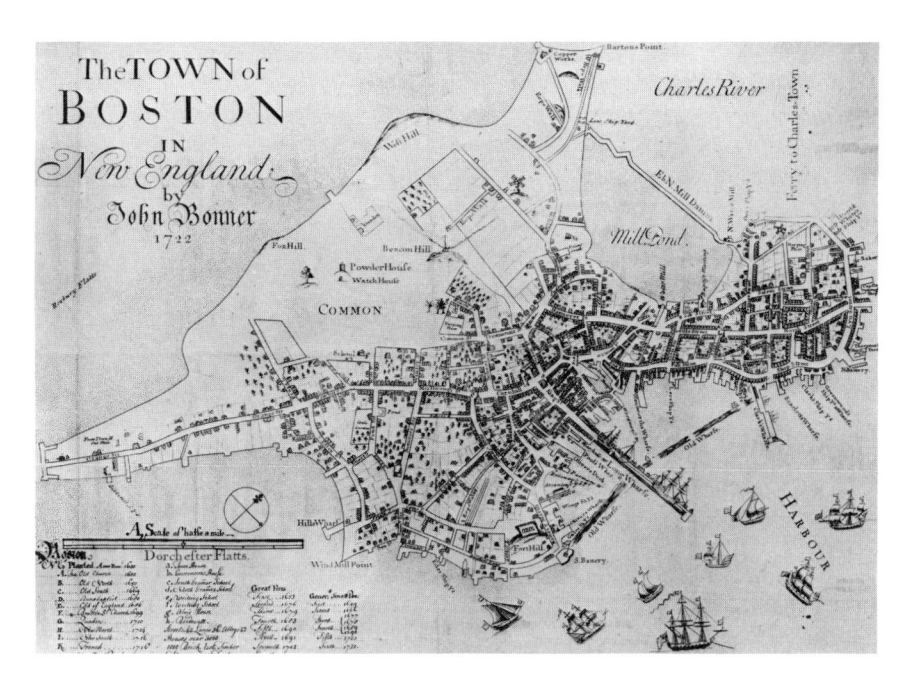

Boston in 1722. In many ways a typical colonial town, Boston survived on commerce, as evidenced by the numerous wharves along the shoreline. ("Town of Boston in New England," by John Bonner, 1722. I. N. Phelps Stokes Collection, Prints Division, The New York Public Library, Astor, Lenox and Tilden Foundations)

once the Carolinas became valuable, with Georgia as a buffer. The English also took over the Dutch colony of New Netherland, and then completed their chain of colonies by settling New Jersey, Pennsylvania, and Delaware. Still another, less dramatic form of expansion occurred as the established colonies pushed westward, settling territory that had been virgin wilderness and the domain of the Indians.

New Ethnic Streams

Near the close of the seventeenth century, America had fulfilled Sir Walter Raleigh's earlier prediction by becoming a collection of little Englands. Most settlers had come from the mother country, with only a scattering of other nationalities, such as the Dutch and Swedes in the middle colonies. However, after 1680, the main stream of immigrants shifted, and great numbers began arriving from Germany, Ireland, Scotland, France, Switzerland, and especially Africa. In 1780 foreign-born inhabitants (i.e., those not born in England or the colonies) comprised one out of every three colonists. In 1921, when America first limited large-scale immigration, the foreign-born represented only one out of every six inhabitants. More significant than the ratio itself was the dimension of the increase, for the colonial population jumped from 250,000 in 1690 to 2.8 million in 1780, including 575,000 slaves.

Religious persecution loomed large in motivating migration to America. In Germany, Catholic princes oppressed pietistic sects, and compulsory military service violated pietistic religious beliefs. Moreover, western Germany became a battlefield during the Thirty Years War, Louis XIV's campaigns against the Dutch, the War of the League of Augsburg, and the War of Spanish Succession. In France, Louis XIV revoked the Edict of Nantes in 1685, thereby destroying the Huguenots' political security. This Calvinistic group, important economically, could not legally leave France, but many escaped to Holland, Germany, Denmark, and England, often taking their wealth with them, and later found their way to America.

Two important new streams of migrants came from the British Isles in the eighteenth century. The Scotch-Irish had first become colonists when they migrated to Northern Ireland after Cromwell pacified it in the seventeenth century. There they competed with the English, first in cattle and dairy products, and then in wool and cloth manufacturing, leading Parliament to restrict Scotch-Irish economic activity severely. The ensuing economic decline caused a large-scale migration beginning early in the eighteenth century. Not to be confused with the Scotch-Irish were Highland Scots, who came to America for different political and economic reasons. They had never abandoned their Stuart loyalty, and in 1715 and 1745 they participated in abortive uprisings against the Hanoverians, only to be harshly repressed and often deported to the colonies. Other Highlanders left Scotland because of economic distress as landlords enclosed farmland for sheep grazing.

Perhaps the single largest source of immigrants, frequently overlooked in such descriptions, was Africa. The eighteenth century was the heyday of the slave trade, and its flow shifted from Caribbean islands to English mainland colonies. The Royal African Company, headed by the Duke of York, became in the late seventeenth century the dominant slave trading operation, selling over 2,000 slaves a year in Jamaica alone. Parliament broke its monopoly in 1697 and opened the trade to all Englishmen. Loss

A VIRGINIAN EXPLAINS SLAVERY, 1757

LIKE ADAM we are all apt to shift off the blame from ourselves and lay it upon others, how justly in our case you may judge. The Negroes are enslaved by the Negroes themselves before they are purchased by the masters of the ships who bring them here. It is to be sure at our choice whether we buy them or not, so this then is our crime, folly, or whatever you will please to call it. But, our Assembly, foreseeing the ill consequences of importing such numbers amongst us, hath often attempted to lay a duty upon them which would amount to a prohibition, such as ten or twenty pounds a head, but no governor dare pass such a law, having instructions to the contrary from the Board of Trade at home. By this means they are forced upon us whether we will or will not. This plainly shows the African Company hath the advantage of the colonies, and may do as it pleases with the ministry. Indeed, since we have been exhausted of our little stock of cash by the war, the importation has stopped, our poverty then is our best security. . . .

This is our part of the grievance, but to live in Virginia without slaves is morally impossible. Before our troubles, you could not hire a servant or slave for love or money, so that unless robust enough to cut wood, to go to mill, to work at the hoe, etc., you must starve, or board in some family where they both fleece and half starve you. There is no set price upon corn, wheat and provisions, so they take advantage of the necessities of strangers, who are thus obliged to purchase some slaves and land. This of course draws us all into the original sin and curse of the country of purchasing slaves, and this is the reason we have no merchants, traders, or artificers of any sort but what become planters in a short time. (From A. Maury, ed., Memoirs of a Huguenot Family *[New York: George P. Putnam, 1853], pp. 351-352)*

☆☆☆☆☆☆☆☆☆☆☆☆☆☆☆☆☆☆☆☆☆☆☆☆☆☆☆☆☆☆☆

of central control resulted in even worse conditions for the Africans being transported, and the horrors of the slave ships cannot be imagined. By mid-eighteenth century, an estimated 70,000 slaves were taken from Africa each year; more blacks than whites sailed across the Atlantic. Not all Africans ended up in the English mainland colonies — one estimate was that less than 10 per cent did so — but by the 1760s some 300,000 blacks lived south of Pennsylvania and another 90,000 lived in the northern colonies.

Slave ship. This late eighteenth-century sketch indicates the tightly-packed conditions on slave ships throughout the period. New England vessels were among the most notorious that plied this trade between the Guinea Coast of Africa, the West Indies, and the mainland colonies. (From the collections of The Library Company of Philadelphia)

Importation of large numbers of slaves caused some concern about controlling an ungovernable and alien population under frontier conditions. Nonetheless, black slaves solved the labor shortage even though the white colonists had to pay heavily for the system. Mixing of races and slave conspiracies exacerbated the problem of social stability. Uprisings occurred in Virginia in 1687, New York in 1712 and 1741, and South Carolina in 1720 and 1739. In response to these uprisings, colonial assemblies enacted slave codes which restricted black activity. Although the codes varied in severity from colony to colony, even minor offenses frequently called forth harsh penalties.

Conversion of blacks to Christianity raised complex problems for colonists. Some argued that conversion automatically ended their servitude, for a Christian could not be a slave. Others reacted differently, and colony after colony legislated against any change in status resulting from conversion. The dichotomy of accepting the black as a person with a

QUAKERS OPPOSE SLAVERY, 1688

THESE ARE THE REASONS why we are against the traffic of mens-body as follows . . . Now, though they are black, we cannot conceive there is more liberty to have them slaves as it is to have other white ones. There is a saying that we shall do to all men like as we will be done ourselves; making no difference of what generation, descent or colour they are. And those who steal or rob men, and those who buy or purchase them, are they not all alike? Here is liberty of conscience, which is right and reasonable; here ought to be likewise liberty of the body, except of evil-doers, which is another case. But to bring men hither, or to rob and sell them against their will, we stand against. In Europe there are many oppressed for conscience sake; and here there are those oppressed which are of a black colour. . . . Therefore, we contradict, and are against this traffic of mens-body. And we who profess that it is not lawful to steal, must, likewise, avoid to purchase such things as are stolen, but rather help to stop this robbing and stealing, if possible. And such men ought to be delivered out of the hands of the robbers and set free. . . .

If once these slaves (which they say are so wicked and stubborn men), should join themselves — fight for their freedom, and handle their master and mistresses as they did handle them before; will these masters and mistresses take the sword at hand and war against these poor slaves, like we are able to believe, some will not refuse to do? Or, have these Negroes not as much right to fight for their freedom as you have to keep them slaves? *(From* Pennsylvania Magazine of History and Biography, *IV [1880], 28-30)*

☆☆☆☆☆☆☆☆☆☆☆☆☆☆☆☆☆☆☆☆☆☆☆☆☆☆☆☆☆

soul in God's eyes, but as a chattel in man's eyes, plagued Americans for many generations.

By mid-eighteenth century, slavery with all its problems had become an indelible part of the colonial scene. Protests against the institution, led by Quakers such as John Woolman and Anthony Benezet, found allies among such men as Benjamin Franklin and Benjamin Rush, but the system's economic imperative and the colonists' prejudice against blacks prevented any effective action. Attempts to solve the slavery problem would have to wait until the nineteenth century.

THE STATUS OF BLACKS, 1750's

THE NEGROES, OR BLACKS ... are in a manner slaves; for when a Negro is once bought he is the purchaser's servant as long as he lives. However, it is not in the power of the master to kill his Negro for a fault, but he must leave it to the magistrates to proceed according to the laws. A man who kills his Negro is, legally, punishable by death, but there is no instance here of a white man ever having been executed for this crime....

Formerly the Negroes were ... bought by almost everyone who could afford it, the Quakers alone excepted. But the latter are no longer so particular and now they have as many Negroes as other people. However, many people cannot conquer the idea that it is contrary to the laws of Christianity to keep slaves....

At present Negroes are seldom brought to the English colonies, for those already there have multiplied rapidly.... In case you have not only male but likewise female Negroes, they may intermarry, and then the children are all your slaves. But if you possess a male only and he has an inclination to marry a female belonging to a different master, you do not hinder your Negro in so delicate a point; but it is of no advantage to you, for the children belong to the master of the female. Therefore it is in practice advantageous to have Negro women....

The Negroes in the North American colonies are treated more mildly and fed better than those in the West Indies. They have as good food as the rest of the servants, and they possess equal advantages in all

☆☆☆☆☆☆☆☆☆☆☆☆☆☆☆☆☆☆☆☆☆☆☆☆☆☆☆☆

Immigration sharply stimulated colonial development. Productivity expanded rapidly because of the enlarged labor force and increased market, and colonial merchants accumulated capital more readily. Philadelphia rose from a small village in 1689 to become the largest colonial city by 1770 because it served as the entrance port for most immigrants. Many of the immigrants found their way into the Pennsylvania interior and the backcountry of Maryland, Virginia, and the Carolinas, following the Shenandoah River southwestward from Pennsylvania.

Newcomers attracted by William Penn's promotional literature found his "Holy Experiment" most attractive. Pennsylvania's climate, topography, and soil resembled the Old World's, and the colony contained a

things, except that they are bound to serve their whole lifetime and get no other wages than what their master's goodness allows them. They are likewise clad at their master's expense. On the contrary, in the West Indies, and especially in the Spanish Islands, they are treated very cruelly; therefore no threat makes more impression upon a Negro here than that of sending him over to the West Indies in case he will not reform.

To prevent any disagreeable mixtures of the white people and Negroes, and to hinder the latter from forming too great opinions of themselves, to the disadvantage of their masters, I am told there was a law passed prohibiting the whites of both sexes to marry Negroes, under pain of capital punishment, with deprivation of privileges and other severer penalties for the clergyman who married them. But that the whites and blacks sometimes copulated appears in children of a mixed complexion who are sometimes born.

It is greatly to be pitied that the masters of these Negroes take little care of their spiritual welfare, and let them live on in their pagan darkness.... To this they are led partly by the conceit of its being shameful to have a spiritual brother or sister among so despicable a people; partly by thinking that they would not be able to keep their Negroes so subjected afterwards.... (From: Peter Kalm, En Resa til Norra America *[Stockholm: Tryckt pä L. Salvii Kosfnad, 1753-61])*

☆☆☆☆☆☆☆☆☆☆☆☆☆☆☆☆☆☆☆☆☆☆☆☆☆☆☆☆

seemingly limitless amount of cheap fertile lands. Beyond Pennsylvania stretched the Great Valley leading southwestward into Virginia and the Carolinas, offering even more cheap, fertile lands and a highway into the continent's interior. Penn's colony offered other advantages: no tax-supported church, an affinity between Quakers and German pietist sects, and peaceful Indian relations. The new immigrants brought with them into Pennsylvania and the southern backcountry attitudes that would later create serious internal dissensions: hatred of landlords, state churches, compulsory military service, and taxation.

New England, on the other hand, attracted few immigrants. Its poor soil matched its inhospitable attitude toward newcomers. The most accessible and desirable areas had been preempted by earlier settlers, and its history of religious persecution did not lure those seeking greater freedom. By 1760, only one out of twenty in New England was foreign-born, against a ratio in all the colonies of one out of three. New York, too, failed to draw large numbers of immigrants because of unhappy experiences of German settlers there in the early eighteenth century and because its best lands were granted in large tracts, whose owners generally refused to sell, but insisted on rental arrangements.

The Philanthropic Experiment: Georgia

In all but one instance this migration was unorganized and without direction. The exception was Georgia, which began in 1732 as an effort by humanitarian and imperialistic groups in England. England faced a serious situation in its increasing prison population. Those convicted of crimes and those incarcerated for debt cost the English taxpayers, basically the landed gentry, a goodly amount, and during the eighteenth century criminals had the choice of execution or transportation to the colonies for fourteen years of indentured servitude. Some 50,000 convicts found their way to the colonies under these terms, much to the disgust of many Americans, but this did limit English prison costs and did offer felons the chance to become productive workers. Another use for convicts, the defense of existing, profitable colonies, came under discussion in England in the 1730s. The southern frontier needed bolstering especially, since it faced the French in Louisiana and the Spanish in Florida. That area could be a potential source of silk, wine, rice, naval stores, and perhaps even gold, making the idea even more attractive.

In 1732 George II issued a charter to General James Oglethorpe and his associates for a colony which differed from any other English grant. Georgia was established under the control of trustees who could raise money, grant lands, and levy taxes, but could not profit from the venture, and who would lose their authority after twenty-one years. This colony would relieve British prisons, reduce the poor tax, and protect South Carolina from possible attack. A vast philanthropic outpouring financed Georgia's establishment and development, together with an annual parliamentary subsidy for its defense.

The trustees envisaged a paternalistic economy and society because the settlers would be those who had failed in England and must therefore be protected against temptations. Land grants were limited to 500 acres, and settlers could not dispose of their holdings. The trustees established wage rates for free servants, prohibited slave labor, and encouraged production of staple crops. Since "demon rum" tempted men sorely, liquor was forbidden. Few debtors took advantage of the opportunity to settle in Georgia, and these idealistic policies collapsed. Consequently, Georgia developed a plantation pattern of agriculture similar to its neighbors. However, it differed in one way: not until the Crown took it over in the early 1750s did the colony acquire a legislative assembly. Thus, Georgia's political maturity lagged behind that of other colonies.

Growing Economic Sophistication

Americans aped the British commercial system to the point where, by the 1760s, a competitive American commercial system had been created. Americans, like Englishmen, accumulated surplus capital and then sought opportunities to employ it. However, they did not have the same freedom of investment as their British models. Certain trade patterns were prohibited, as were various manufactures, leaving land speculation as their sole major outlet. Of course, Americans did not obey all British injunctions regarding trade and manufacturing but such restrictions made life difficult for enterprising colonials.

Surplus colonial capital was initially absorbed in expanding tobacco, rice, and indigo culture in the South, shipping and permissible manufacturing in the North, and fur trade and land speculation in the West. By the 1760s, however, tobacco production reached its natural limits and actually started declining due to soil depletion, excessive planter indebtedness, increasing labor costs, and artificial market restrictions imposed by the Navigation Acts. Some Virginia planters began shifting from tobacco production to grain crops and diverting funds into plantation manufacturing and land speculation. Northern commerce by the 1760s had also reached its limits under the Navigation Acts, although New England shippers frequently ignored legal restraints in penetrating profitable markets such as the French and Spanish West Indies.

English efforts to curtail manufacturing were only partially successful. As a comptroller of the customs once reported: "It would be ridiculous to imagine that people bred in all the improvements of Europe should, by crossing the Atlantic, so unaccountably lose all remembrance of former skill and knowledge, as to betake themselves entirely to agriculture, and not once dream of improving these advantages, or applying

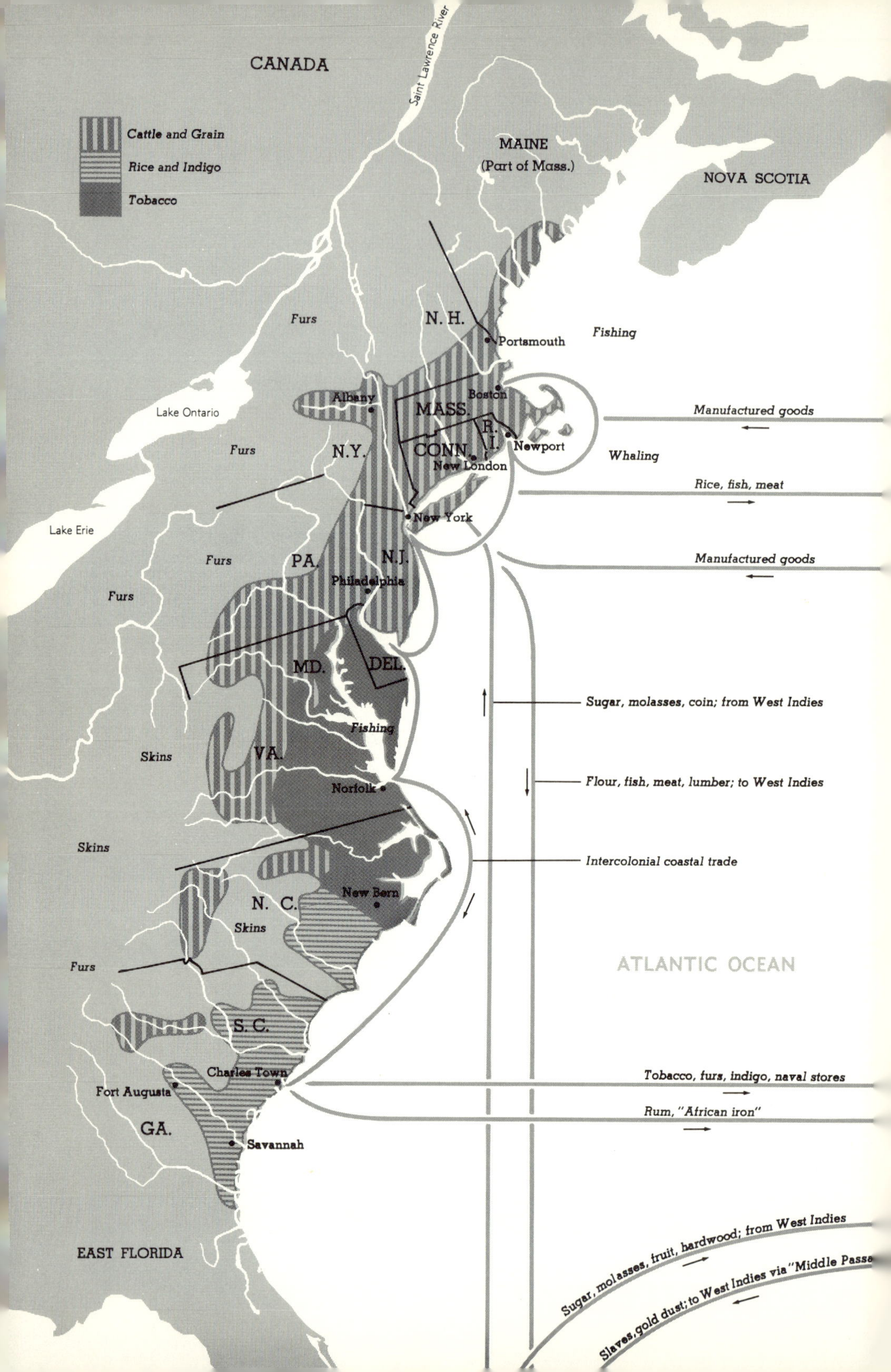

CANADA
Saint Lawrence River
Cattle and Grain
Rice and Indigo
Tobacco
MAINE
(Part of Mass.)
NOVA SCOTIA
Furs
N. H.
Portsmouth
Fishing
Albany
Boston
Lake Ontario
MASS.
R. I.
Newport
Manufactured goods
Furs
N.Y.
CONN.
New London
Whaling
Rice, fish, meat
Lake Erie
New York
Furs
PA.
N.J.
Manufactured goods
Furs
Philadelphia
MD.
DEL.
Sugar, molasses, coin; from West Indies
Fishing
Skins
VA.
Flour, fish, meat, lumber; to West Indies
Norfolk
Skins
Intercolonial coastal trade
New Bern
N. C.
Skins
ATLANTIC OCEAN
Furs
S. C.
Charles Town
Tobacco, furs, indigo, naval stores
Fort Augusta
Rum, "African iron"
GA.
Savannah
Sugar, molasses, fruit, hardwood; from West Indies
EAST FLORIDA
Slaves, gold dust; to West Indies via "Middle Passa

COLONIAL ECONOMY AND TRADE ROUTES

American colonies are shown here on a much larger scale than Europe.

WILLIAM FITZHUGH'S ESTATE IN VIRGINIA, 1686

... *THE PLANTATION WHERE I now live contains a thousand acres, at least seven hundred acres of it being rich thicket, the remainder good, hearty, plantable land, without any waste either by marshes or great swamps. The commodiousness, convenience, and pleasantness yourself well knows. Upon it there is three quarters well-furnished with all necessary houses, ground, and fencing, together with a choice crew of Negroes at each plantation, most of them this country born, the remainder as likely as most in Virginia, there being twenty-nine in all, with stocks of cattle and hogs at each quarter. Upon the same land is my own dwelling house, furnished with all accommodations for a comfortable and genteel living, as it is a very good dwelling house, with thirteen rooms in it, four of the best of them hung, nine of them plentifully furnished with all things necessary and convenient, and all houses for use well-furnished with brick chimneys, four good cellars, a dairy, dovecote, stable, barn, henhouse, kitchen, and all other conveniencies, and all in a manner new; a large orchard of about twenty-five hundred apple trees, most grafted, well fenced with a locust fence, which is as durable as most brick walls, a garden a hundred foot square, well paled in, a yard wherein is most of the aforesaid necessary houses pallisadoed in with locust puncheons, which is as good as if it were walled in, and more lasting than any of our bricks; together with a good stock of cattle, hogs, horses, mares, sheep, etc., and necessary servants belonging to it for the supply and support thereof. About a mile and half distance*

☆☆☆☆☆☆☆☆☆☆☆☆☆☆☆☆☆☆☆☆☆☆☆☆☆☆☆☆

those materials with which the country abounds, to the common use of human life." Colonial manufacturing particularly concerned the Board of Trade, which often asked governors for detailed estimates of such activity. New York in the 1740s manufactured linseed oil, refined sugar, distilled rum, and had an iron furnace operating. New England engaged in shipbuilding, of course, but also distilled rum and manufactured ironware. Pennsylvania reportedly manufactured nine-tenths of its own wearing apparel.

Colonial manufacturing potential aroused even greater concern in the 1760s when, in consequence of the Stamp Act, Americans talked of self-sufficiency. The Board of Trade demanded that governors provide a

a good water grist mill, whose toll I find sufficient to find my own family with wheat and Indian corn for our necessities and occasions.
Up the river in this country three tracts of land more. One of them contains 21,996 acres, another 500 acres, and one other 1,000 acres, all good, convenient, and commodious seats, and which in a few years will yield a considerable annual income. A stock of tobacco with the crops and good debts lying out of about £250,000, besides sufficient of almost all sorts of goods to supply the family's and the quarter's occasions for two if not three years.
Thus I have given you some particulars, which I thus deduce: the yearly crops of corn and tobacco, together with the surplus of meat, more than will serve the family's use, will amount annually to sixty thousand pound tobacco, which at 10s. per hundredweight, is £300 annum, and the Negroes' increase, being all young and a considerable parcel of breeders, will keep that stock good forever. The stock of tobacco managed with an inland trade will yearly yield about sixty thousand pound tobacco without hazard or risk, which will be both clear without charge of housekeeping or disbursements for servants' clothing. The orchard in a very few years will yield a large supply to plentiful housekeeping or if better husbanded yield at least fifteen thousand pound tobacco annual income. *(From Richard Beale Davis, ed., William Fitzhugh and His Chesapeake World, 1676-1701 [Charlottesville: University Press of Virginia, 1963], pp. 175-76)*

☆☆☆☆☆☆☆☆☆☆☆☆☆☆☆☆☆☆☆☆☆☆☆☆☆☆☆☆☆☆

detailed statement of all new manufacturing. The list's variety suggested the impossibility of effectively restricting the colonials. It ranged from New Hampshire, which made a better linen than that imported from Ireland, to Rhode Island which admitted to ten iron forges, six spermaceti candle works, three ropewalks for the manufacture of cordage, and a papermill. Even the southern colonies engaged in manufacturing. South Carolina refined sugar and manufactured silk textiles, Virginia had blast furnaces and hatmaking under way, and Maryland had four ropewalks. As impressive as these accomplishments may seem, colonial industry was hampered by high labor costs, poor marketing and transportation facilities, as well as English regulations. Most industries tended to be extractive, using unskilled or semiskilled labor with little machinery to prepare raw materials for overseas shipment.

England attempted to keep colonial economic activity within bounds by means of subsidies, as well as restrictions. Hemp and flax production, development of naval stores, and cultivation of indigo are excellent examples of activities which were given financial encouragement. Subsidies, combined with restrictions such as prohibition of foreign shipping between England and the colonies, and the juggling of English customs duties to regulate trade patterns, were practical applications of mercantilism.

America's basic economic activity remained agriculture. New England had the poorest soil in the English colonies, and agriculture there emphasized diversified crops grown for local consumption. The Middle Atlantic region offered some of the best farmland and served as a breadbasket for the West Indies. The southern colonies produced staple crops: tobacco in Virginia and Maryland, rice and indigo in South Carolina, and lumber and naval stores in North Carolina. By the 1760s, England's colonies had developed complex and sophisticated economic patterns based upon agriculture, commerce, and limited manufacturing. Not only were they tied to the mother country's mercantilistic system, but they had created one of their own — one that would soon complicate Anglo-American relations.

Intellectual and Cultural Growth

In suggesting the formation of an American Philosophical Society, Benjamin Franklin observed in 1743 that "the first drudgery of settling new colonies which confines the attention of people to mere necessaries is now pretty well over; and there are many in every province in circumstances that set them at ease, and afford leisure to cultivate the finer arts and improve the common stock of knowledge." Development of American science had been hindered by lack of libraries, absence of an aristocracy to provide patronage and support for scholars, and a shortage of great universities with long traditions in the pursuit of knowledge. But by the 1770s a number of Americans participated actively in an international community of scientists who corresponded regularly and formed organizations for the exchange of information.

Newtonian science, which dominated European thought at this time, also colored and conditioned Americans' outlook on life. Descartes's *Discourse on Method* contained the inductive method, the germ of New-

CRIMINAL PUNISHMENTS IN BOSTON, 1740

AS TO CRIMINAL MATTERS, they are very tender in punishing of them; and very rarely put any to death, unless it be for murder. By their law, robbing on the highway, or burglary, for the first offence, branding on the forehead only; for the second offence, branding again and whipping; and, for the third offence, death. Blasphemy is punished with death. A child, for striking or cursing a parent, to be punished with death, if upwards of sixteen years of age. Cruel punishments or correction of either children, servants, or slaves, prohibited. Nor may any court of justice condemn any offender to receive more than forty stripes. No orphan may be disposed of by their guardian, without the consent of one of the courts. The minority of women, in respect of marriage, is determined to be under sixteen. They have many other laws relating to their religious and civil government; but I take those already mentioned to be the most material. (From Joseph Bennett, History of New England, *in Massachusetts Historical Society* Proceedings, *1st series, V, 119-122)*

☆☆☆☆☆☆☆☆☆☆☆☆☆☆☆☆☆☆☆☆☆☆☆☆☆☆☆

tonian thought: "It is possible to attain knowledge which is very useful in life, and instead of that speculative philosophy which is taught in the schools [scholasticism] we may find a practical philosophy by means of which, knowing the force and action of fire, water, the stars, heavens, and all other bodies that environ us, as distinctly as we know the different crafts of our artisans, we can in the same way employ them in all those uses to which they are adapted, and thus render ourselves the masters and possessors of nature." If every secret of the universe could be understood by man, if knowledge was power for good, then man could live in accord with the laws of nature and attain perfect harmony. Moreover, if this could be done in physical terms, some argued it could also be done in social terms, and man could finally perfect his own innate goodness.

Eighteenth-century Americans participated in the Enlightenment's scientific developments, although their contributions were more often descriptive rather than experimental. However, they had the perfect opportunity to add to scientific knowledge, for they lived on a new continent which contained many wonders previously unknown to Europeans. In astronomy, for example, Americans excelled because they could provide Europe with data for correlation with continental findings, and because they had a clearer atmosphere for their observations. John Winthrop IV, who at twenty-three held a chair of Mathematics and Natural Philosophy at Harvard, observed the transit of Venus across the sun in 1761 and again in 1769. His data, communicated to English astronomers, enabled them to calculate with extraordinary accuracy the distance between the earth and the sun, an immense step toward determining the dimensions of the Newtonian universe. Similar activity occurred in botany where John Bartram of Philadelphia and Dr. Alexander Garden of Charleston collected specimens of New World plants and communicated their findings to the Swedish classifier, Carolus Linnaeus (who rewarded Dr. Garden by naming the gardenia after him).

The ingenious Dr. Franklin, America's outstanding scientist, encompassed within his interests the full spread of colonial scientific endeavors. Self-trained, an amateur and pragmatist, Benjamin Franklin dabbled in oceanography, physics, chemistry, electricity, geography, and medicine. His famed electrical experiments developed the thesis of positive and negative electricity which he pragmatically applied by inventing a conductive rod to provide protection from lightning. His other important contributions, such as the Franklin stove and bifocal glasses, had obvious practical uses. These scientific developments were not the property of an esoteric few, but belonged to the population at large, and were disseminated widely by newspaper essays, almanacs, and other printed materials. Newtonian science fired men's imagination and colored their attitudes toward all problems. The potential of finding general laws which guided all of the universe stimulated rationalism and optimism in American life.

American literature reflected this, for while colonists never lost their Calvinist inheritance, they added to it the rationalist impulse. Old florid literary styles gave way to sharper, clearer prose, even among preachers. The Reverend Mather Byles wrote: "A preacher must study an easy style, expressive diction, and tuneful cadences.... Rattling periods, uncouth jargon, affected phrases, and finical jingles, let them be condemned; let them be hissed from the desk and blotted from the page." The Reverend Charles Chauncy so strongly opposed florid oratory that he reportedly prayed he might never be an orator. One of his parishioners, overhearing him, responded that his prayer had been granted.

A colonial self-consciousness also emerged in the eighteenth century, as suggested by the number of histories written by Americans. In many,

B. FRANKLIN ON FELONS AND RATTLESNAKES

> ... *I UNDERSTAND* that the Government at home will not suffer our mistaken Assemblies to make any Law for preventing or discouraging the Importation of Convicts from Great Britain, for this kind Reason, "That such Laws are against the Publick Utility, as they tend to prevent the *IMPROVEMENT* and *WELL PEOPLING* of the Colonies."
>
> ... this Exporting of Felons to the Colonies, may be consider'd as a Trade, *as well as in the Light of a Favour. Now all Commerce implies Returns: Justice requires them: There can be no Trade without them. And* Rattle-Snakes *seem the most* suitable Returns *for the* Human Serpents *sent us by our* Mother Country. In this, however, as in every other Branch of Trade, she will have the Advantage of us. She will reap equal Benefits without equal Risque of the Inconveniencies and Dangers. For the* Rattle-Snake *gives Warning before he attempts his Mischief; which the Convict does not.* (Pennsylvania Gazette, May 9, 1751)

☆☆☆☆☆☆☆☆☆☆☆☆☆☆☆☆☆☆☆☆☆☆☆☆☆☆

such as the Reverend Thomas Prince's *Chronological History of New England* (1736), the dominant idea was that God peculiarly sanctioned America, that New Englanders were God's chosen people. A later historian, Dr. William Douglass of Boston, argued the same point, though in secular terms, when he insisted that America was novel in world history, and its uniqueness made it worthy of study. Americans in all the colonies were clearly developing a sense of their own destiny, of their own special identity apart from that of Englishmen.

Newspapers and magazines became important factors in colonial literature and began to multiply after 1720. England provided the original idea and form, and they began as newssheets reprinting material from English publications. Here, too, Benjamin Franklin innovated by publishing the "Silence Dogood" essays in the *New England Courant*. These critical commentaries on Boston's manners and morals set the pattern for future American newspapers, and as the concept of freedom of the press expanded, they became more and more courageous and critical. Newspapers, as reading matter for the general public, sounding boards for literary expression, and critics of American society, secularized the colonial mind and made it aware of contemporary ideas. They stimulated a cultural self-consciousness reflected in other aspects of colonial life. Provincial self-government, economic maturity, and development of strong social institutions were all part of the same pattern.

Religious Variations

Creation of an American identity, a sense of uniqueness, was most evident in religion. Seventeenth-century Calvinism gradually gave way, and the introspective mood based upon man's sinfulness and depravity was replaced by an optimism founded on man's potential for perfection. This change can first be seen in adoption of the Halfway Covenant (1662) by Bay Colony Puritans. The Covenant enabled church members to have their grandchildren admitted to partial church membership (but not to the sacraments) after baptism but without a public confession of faith. This indicated that succeeding generations did not always share the founders' religious enthusiasm. The first generation's attitude had been predicated on their experience of persecution; later generations often found their religion too comfortable, for they suffered no hardships because of it. The Puritan church would no longer be composed only of visible saints, but would include second and third generation Puritans lacking the conversion experience.

By the 1680s Bay Colony Puritanism had weakened. Congregational Church membership no longer depended exclusively upon an experience of personal regeneration and a public confession of faith. The Reverend Solomon Stoddard argued that permitting the unregenerate to join the Church might induce in them the desired conversion. Soon the Brattles, Thomas and William, urged that all persons "of visible sanctity" be admitted as full church members, thereby substituting good works for grace, as Anne Hutchinson had feared half a century earlier. This liberalization and humanization of Puritanism moved from the rigor and inflexibility of God's justice to the broadness of His mercy.

The Brattles met with sharp hostility from old-line Puritans who now argued for a Presbyterian-type of church government which could repress such deviations. However, they proposed one heresy to combat another, and the Reverend John Wise forcibly denounced Presbyterianism in his famous *Vindication of the Government of New England Churches* (1715). He supported church autonomy, though he justified it by still another heresy. A church, he argued, was a religious society designed "to cultivate humanity and promote the happiness of all and the good of every man in all his rights." This was a far cry from John Cotton's Puritanism.

The Reverend Jonathan Mayhew expressed an eighteenth-century view of religion and God, which was remarkably close to Newtonianism. God, he said, "governs His great family, His universal Kingdom, according to those general rules and maxims which are in themselves most wise and good, such as the wisest and best Kings govern by ... perfect goodness, love itself, is His very essence, in a peculiar sense; immeasurable, immutable, universal and everlasting love." Ministers now insisted that man was "an intelligent moral agent, having within himself an ability and freedom to will, as well as to do." God operated "by general laws, whose operation He does not counteract, but concurs with, in a regular uniform course." The old Puritan Deity, arbitrary, self-centered, and glory-loving, became the God of love and benevolence who worked from a dependable plan. Man, no longer contemptible in God's eyes, simply had to learn the rules and operate accordingly.

Not only was Puritanism changing, but so too were other religious groups. As America rediscovered England in the eighteenth century, Anglicanism gained strength. It was the established church in Virginia, where it was dominant, and in New York, North and South Carolina, Georgia, and Maryland. As its adherents increased in the eighteenth century, the question of appointing a colonial bishop became a critical and unresolved issue that inflamed men's passions. The Bishop of London exercised nominal control over the colonial Church of England, but he was 3,000 miles away. Under an episcopal organization, only a bishop could ordain ministers, and prospective colonial clergymen had to journey to England for ordination. One of every five died while making the journey to England for holy orders. More important than this difficulty, however, Anglicans in the northern colonies most strongly urged the appointment of an American bishop because they were weak and needed his support. In Virginia, Anglicans strongly opposed such an appointment because local parishes had established a strong congregational system and taken control of the Church, a situation which a bishop would upset.

Still another variation in eighteenth-century religion, which appealed to intellectual leaders, was deism. An attitude rather than an organized worship form, deism held that religion should conform to scientific reason, and only three basic concepts withstood that test. First, there was one omnipotent God; second, God's plan for the universe included virtuous living for men; and third, life after death provided a reward for virtue and a punishment for evil. Benjamin Franklin epitomized this creed when he wrote: "I believe in one God, creator of the universe. That He governs it by His providence. That He ought to be worshipped. That the most acceptable service we render to Him is doing good to His other children. That the soul of man is immortal, and will be treated with justice in another life respecting its conduct in this."

These attitudes softened religion, but they did not pass unchallenged. A conservative reaction set in, and efforts were made to revive the old Calvinism. Jonathan Edwards, one of America's great theologians, led this move in the 1730s and 1740s. He accepted Newtonian science and its wonders, but contended that they paled into insignificance when compared to God's revealed wonders. Edwards reminded his generation that God is all-powerful and man's happiness depended upon showing God's glory, not man's presumption.

Reaction against the new religion came into sharp focus with the Great Awakening, a revivalist wave which swept over America in the 1730s and 1740s. This attracted people from all classes who needed a more emotional religion, for whom an exclusively intellectual faith had no relevance. On the frontier in particular, and among lesser educated colonials in general, deism and intellectually-oriented religion did not provide answers. It seemed cold, uninspiring, and impersonal, while these people believed in an unquestioned obedience to God's inscrutable will.

The Great Awakening began with Theodore Frelinghuysen's work in the Dutch Reformed Church and William Tennent's in the Presbyterian, and quickly spread to other sects. The new emotional techniques split existing churches into Old Lights and New Lights. Both believed in individual salvation for repentant sinners and hellfire and damnation for the unregenerate, but the New Lights placed more emphasis upon emotion and less upon intellect. Two English figures, John Wesley and George Whitefield, gave further impetus to this movement and accomplished within the Church of England precisely what Frelinghuysen and Tennent did in their churches. The movement led by Wesley and Whitefield developed into Methodism, which for a time remained within the folds of Anglicanism.

Whitefield arrived in America in 1738 and quickly became the most popular revivalist preacher. He spoke before enormous crowds from Massachusetts to Georgia, and even managed to sway the confirmed deist,

George Whitefield (1715-1770), English evangelist, associated with the Wesley brothers and a founder of Methodism. Adept at outdoor sermons to large crowds, Whitefield sparked the Great Awakening in the American colonies in 1739. (Fogg Art Museum, Harvard University Portrait Collection. Given by Mrs. H.P. Oliver to Harvard College, 1852)

Benjamin Franklin, who recorded his spell. "The multitudes of all sects and denominations that attended his sermons were enormous," wrote Franklin the scoffer of Whitefield's visit to Philadelphia, "and it was a matter of speculation to me, who was one of the number, to observe the extraordinary influence of his oratory on his hearers, and how much they admired and respected him, notwithstanding his common abuse of them, by assuring them they were naturally half beasts and half devils.... I happened to attend one of his sermons in the course of which I perceived he intended to finish with a collection, and I silently resolved he should get nothing from me. I had in my pocket a handful of copper money, three or four silver dollars, and five pistoles in gold. As he proceeded, I began to soften, and concluded to give the copper. Another stroke of his oratory made me ashamed of that, and determined to give the silver; and he finished so admirably, that I emptied my pocket wholly into the collector's dish, gold and all."

The Great Awakening concerned itself not with the fine points of theology, but with inducing an uncritical conversion in its listeners, much in the tradition of the early seventeenth-century Puritan ministers. Whitefield appealed to a multitude of diverse faiths and used emotion to combat "pernicious intellectualism and rationalism." This led to a religious democratization which would have unforetold consequences, for emotionalism involved a leveling tendency. Indeed, revivalists preached the salvation of blacks and rebuked slaveowners for keeping their charges in spiritual darkness. More important, perhaps, was the assault upon the authority of the clergy and of formal religion. These two props of the established order could no longer be viewed as exclusive interpreters of man's relationship to man, to society, or to authority. If ministers could err in determining man's proper relationship to God, they could be mistaken in all other things. From this emerged a powerful impulse toward the separation of church and state, toward a realization of the fallacy of government support for one particular sect. The Great Awakening, at the same time that it stimulated a new religious enthusiasm, also began a challenge to the existing social order in all its dimensions.

Political Ideas and Attitudes

Eighteenth-century Americans developed working concepts of the British Empire and of their own political systems based upon empiricism, upon rational explanations of their actual operation. To Americans, the colonies were separate states bearing close but ill-defined relationships to England, and the empire functioned as a series of dependencies rather than a coherent whole. These ideas resulted from Americans' acceptance for over a century of responsibilities which the English had failed to assume. Americans often developed their own mechanisms of government and formulated political ideas as justifications. Sometimes American patterns and concepts did not agree with those held in England.

To Americans, the greatest political theorist was John Locke, whose ideas had perfectly explained the Glorious Revolution of 1688-89. Colonials found him appealing because their situations so nearly paralleled the general theory he espoused. They had found themselves in a wilderness with no legal authority to govern and had fallen back upon a social contract before he had enunciated that idea. Yet, all English ideas did not adapt themselves perfectly to the American environment.

Identical terms often carried different definitions, as was the case with representation and constitutionalism. In England, representation imme-

John Locke (1632-1704), English philosopher, who founded the empirical school and laid the basis for nineteenth-century liberalism. His justification of the Glorious Revolution provided Americans a coherent political philosophy, and for them it outweighed his other contributions. (Crown copyright, Victoria and Albert Museum, London)

diately connoted a class system, with Lords Spiritual, Lords Temporal, and the Commons, but no such divisions existed in the colonies. In America, representation was geographically based, since they had no lords and the social structure was fluid and constantly changing. Thus Englishmen elected representatives from shires and boroughs without requiring actual residence in the district, and by statute abolished the legal fiction of residence. At the same time, Americans moved in the opposite direction and instituted strict residence requirements.

Constitutionalism offered another example of divergent political definitions in the mother country and its colonies. The English had no written constitution, relying instead on precedent, custom, and parliamentary statutes. However, the colonies had known written limits on governmental power from their earliest days. Their charters, frames of government, and even Crown instructions to governors were written constitutions. And such precisely defined limits, of course, followed the Lockean tradition, for the constitution is a formalized social contract which enables

JOHN ADAMS ON THE PURPOSE OF GOVERNMENT

WE OUGHT TO CONSIDER what is the end of government, before we determine which is the best form. Upon this point all speculative politicians will agree, that the happiness of society is the end of government, as all divines and moral philosophers will agree that the happiness of the individual is the end of man. From this principle it will follow, that the form of government which communicates ease, comfort, security, or, in one word, happiness, to the greatest number of persons, and in the greatest degree, is the best....

Fear is the foundation of most governments; but it is so sordid and brutal a passion, and renders men in whose breasts it predominates so stupid and miserable, that Americans will not be likely to approve of any political institution which is founded on it....

The foundation of every government is some principle or passion in the minds of the people. The noblest principles and most generous affections in our nature, then, have the fairest chance to support the noblest and most generous models of government.... (From: John Adams, Thoughts on Government *[Philadelphia: John Dunlap, 1776])*

☆☆☆☆☆☆☆☆☆☆☆☆☆☆☆☆☆☆☆☆☆☆☆☆☆☆☆☆☆☆

the parties to it to understand precisely their rights and duties and to determine violations of the agreement.

Variations in the meaning of representation and constitutionalism would have major consequences for Anglo-American relations after 1763 as debates developed over the nature of the empire and the status of its components. American versions of these ideas went unchallenged until after 1763, largely because the English made little effort to rationalize the political empire. Standard governmental forms had been created and applied after 1689 for pragmatic reasons, not philosophical ones. The earliest exposition of a political theory of empire was probably a statement made by Sir William Keith, Governor of Pennsylvania, in 1728, but his views gained neither acceptance in the colonies nor support in England. Not until 1766 with the Declaratory Act, which cancelled the Stamp Act but reaffirmed Parliament's right to levy such taxes, did Parliament spell out the political nature of empire, but it was then too late, for Americans rigidly adhered to their own ideas.

The Web of Empire

By 1763, the English had established and strictly applied certain political standards for the empire. Each colony had to have a representative assembly, whether feasible or not. When the Privy Council learned that only a governor and council ruled Nova Scotia, recently acquired from France, it ordered an immediate assembly election. The governor protested that not enough Englishmen lived in the colony to elect two representatives and that French Acadians did not know how to use a legislature, but the Privy Council remained adamant. None could challenge the idea that English forms followed the flag to all corners of the empire.

Although England insisted upon assemblies in all colonies, it also tried to curb their aggressiveness and keep them within strict limits. The English looked upon the commission and instructions given to a royal governor as a colonial constitution from which there was no appeal, as a mandate from a higher authority. Governors, more than once, reminded assemblies that local legislatures were royal creations which could be modified or destroyed at will. Colonials viewed such threats with dismay, but they were usually made only under great stress and before 1763 they were never carried out.

Even in the critical area of taxation, rigidities had set in. In 1724 Sir Philip Yorke, England's Solicitor General, ruled that colonials could only be taxed by their own representatives or by Parliament. Since Parliament failed to act in this area from 1603 to the 1760s, local assemblies filled the void. Parliament's resignation of power by inadvertent omission proved to be a serious mistake, since Americans assumed their assemblies had exclusive tax power and erected this into an ideological principle.

That assumption placed royal and proprietary governors between two diametrically opposed forces — local power and royal or proprietary commands — and they sought vainly to bring them together. This required great tact and diplomacy, qualities that governors often lacked. A British journal in 1770 aptly described many of those who became colonial executives: "Whenever we find ourselves encumbered with a needy Court-Dangler, whom, on account of connections, we must not kick downstairs, we kick him upstairs into an American government." Not all governors, of course, were broken-down rakes and bankrupt plungers, but the office's very awkwardness made it difficult for even a qualified official to govern in tranquility. Faced with a choice of supporting royal

VIRGINIA'S PLACE IN THE EMPIRE, 1764

IF THEN THE PEOPLE of this colony are freeborn and have a right to the liberties and privileges of English subjects, they must necessarily have a legal constitution, that is, a legislature ... who may enact laws for the INTERNAL government of the colony. ...

By the term INTERNAL government ... I exclude from the legislature of the colony all power derogatory to their dependence upon the mother kingdom; for as we cannot lose the rights of Englishmen by our removal to this continent, so neither can we withdraw our dependence without destroying the constitution. In every instance, therefore, of our EXTERNAL government we are and must be subject to the authority of the British Parliament, but in no others; for if the Parliament should impose laws upon us merely relative to our INTERNAL government, it deprives us ... of the most valuable part of our birthright as Englishmen, of being governed by laws made with our own consent. As all power, therefore, is excluded from the colony of withdrawing its dependence from the mother kingdom, so is all power over the colony excluded from the mother kingdom but such as respects its EXTERNAL government. ... Parliament, as the stronger power, can force any laws it shall think fit upon us; but the inquiry is not what it can do, but what constitutional right it has to do so. ...

But it may be objected that this general position excludes all the laws of England, so as that none of them are obligatory upon us in our INTERNAL government. The answer to this objection is obvious: the common law, being the common consent of the people from time immemorial, and the "birthright of every Englishman, does follow him wherever he goes," and consequently must be the GENERAL law by which the colony is to be governed. ... (From: Richard Bland, The Colonel Dismounted: or The Rector Vindicated *[Williamsburg: Joseph Royle, 1764], pp. 22-23).*

☆☆☆☆☆☆☆☆☆☆☆☆☆☆☆☆☆☆☆☆☆☆☆☆☆☆☆☆☆

directives he had sworn to enforce or living on peaceful terms with Americans who controlled fiscal affairs, governors were indeed in a dilemma.

Although weakened by grasping legislatures, colonial governors still retained great theoretical power, for their authority came not from within the colony, but from the Crown, though 3,000 miles away. This dichotomy between practical limits and theoretical potential left many colonial executives unable to operate effectively. Governors fought assemblies every step of the way, but it was a losing battle. Every time a governor challenged the legislature for aggressively seeking complete dominance of government, the legislators claimed to be imitating the Commons of England. But a basic difference existed between assemblies and Parliament. In England the executive controlled a working majority in Commons and was thus responsible to the legislature; in America the executive was independent of the assembly and therefore could survive, happily or otherwise, a hostile legislature. Americans refused to accept or understand this difference and its implications.

Only his council's cooperation made a governor's tenure bearable, but members of the governor's council found themselves in an equally awkward position. Most were politicians of some consequence and tried to bridge their own local interests and those of the Crown. Councillors, by virtue of their positions, served two masters and were thus more uncomfortable than governors who only served one, the king, and appeased another, local politicians.

The crux of the difficulty facing both governor and council was the assembly's assumption that it reflected popular will and had an exclusive right to governmental power. Americans patterned their political attitudes upon Parliament's, and especially those of the House of Commons. By thus imitating English methods, colonials sought for themselves that which the Commons had accomplished in England — an executive responsible to the legislature — and they used the same power of the purse. By the 1680s assemblies claimed exclusive power to initiate legislation, although governors occasionally presented them with draft laws, especially those formulated in London. They soon won the right to levy taxes, appropriate money, decide its uses, and supervise its expenditure by their own treasurer. Indeed, they lost only one major battle: appointment of judges for life during good behavior (e.g., therefore subject to dismissal only for improprieties) instead of at the king's pleasure. Crown insistence upon retaining control over the courts prevented an otherwise completely independent local power.

These assembly powers did not go unchallenged. Legislative financial control posed serious problems. The Crown sought to establish a civil list, a dependable revenue immune from assembly interference, from which Crown officers could be paid. American legislatures as bitterly opposed efforts to secure permanent salaries for royal appointees as had Parliament in the seventeenth century. Assemblies usually made annual grants and carefully doled out funds. If they trusted a governor, they might authorize funds for as long as five years, but never permanently. This may offer a partial explanation of differences between mainland and West Indian colonies. Several island assemblies had dedicated permanent revenues for Crown use in the seventeenth century, taxing cash crops and thereby passing the burden to English consumers, and those legislatures thereafter became moribund, while mainland assemblies remained vigorous and resisted encroachments.

Patterns of legislative development varied among colonies, however, because institutional stability differed from one to another. Massachusetts and Virginia, the two oldest, certainly had the most advanced self-government, although their economic basis for social and political maturity differed sharply. Yet despite variations, colonists were developing, however subtly, into something distinguishable as Americans. Even those whose ancestors came from the mother country had no first-hand knowledge of English life and society, and newcomers of other backgrounds simply did not understand the English. Although they imitated English ways, Americans frequently mimicked form rather than substance and sometimes put their emphasis in the wrong places. As early as 1701 an anonymous *Essay Upon the Government of the English Plantations* bewailed: "But the last and greatest unhappiness the plantations labor under is that the King and Court of England are altogether strangers to the true state of affairs in America, for that is the true cause why grievances have not been long since redressed." This source of mutual irritation increased over the years.

As the colonists, unaware of the ultimate consequences of their position, sought protection for what they understood to be their rights as Englishmen, they increasingly created an unstable political system in the colonies. During most of the eighteenth century, at least until 1763, the instability of colonial politics could be overlooked because of the more pressing problems of the French menace. Many of the difficulties after 1763, however, originated in earlier conflicts which were ignored because of pressures created by imperial warfare.

THE IMPERIAL WARS

The imperial wars, which began as a trade rivalry between England and The Netherlands in the 1650s, shifted focus by the 1680s. By then, the English had eliminated their Dutch rivals and subordinated them in many ways to England's mercantile system. France now rivalled England and planned a mercantilism of its own in the general area which most interested England — the West Indies and North America. Consequently, conflict between the two commercial competitors was very likely.

Agricultural prosperity in the West Indies depended on the mainland colonies, because the islands, which grew staple crops such as tobacco and sugar, did not produce horses, lumber, or enough food for their own needs. The mainland colonies therefore served as storehouses for the West Indies and became valuable prizes in the contest for empire. Other centers of conflict between French and English mercantilism were the Great Lakes basin, source of the fur trade, and the Newfoundland fisheries, valuable for supplying the West Indies and southern Europe.

This Anglo-French rivalry did not erupt until 1689 because both Charles II and James II sympathized with Catholicism and allied themselves with Louis XIV's policies. However, William and Mary's accession to the throne changed matters, for England now allied itself with The Netherlands and the German Rhineland principalities to halt Louis XIV's plans for eastward expansion in Europe. William only accepted the English Crown in order to complete his alliance against France, while the English had their commercial reasons for opposing Louis XIV.

The immediate impact of King William's War (1689-1697) in America fell upon New York. France planned to conquer that colony, thereby gaining complete control of the fur trade, eliminating the breadbasket of the English West Indies, and driving a wedge into the chain of English colonies. When Governor Frontenac of New France arrived on the St. Lawrence, however, he found his Indian allies demoralized by Iroquois raids. Thus border skirmishes replaced the proposed invasions. These stimulated a new unity among the English colonies, led by Jacob Leisler of New York who called an intercolonial congress to consider action against Canada. His expedition failed, and England's inability to offer aid dashed any hopes of effective action. King William's War ended with the Peace of Ryswick in 1697 on the basis of the *status quo ante bellum*.

However, Ryswick was merely a truce. In 1701 war erupted again, this time over the succession to the Spanish throne. This involved the complex disposition of the wealthy Spanish empire claimed by both Philip of Anjou, grandson and heir to Louis XIV, and the Archduke Charles of Austria. England could not accept Philip as monarch because he would unite Spanish America's wealth to Louis XIV's power. Known in America as Queen Anne's War, this conflict centered on control of Spanish America's lucrative trade, long prized by Dutch, French, and English merchants for its bullion.

The Spaniards sold the right to trade with their colonies on a contractual basis known as the *Asiento*. The English Royal African Company, first chartered in the 1660s, wanted to monopolize the slave trade with Spanish America, for it provided an excellent cover for the illicit sale of European goods. France, too, desired this opportunity for greater profit. When Philip of Anjou took the Spanish throne as Philip V, he gave the French Guinea Company a ten-year slave trade monopoly in the Spanish Indies, plus a share of the general trade.

Queen Anne's War had little effect in New York because the Iroquois, badly assaulted by the French and their Indian allies, desired neutrality and refused to become involved again. The Iroquois reinforced their position by signing a peace treaty with Canada in 1701, and another with New York in the same year. The latter treaty, incidentally, granted all western lands of the Iroquois to New York, and gave that colony its only claim to the region south of the Great Lakes. The neutrality policy of the Iroquois accorded with the desires both of New Yorkers, who did not want their fur trade interrupted, and of Canadians, intent on rebuilding their strength.

Consequently, New England bore the brunt of Queen Anne's War. The French had great influence among the Algonquin Indians along the New England frontier, and instigated constant border raids. By 1708, New Englanders, bent on ending this harassment, turned to England for assistance. England, more secure because of victories in Europe, promised a naval expedition to work with a land force from Albany. However, the situation in Europe changed and England reneged on its promise. Nevertheless, the colonials, under General Francis Nicholson's command, attacked and captured Port Royal in Nova Scotia (Acadia according to the French). Finally, in 1711, an English fleet left Boston for the St. Lawrence River, but it was wrecked before it could accomplish its purpose.

When the Treaty of Utrecht ended Queen Anne's War in 1713, the French relinquished Nova Scotia and Hudson's Bay, making England dominant in the fur trade, and they recognized the English title to Newfoundland. England accepted Philip of Anjou as King of Spain, but denied France the benefits of Spain's empire by securing a thirty-year monopoly of the Spanish slave trade and a share in the general trade.

England gave the *Asiento* to the South Seas Company, a speculative corporation organized in 1711 for trade in the Pacific.

The unstable Peace of Utrecht left unresolved the real problems of Anglo-French hostility, British-Spanish rivalry, and the Franco-Spanish alliance, but dynastic reasons temporarily imposed peace. Queen Anne died in 1714, leaving no direct descendants, and the English throne passed to the Hanoverians, distant relatives of the Stuarts. George I, a German with little real interest in English development, succeeded to the throne, but England remained vulnerable to efforts to restore the Stuarts, and invasions for that purpose occurred in 1715 and 1745. Thus, England preferred peace until the new monarchs were firmly established. The French, too, wanted peace, because Louis XV, a five-year-old, had succeeded to the throne, and domestic rivalries threatened to blow up into civil war.

From 1714 to 1739, both sides continued their basic policies, but by peaceful means. Britain consolidated its gains from the previous war, about a £300,000 annual increase in trade, while France stabilized Europe through alliances, beginning with the Triple Alliance, then the Quadruple, and finally the Quintuple. The French also strengthened their position in America, building Fort Louisbourg on Cape Breton Island, reputedly the most powerful fortress in America, to protect its fisheries. France also used the Acadians to sabotage the English position in Nova Scotia, and only the expense involved and the fear of provoking hostilities prevented England from deporting the entire French population of Nova Scotia in the 1730s.

The uneasy truce finally collapsed in 1739 because of demands by British merchants for a still larger share of Spanish American trade. The need for Mexican and Peruvian silver, increasingly important in the China trade, led the British to expand their smuggling with Spanish America. Spanish authorities used coast guard vessels with some success to stop illegal trading, but this incited English protests because of a bullion shortage. When a Captain Robert Jenkins claimed to have lost his ear to a Spanish guardship captain, English merchants and the South Seas Company had their pretext for war. Spain suspended the *Asiento* in May 1739, pressure built up rapidly, and by October England declared war.

The War of the Austrian Succession (1739-1748), like its predecessors, was an international conflict involving many issues. England and Spain began the war, and it spread into a general conflagration over succession

VICTORIOUS BRITISH EMPIRE AFTER 1763

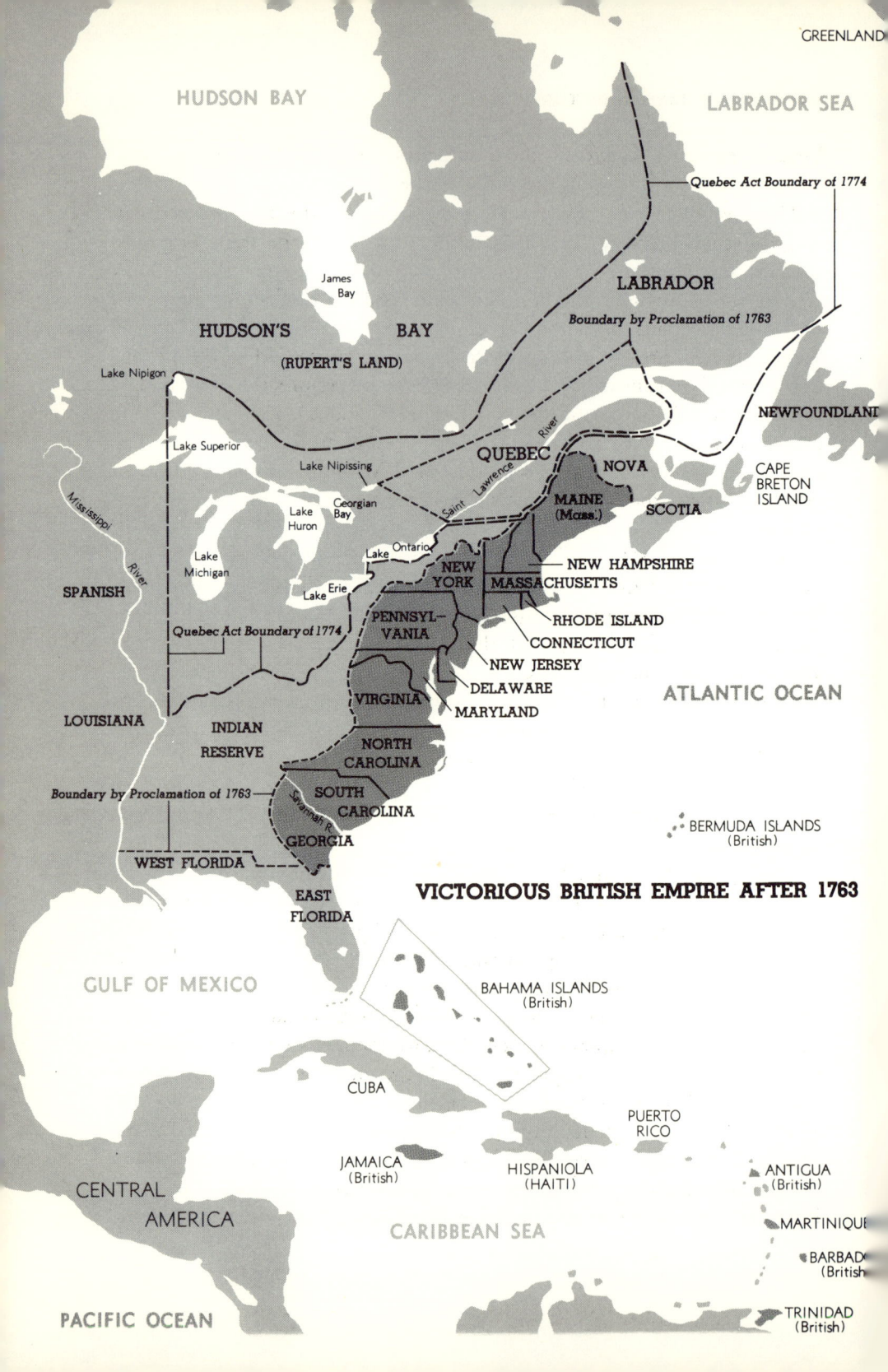

to the Austrian throne. Before it ended, France and Spain fought against Austria, The Netherlands, Russia, Saxony, and England. In America the colonials, under William Pepperell and Sir Peter Warren, captured the supposedly impregnable fortress of Louisbourg in 1745. When the war ended in 1748, however, Louisbourg's restoration to France in exchange for Madras in India dashed American enthusiasm. Again, the peace treaty provided for the *status quo ante bellum*.

The Treaty of Aix-la-Chapelle provided an even briefer truce than its predecessors. Anglo-French rivalry now centered on the Ohio Valley area south of the Great Lakes. The Ohio River gave its possessor control of the whole interior of America. France needed it as a link for its far-flung settlements. England wanted it to accommodate the settlers already spilling over the Appalachian ridge. Americans viewed it as a key opportunity for land speculation, increasingly important since their surplus capital could not legally be employed in expanding manufacturing or trade. Frontier skirmishes between English colonists and the French continually marred the fragile Peace of Aix-la-Chapelle.

Learning that the French contemplated construction of a fort at the forks where the Monongahela and the Allegheny join to form the Ohio, Governor Dinwiddie of Virginia dispatched George Washington with 200 militiamen to demand removal of the French from the area south of Lake Erie. Washington was defeated and forced to surrender near Fort Duquesne (modern Pittsburgh) that summer, and Virginia and Canada were at war. This incident was so serious that the Board of Trade called a conference at Albany to stabilize Indian relations and establish a unified colonial policy. At this meeting Benjamin Franklin proposed a Plan of Union, not completely original with him, and tried unsuccessfully to unite the colonists in their own defense.

Responding to Virginia's call for help, the British sent two regiments of redcoats under General Braddock to oust the French. Braddock, however, stubbornly refused colonial advice, Washington's included, about frontier fighting and the French and their Indian allies ambushed the British, slaughtered the hapless soldiers, and fatally wounded Braddock himself. English prestige was badly damaged, for the Indians believed France to be stronger and became its allies.

In May 1756, war was formally declared. The French and Indian War, or the Seven Years' War, became an international conflict with Britain and Prussia fighting France and Austria, while Spain entered on the side

Death of General James Wolfe. Wolfe (1727-1759) had led a force of 9,000 British troops in 1759 up the St. Lawrence River, landed in Île d'Orléans, and then led the surprise attack against the Plains of Abraham, a plateau above Quebec, where he met the French forces of Montcalm. The superior discipline and arms of the British won the day, but both Wolfe and Montcalm were fatally wounded. The British captured Quebec on September 18, 1759. (By Benjamin West, The Public Archives of Canada)

of France near the end. During the first year England suffered many serious reverses. When William Pitt became prime minister in 1757, however, he reinvigorated British efforts and the tide turned. In 1758, England conquered Fort Louisbourg, Fort Duquesne, and Fort Frontenac; in 1759 Niagara, Ticonderoga, Crown Point, and Quebec fell, and the French navy was shattered; in 1760, Montreal surrendered, and French Canada was no more.

Pitt's successes aroused George III's jealousy. He came to the throne in 1760 determined to have no rival, and he organized a peace party that forced Pitt's resignation. In the meantime, British arms took Martinique, Guadeloupe, Havana in Cuba, and Manila in the Philippines. But George III sued for peace, and in the ensuing negotiations England had to choose which of France's possessions it would retain. England could not have them all, for France was not truly defeated.

In England and the colonies, a great debate developed over which French possessions should be acquired. England finally narrowed the choice to the West Indies islands of Guadeloupe and Martinique, or Canada. The sugar islands grew a valuable product and needed food, lumber, and horses supplied by mainland colonies. Proponents of acquiring the islands also noted that taking Canada would eliminate the French threat, a major tie between England and its colonies. However, acquisition of Canada also had strong support. It would permit England to monopolize the fur trade, eliminate France from the Ohio Valley, and guarantee colonial expansion, all of which would enhance the market for English manufactures. British West India planters helped shape the final decision by arguing for Canada rather than competing sugar islands with greater productivity than their own. They were aided by British merchants greedy for the fur trade and interested in expanding their markets, and by colonists whose blood and treasure went into the victory and who rejected the thought of the great prize slipping from their grasp. The Treaty of Paris of 1763 gave the British all of Canada and the territory west to the Mississippi. Spain traded Florida to England for Cuba and the Philippines, and France compensated Spain with Louisiana west of the Mississippi.

End of An Era

England's victory in 1763 ended an era, created new demands, and presented new problems. Imperial authorities no longer needed to make concessions to secure colonial cooperation against the common enemy, France. Such concessions, however grudgingly and sparingly granted, had over three-quarters of a century gradually eroded England's authority in America while ultimate victory over France expanded England's domain and responsibilities. Now England governed and protected not just thirteen mainland colonies between the Atlantic and the Appalachians, but all of Canada and the area from the Atlantic to the Mississippi. Although France no longer posed a threat, the Indians, who had lost their bargaining position between the two contending forces, menaced English expansion.

THE BLESSINGS OF PEACE, 1763

THE FIRST THING that will naturally present itself to us in our reflecting upon the happy Consequences resulting from the Blessing now given us, is the Security of our Civil Liberty, a Happiness we justly glory in; For Britons have preserv'd it pure and uncorrupted thro' all the Struggles of Ambition and the most dangerous Attacks of Power: They have set the World a fair Example that the highest Ambition of Princes shou'd be to govern a free People, and that no People can be great or happy but such as are so; whilst other Nations have bow'd their Necks to the Yoke of Power and have basely given up this indisputable Right of Man deriv'd to Him from the first Law of Nature, and daily feel that Misery, which ever waits on Slaves. Oh Liberty! Thou are the Author of every good and perfect Gift, the inexhaustible Fountain, from whence all Blessings flow. Without Thee, what avails the Sweetness of Climate, or the most delightful Situation in the World? what avail all the Riches of Nature, the various Production of the Earth, the Mine bringing forth a thousand Treasures, the Olive and the Vine blooming upon the Mountains, if Tyranny usurps the happy Plains, and proud Oppression deforms the gay-smiling face of Nature. . . . (From: **James Horrocks,** Upon the Peace *[Williamsburg: Joseph Royle, 1763], p. 7)*

☆☆☆☆☆☆☆☆☆☆☆☆☆☆☆☆☆☆☆☆☆☆☆☆☆☆☆

New policies were required which included consideration of fur trading interests, land speculators, both English and colonial, prospective settlers, English merchants, and West India planters — to name a few.

France's elimination left England supreme in North America, for Spain, which shared the continent west of the Mississippi, was too weak to constitute a challenge. England now fixed its attention on problems glossed over earlier: commercial rivalry from its own colonies which had long traded illegally with Canada and the foreign West Indies, and fiscal responsibility previously ignored while the empire engaged in a life and death struggle with France. Both were high on the list of immediate projects. To benefit fully from an expanded empire, England intended to regulate trade for its own exclusive advantage. And, as English authorities contemplated the ruinous debt incurred because of warfare since 1689, they determined that those who benefited from the war would share its burdens.

Efforts to establish a western land policy, regulate trade, and reorganize imperial finance would shatter Americans' sense of community by challenging their suppositions about the empire's foundations. In 1763 Anglo-Americans congratulated themselves on the success of their arms and, more importantly, their ideas. The eighteenth century was an ideological era, and Americans certainly looked upon England's victory and France's defeat as the triumph of good over evil, of liberty over tyranny. As a people who probably enjoyed a greater freedom than any other colonial group in the world, Americans were exceptionally sensitive about their liberties and had guarded them jealously for a long time. Thus efforts to curtail them, efforts which emanated from the nation so thoroughly identified in American minds with freedom, proved doubly shocking after 1763.

This English empire which would so soon be ripped asunder had become the envy of all Europe by 1763. No one quite knew how or why it worked, nor could anyone deny its success. The empire was founded upon a variety of motives which should have been mutually hostile — commercial expansionism, land speculation, royal greed for increased revenues, and religious purism — but these somehow amalgamated into a coherent structure that benefited the mother country as well as the colonies. England's trade and manufacturing expanded as American markets grew, and the colonists also prospered, a phenomenon not necessarily a part of mercantilism's philosophy or operation.

Along with economic success, colonies developed a political self-control which was admittedly unplanned by royal authorities. Americans thoroughly considered themselves Englishmen and enthusiastically adopted English techniques, particularly in politics. Imperial authorities paid little heed to dangers inherent in this imitativeness; indeed, they often encouraged it when it served their purposes. But they expressed amazement after 1763 when Americans threw back in their faces old, established, and sometimes forgotten principles of English government. Colonial devotion to English ideas and practices came in part from the variety of immigrants America absorbed and converted into Englishmen. These converts became more dogmatically determined to preserve their new heritage than those who had grown up in it. If anything, Americans became more English than the English themselves.

Disruption of a working empire in which both partners profited and in which the colonists slavishly emulated the mother country's ways contained all the ingredients of tragedy. But the English, in reshaping imperial policies after the Peace of Paris, inevitably alienated Americans and forced them to reassess their place within the empire. Suddenly the colonists discovered that things they took for granted were neither as firm nor as secure as they had imagined. Consequently, they demanded a specific enunciation of the imperial constitution which would guarantee that the empire they had known would remain unchanged.

A portent of these demands was heard in Virginia when Patrick Henry argued the Parson's Cause in 1760. Ministers of the established Church of England in that colony were paid, by law, in tobacco by their vestries. Poor crops in 1755 and 1758 drove prices up and brought unexpected prosperity to the clergy, and this seriously concerned vestrymen who feared for their ministers' souls. Consequently the assembly passed the Two Penny Act in 1758, permitting vestries to commute the salary to cash at a fixed value of 2d. per pound weight of tobacco, which was well below market price. The clergymen appealed, and the Privy Council disallowed the law in 1760. The Reverend James Maury then began suit to collect his back salary, and his vestry hired young Patrick Henry to defend the case. Since Henry had no legal grounds, he resorted to emotion, challenging the Privy Council disallowance of a beneficial statute as a violation of the compact establishing government. His oratory proved persuasive and, although Henry lost the case, Maury won damages of only one penny.

A similar discordant note was struck in Massachusetts in 1760 by another young lawyer, James Otis, seeking to prevent reissuance of Writs of Assistance. These legal devices, first authorized in 1662, gave their possessors the right, with few restrictions, to search for and seize smuggled goods. As perpetual warrants, they expired only with the death of the monarch in whose name they were issued. In 1760 George II died, and customs officers in Boston sought new writs in George III's name. A group of merchants, unhappy over suppression of illegal trading, hired Otis to argue against their reissuance. He, too, had no ground in legal precedent and so took an emotional position, challenging Parliament's right to authorize unreasonable searches and seizures, and alleging that a man's home was his castle. Otis lost his case without winning a moral victory as had Patrick Henry.

Yet these two challenges — one of Crown authority and the other of parliamentary authority — were omens of trouble which lay ahead for the empire. These questions seemed minor and even foolish in 1760, but within a few years they would assume larger proportions. Americans and Englishmen had developed divergent concepts of rights, and this divergence would split the empire. Tempests in the 1760s and storms in the 1770s would swirl around American contentions for rights which, to Englishmen, were destructive of the empire as they understood it. But to Americans, the empire seemed insupportable without those same rights. Clearly one era ended and another began in 1763.

Selected Bibliography

The maturation of colonial society is dealt with in Max Savelle's *Seeds of Liberty* (1948), Thomas Jefferson Wertenbaker's *Golden Age of Colonial Culture* (1959), Louis B. Wright's *The Cultural Life of the American Colonies* (1956), and Brooke Hindle's *Pursuit of Science in Revolutionary America* (1956).

Eighteenth-century politics are described in Michael Kammen's *Empire and Interest* (1970), Stanley N. Katz's *Newcastle's New York* (1968), John A. Schutz's *Thomas Pownall* (1951) and his *William Shirley* (1961). Leonard W. Labaree's *Royal Government in America* (1930) describes the nature of imperial authority. The ideas behind imperial relationships are discussed in Jack P. Greene's *The Quest for Power* (1963), Lawrence H. Leder's *Liberty and Authority* (1968), Trevor Colbourn's *The Lamp of Experience* (1964), and Bernard Bailyn's *The Ideological Origins of the American Revolution* (1967).

Indian relations are discussed in Nicholas B. Wainwright's *George Croghan: Wilderness Diplomat* (1959), Wilbur Jacobs's *Wilderness Politics and Indian Gifts* (1962), and Douglas Leach's *The Northern Colonial Frontier, 1607-1763* (1966).

Religion has been treated extensively. Some important works are Edwin S. Gaustad's *The Great Awakening in New England* (1957), Ola Winslow's *Jonathan Edwards* (1940), Frederick B. Tolles's *Quakers and the Atlantic Culture* (1960), Sidney V. James's *A People Among Peoples: Quaker Benevolence in Eighteenth Century America* (1963), and Carl Bridenbaugh's *Mitre and Sceptre* (1962).

A basic work, essential to any understanding of eighteenth-century America, is Lawrence Henry Gipson's monumental *The British Empire Before the American Revolution* (15 vols., 1936-70).

CHAPTER 5

A BROODING VIGILANCE, 1763-1776

Peace in 1763 released a series of tensions which had accumulated over three-quarters of a century, and these presented the colonies with grave internal problems. Frontier violence and turbulence, dissatisfaction with established governmental practices, and ill-will between social classes made many on both sides of the Atlantic wonder about American society's future. Fortunately for colonial unity, these resentments soon centered upon England, thereby foreshadowing a standard American practice — the use of an external enemy to distract people from domestic crises.

England became the enemy because it sought to exercise authority in the colonies more effectively than it ever had before. Americans understood the innate conflict between liberty and authority. The former was man's by divine gift or by natural right; the latter was society's by necessity at best and by usurpation at worst. Government, as Thomas Paine so eloquently phrased it, "like dress, is the badge of lost innocence; the palaces of Kings are built on the ruins of the bowers of paradise." Viewing authority as a necessary evil, seeking to preserve the maximum expanse of liberty, Americans in the 1760s were wary of any effort to extend the former at the expense of the latter. Their concern was compounded by their inability to control the central authority of the empire — the king and the Parliament. England before it exerted its authority represented benevolence; once it became the locus of effective authority, it represented disaster in colonial eyes to American liberty.

England sought to increase its role in governing the colonies at a time when social conflict in America was accelerating as a natural result of rapid expansion. Within half a century, population had jumped nearly 600 per cent, whole new areas had been settled, and governmental processes frequently failed to keep pace with this growth. Yet colonial society still patterned itself upon the relatively stable mother country. Americans, like Englishmen, had their gentry and lower classes, but they did not clearly understand the relative positions of the two, and lower classes often seemed to lack a knowledge of their proper place. A key to variations between English and American social systems was land, scarce in the Old World but acquired with relative ease in the New. Land, therefore, did not carry the same aristocratic connotation in America as it did in England. Consequently, the lower classes rejected the colonial gentry's occasional arrogance as unwarranted. Moreover, the fluidity of society deprived Americans of the traditional certainties of life; opportunity opened the door to failure as well as success, thereby creating different tensions in colonial society from those in England and often stimulating exaggerated reactions to new and challenging developments.

Lack of class stratification in America existed not just on the frontier, but in urban areas as well. Boston, New York, Philadelphia, and Charleston by 1760 had become important commercial centers with many opportunities for middle-class artisans and merchants. The career of "Poor Richard" (Benjamin Franklin) suggested the opportunities available to enterprising colonials even though his steady rise was exceptional and due more to his personality than his circumstances. Thrift, industry, honesty, and initiative, Franklin argued, led to success. In *Poor Richard's Almanac* and his famous essay, "The Way to Wealth," he emphasized mid-eighteenth century middle-class values. Profoundly pragmatic, Frank-

COLONIAL SETTLEMENT, 1760

lin's writings verged on materialism. For him, inculcation of industry and frugality became "the means of procuring wealth, and thereby securing virtue; it being more difficult for a man in want to act always honestly, as ... *it is hard for an empty bag to stand upright.*"

BRITISH POLICY REVISED

Americans by 1763 had a prosperous, fluid society with established political patterns. Contradictions abounded as in any rapidly growing society, and these created internal tensions and threatened domestic tranquility. Before such disturbances became too widespread or created irreparable divisions, English policy, which reflected both international politics and English domestic crises, intruded and united most Americans against an external foe. England had won the French and Indian War, but almost lost the peace. France had been defeated, but not destroyed as a power, and still threatened revenge for its humiliation. Moreover, England isolated itself by its sacrifice of Prussia in 1763 when it signed a separate peace treaty. Fears of French retaliation led to demands for rearmament and strengthening American defenses.

Need for a reinforced defensive posture lay behind the Earl of Shelburne's announcement of the Proclamation Line in 1763, which marked the westernmost limits of settlement (roughly the Appalachian ridge), thereby reducing the chance of Indian conflicts, keeping colonists near the seaboard and under English control, maintaining the fur trade, and opening the Floridas and Canada to settlement by directing migrants there from both Europe and older colonies. However, Americans saw the Proclamation Line as a betrayal. They had fought for the Ohio country only to have that great prize denied them.

Still another English policy raised serious questions. Stationing British troops in America to strengthen defenses against both France and its potential Indian allies seemed extraordinary (sixteen regiments were mentioned in rumors current in 1763). England had never maintained such a force in America while France had dominated half the continent, and Americans wondered why France's elimination should result in even stronger forces. Besides, colonials shared Englishmen's traditional distrust of standing armies and could see but one purpose in maintaining such a force — to jam taxes and other unwanted parliamentary measures down colonial throats.

Such fears had good foundations, for England had incurred a debt of

£140 million during the long series of wars, and George Grenville, George III's Chancellor of the Exchequer, worried about the nation's fiscal stability. Grenville, passionately devoted to economy and revenue, determined to reduce the drain upon England by creating a colonial revenue. Since Americans had borne little of the financial burden of the French and Indian War, this seemed reasonable. A wartime requisition system to secure needed support from America had been ineffective, and William Pitt finally promised to repay Americans for fighting in their own defense. This had rankled the English. Moreover, during the empire's life and death struggle, colonials freely traded with the enemy and evaded English custom laws. An estimated £700,000 of annual trade never appeared on the custom collectors' books.

The colonial customs service first caught Grenville's eye, and he determined to revise it, eliminating sinecures which cost England four times more than the duties produced. He insisted upon tighter procedures to make the existing system more effective. Posting bonds after loading a ship made checking by collectors impossible. Now, bonds would be signed before loading so actual cargoes could be checked against manifests. Customs officials, who resided in London while deputies executed their offices in the colonies at half pay, now had to go to their posts or resign. Admiralty Courts, used since the Navigation Act of 1696 to enforce trade laws, were expanded and given greater authority.

Smuggling continually bothered Englishmen. During the French and Indian War, Americans had nullified the blockade of the French and Spanish West Indies by sending them provisions in return for sugar and molasses, Spanish coins, and slaves. New Englanders used ingenious tricks for this purpose, including the flag-of-truce meant for exchange of captives. They secured passes to rescue "relations lying in French dungeons," but their vessels came back with more molasses than relatives. Ships sailed for Jamaica, but winds and storms inevitably carried them into alien ports, as they had for decades.

George Grenville, in all innocence, thought only to improve England's existing mercantilism and make it more profitable. He had no desire to antagonize colonists, but he accomplished just that. James Burgh in his *Political Disquisitions* (1774) reflected: "Our prime-minister's grey-goose quill governed the colonies till that fatal hour in which the evil genius of Britain whispered in the ear of George Grenville, 'George! erect thyself into a great financier.'" Yet, in retrospect, Grenville was being reasonable, for the colonies, unlike the mother country, had no heavy debts, had gained greatly from the war, and certainly had some obligations to the empire that protected and benefited them. Grenville's initial actions did not change traditional patterns, but merely tightened them up. Even alterations in customs duties involved more detail than substance. A higher duty on French cottons gave British merchants a stronger hold on American textile markets, and additional commodities — lumber, raw silk, potash, and logwood — were enumerated and so could only be shipped from the colony of origin to England. Logwood was included because New Englanders used this dyestuff in their smuggling trade with the Dutch.

Grenville assumed that Americans should bear their share of imperial burdens as readily as they accepted its benefits, and so cast about for a new tax. The total colonial public debt was estimated at £2.6 million, but England paid £5 million in annual interest alone. Per capita public debt in the colonies amounted to 18 shillings, in England to £18. To ask Americans to aid with part of their wealth did not seem at all unreasonable since they now monopolized the fur trade, their fisheries were safe from attack and, most important, they themselves were secure for the first time since their settlement.

Parliament's only dilemma was to determine how Americans should participate. The idea of a new tax met with general agreement in Parliament, but what kind? George Grenville finally proposed a tax on molasses which would convert an earlier prohibitory measure of 1733 into a revenue-producing one. After all, if Americans insisted upon trading with the foreign West Indies for prohibited goods, why not accept the trade and make it profitable for England? Grenville's brilliant idea proved disastrous. British West Indies planters and New England colonists had long been rivals, and Americans immediately assumed that Grenville's Sugar Act of 1764 was a West Indian plot. In reality it hurt the West Indies almost as much as it did the New England and Middle Atlantic colonies.

Mainland colonies sold their grain, lumber, horses, and fish to the foreign West Indies, for the British islands could not absorb the full output of those products. In return, the foreign islands provided sugar and molasses at much lower prices than the British West Indies because France, fearful of competition for its domestic wine and brandy industry, would not allow the shipment of molasses to Europe. The foreign islands also provided Spanish gold and silver coins which currency-short mainland colonies always welcomed. British sugar planters had tried to prohibit this trade by the Molasses Act of 1733 which put a prohibitive duty of six pence a gallon on foreign molasses, but extensive smuggling resulted and the British West Indies received little protection.

Now, Grenville proposed to legitimize this trading and make it profitable for the Crown. The Sugar Act of 1764 reduced the tax on foreign molasses to three pence, thereby making British and foreign molasses competitive with each other. Since the Americans had insisted upon trading with the French and Spanish West Indies, and since England needed this revenue, this Act seemed a perfectly obvious reconciliation. However, the preamble stated: "It is expedient that new provisions and regulations should be established for improving the revenue of this kingdom — for defraying the expenses of defending, protecting and securing" the empire. This bothered Americans, for it implied a revenue for colonial purposes independent of colonial control. Moreover, stationing warships in America and a rejuvenated customs service meant enforcement of the tax. And reduction of the tax from six to three pence destroyed the rum distillers' profit margin. Americans immediately organized opposition: Boston merchants set up corresponding committees and the Massachusetts General Court wrote to other assemblies. Meanwhile, economic chaos descended on the northern colonies as prices of provisions fell sharply, molasses rose to the legal price level, and specie suddenly disappeared.

British West Indian planters had finally triumphed at New England's expense, or so the New Englanders assumed. However, Parliament adopted the Sugar Act, not to protect or harm any section of the empire, but solely to raise a revenue. Samuel Adams understood its real purpose and persuaded the Massachusetts General Court to denounce it for levying taxes without local consent in violation of the colony's charter. However, most colonial reaction remained moderate: critics pointed to possible decay of British trade, bemoaned departures from the empire's fundamental principles to benefit West Indian planters, and believed that Parliament would listen to reason. As a tax on trade, it seemed within traditional parliamentary authority. Since the law affected only New England and New York, no continental unity emerged.

Stamp Act

When Grenville proposed the Sugar Act, he suggested the necessity of other taxes and specifically indicated a stamp tax. An old device, it had been used occasionally by the colonies themselves. Colonial agents asked him to delay any new measure for a year to permit Americans to propose an alternative tax, and Grenville agreed. However, Americans came up with unacceptable ideas: the old requisition system, taxation by a continental congress, and a levy on Negro slaves. The first had failed during the French and Indian War, the second was unworkable, and the last was discriminatory.

Grenville firmly believed a stamp tax offered many advantages. In England, it was self-executing and yielded £100,000 a year with minimal collection costs. No legal document was valid and no newspaper could be sold without a stamp, and the only expenses were for warehouses and local distributors. When introduced in Parliament, the Stamp Act stirred little debate and no one questioned England's right or power to tax colonials. A few hesitant voices, misunderstanding the true situation, suggested the inexpediency of taxing "debt-burdened Americans," but this made little impression upon English gentry staggering under heavy land taxes.

The stamp duty, English officials anticipated, would produce nearly £60,000 per year, about one shilling per capita, but this was simply the first step, for Grenville hoped eventually to raise £350,000 a year in America. He anticipated little opposition to this tax, but he miscalculated by failing to eliminate other colonial grievances. The Proclamation Line of 1763, the Sugar Act, and the threat of a standing army still disturbed Americans. Colonial governors and others had warned him to clear up these matters first, but he ignored their advice, just as he did an incipient economic depression caused by the war's end and enforcement of the Sugar Act.

However, Grenville did not have to face the consequences of his folly. His ineptitude in domestic politics and his lengthy lectures finally irritated George III so much that the King announced he would as soon see the devil in his chambers as Mr. Grenville, and the Marquis of Rockingham formed a new government. Rockingham would have to contend with united colonial opposition to the stamp duty and find a graceful way out. Most seriously, the group alienated by this tax — lawyers, printers, merchants, and tavern keepers — provided the main props for English rule in America. The stamp measure hit hardest at this natural colonial leadership, which traditionally supported the existing imperial structure, and it was a most vocal group.

Moreover, Americans began questioning their future within the empire.

Would Parliament stop here? What would be the next tax? Would England try to transfer its entire debt burden to America? The stamp duty opened "a pit that will soon swallow up all the wealth of America." Colonists easily fell into their traditional mass paranoia, taking a difficult situation to its logical extremity, and assuming its ultimate potential was England's goal. A successful tax policy could destroy Americans' vaunted liberties, for it would render meaningless the key safeguard of colonial rights. If assemblies no longer had an exclusive tax power, as they had assumed for three-quarters of a century, then Parliament could make governors, judges, and all other officers dependent on it rather than on local legislatures. Parliament could destroy in one blow what it had taken Americans seventy-five years to accomplish.

American fears of the consequences of parliamentary taxation reflected only a surface issue. More important, Parliament claimed the ability to tax Americans because they, like many Englishmen in an age of inequitable apportionment, enjoyed virtual representation in the imperial legislature. Daniel Dulany in 1765 rejected the idea outright; virtual representation, he announced, was a "mere cob-web, spread to catch the unwary and entangle the weak." Englishmen barred from the suffrage shared no similarities with Americans because "the security of the non-electors in [England] against oppression, is that their oppression will fall also upon the electors and the representatives." However, oppressive measures passed by Parliament for Americans fell only on the colonials, not on English electors or members of Parliament. William Pitt, a year later, denounced virtual representation in even stronger terms: "The idea of a virtual representation of America in this House, is the most contemptible idea that ever entered into the head of man. — It does not deserve a serious consideration." Parliament did not accept Pitt's viewpoint, but all future controversies between England and its mainland colonies centered about the problem of "virtual representation," whether or not the disputants used those words.

Americans feared British taxation, but no one knew who would lead the opposition nor what form it would take. Surprising everyone, Patrick Henry blew the trumpet of sedition in the Virginia House of Burgesses. The legislature had petitioned the king in protest, but its leaders intended to do little more. Not so Henry, who waited until all but thirty-nine of the 116 members had left for home and then introduced his inflammatory resolutions. The first five resolutions insisted that Americans had all the

Patrick Henry (1736-1799), patriot, orator, and statesman, served in the Continental Congress, helped draft the Virginia Constitution of 1776, and served as wartime Governor of Virginia. (By Lawrence Sully, courtesy of Amherst College, Amherst, Massachusetts, bequest of Herbert L. Pratt)

rights of Englishmen, including no taxation without representation, and that the Burgesses had an exclusive right to tax Virginians. The last two resolutions announced that Virginians were bound to obey only laws of their own assembly and labeled as a traitor anyone supporting Parliament's right to tax colonials.

Henry's resolves tested radical and conservative strength in the Burgesses. The first five passed by a close majority, but the last two were defeated. Henry then exposed the financial manipulations of Speaker John Robinson, a conservative leader, who, while the colony's treasurer, had illegally reissued £300,000 of provincial notes to his friends. This thoroughly discredited aristocratic dominance of Virginia's government for a time. More important, however, the reprinting of Henry's resolves, including the two defeated ones, throughout the colonies shocked most people. Even James Otis referred to them as treasonable, but they clearly expressed ideas which many colonists accepted but feared to state openly. Colonial rights were now arrayed against parliamentary power.

Rioting erupted in Boston and other towns in August 1765. Groups of radicals organized as Sons of Liberty to terrorize stampmasters and prevent the Stamp Act's operation. These riots differed from those which traditionally plagued American towns, for colonial aristocrats now led them. John Morin Scott of New York, John Hancock of Boston, William Livingston of New York, William Allen, son of Pennsylvania's Chief Justice, and Christopher Gadsden of South Carolina provided a previously unknown respectability to rioting. Grenville had accomplished what even war with France could not do.

Stamp Act Congress

The alliance between town mobs and colonial aristocrats was most alarming. But Grenville had accomplished more than that — he had created a sense of colonial unity, which became most evident (at the same time that Virginia's Burgesses discussed Henry's resolves) in James Otis' proposal for a Stamp Act Congress. The law would go into effect on November 1, 1765, and Otis urged a meeting of delegates of all colonies in New York City for October to consider concerted action. Nine mainland colonies sent delegates. These men, distinguished colonial leaders, provided a clear warning to England of the situation's gravity. The Congress quickly split into radical and conservative factions, with the latter in the majority. They drafted an address to the king, a memorial to the Lords, and a petition to the Commons. Congress acknowledged that colonials owed a due subordination to Parliament, but insisted upon no taxation without representation. Sons of Liberty argued that once stampmasters had been scared off, little more need be done beyond resuming business as usual without stamps. This would truly demonstrate the colonial triumph over English policy.

But America's real weapon would be trade, not violence. The Sugar Act had led to economic pressures by Bostonians and other New Englanders against English merchants, but the Stamp Act expanded the boycott's scope. Merchants cancelled orders for English goods and told creditors not to expect payments until repeal of the detested law. Many English merchants had criticized the stamp duty for requiring payment in gold or silver, because they feared it would damage trade by draining specie from the colonies. Now they pressured the Rockingham government for repeal.

Rockingham took a pragmatic view. If Americans objected to the stamp tax, get rid of it and end interference with normal trade. He used

THE DECLARATORY ACT, MARCH 18, 1766

> ... *THE SAID COLONIES and plantations in America have been, are, and of right ought to be, subordinate unto, and dependent upon the imperial Crown and Parliament of Great Britain; and that the King's Majesty, by and with the advice and consent of the Lords Spiritual and Temporal, and Commons of Great Britain, in Parliament assembled, had, hath, and of right ought to have, full power and authority to make laws and statutes of sufficient force and validity to bind the colonies and people of America, subjects of the Crown of Great Britain, in all cases whatsoever.*

☆☆☆☆☆☆☆☆☆☆☆☆☆☆☆☆☆☆☆☆☆☆☆☆☆☆☆☆

the tax's impact on English merchants to justify its repeal. William Pitt, who had won an empire and did not intend to see it destroyed by Grenville's folly, supported repeal. He denied Parliament's right to tax colonists, but reaffirmed its right to regulate trade and manufacturing. Benjamin Franklin, in London as agent for Pennsylvania and Massachusetts, supported Pitt's concept of a bifurcated tax power, one internal and the other external. But George III cast the decisive vote by choosing repeal rather than physical enforcement. Parliament cancelled the Stamp Act as a concession to English merchants, but simultaneously passed a Declaratory Act reaffirming Parliament's right to levy such taxes. Out of kindness, not justice, as a concession to Englishmen, not Americans, as a matter of strategy, not right, the Stamp Act was removed.

English Reactions

Americans joyously greeted the Stamp Act's repeal, and ignored the Declaratory Act's ominous wording. Their appeal to Parliament as loyal subjects had won a redress of grievances, but Americans understood neither the processes at work nor their implications. However, they had discovered England's weakness — its rule in America depended upon the colonists' willingness to be governed. Lacking that, the empire was but an aircastle.

Rockingham knew that Americans had to be appeased by resolving their outstanding grievances. Without changing the Sugar Act's purpose, he dropped the molasses tax from three pence per gallon to one penny, thereby restoring the rum distillers' margin of profit but making the tax a more effective revenue producer. To encourage American trade with the foreign West Indies and thereby increase royal revenues, he opened free ports to facilitate the now legal and taxable commerce. At the same time, increased bounties on colonial products stimulated their production and distracted American investment from prohibited fields.

This appeasement of colonials proved unpopular among English gentry weighed down by heavy taxation. They complained of being sacrificed by Rockingham to benefit merchants and Americans. Repeal of the American stamp tax and simultaneous repeal of the English cider tax cost an estimated £130,000 a year, a deficit which the gentry feared would be made up by increasing land taxes. George III, finally weary of Rockingham and the growing dissension he stimulated, dismissed the Marquis in August 1766 and somewhat reluctantly turned to William Pitt.

To Americans, Pitt's elevation was a major victory, for he truly understood colonial problems. Having won the empire for England, he would best know how to preserve it. Statues of Pitt had been erected in American towns, colonials drank toasts in his honor, and Ezra Stiles eloquently described him as "the most penetrating political genius, the most upright and sagacious legislator that ever appeared on earth. I am sure Lycurgus, Plato, Cicero, Selden, or the Venetian Paul had not the amazing compass and force of genius." Indeed, the only sour note to Americans was Pitt's acceptance of a peerage as Earl of Chatham. But Pitt or Chatham, great commoner or nobleman, he still seemed the best guarantee of American liberty.

Pitt and Townshend

Pitt's entrance into the prime ministership changed little. He faced the same problems that had plagued Rockingham, plus some of Grenville's leftover difficulties. The colonials particularly objected to the Mutiny Act of 1765, whose importance had been obscured by the Stamp Act, but which now became their chief grievance. This law, as first written, proposed quartering of troops in private homes in America to alleviate the shortage of colonial barracks. Initial American opposition modified it so only empty houses and barns could be commandeered by English officers. But Americans found the whole idea distasteful. Hypersensitive about their liberties, they imagined their homes turned into barracks and their wives and daughters exposed to the bestialities of a rude soldiery. American fears had some foundation, for the army recruited soldiers from the dregs of English and Irish society. Ten thousand of these troops in America combined with the Mutiny Act's quartering provisions presented a dreadful prospect.

Under the Mutiny Act, colonial legislatures had to provide barracks

"Recruits." A satiric commentary on the origins and qualities of the British common soldiers, who were often recruited from the dregs of Irish and London society. (By H. W. Bunbury, Prints Division, The New York Public Library, Astor, Lenox and Tilden Foundations)

and supplies upon request. This added another dimension to the controversy: if Parliament could not tax directly, could it accomplish its purpose indirectly by forcing colonists to bear the costs of a standing army? Perhaps Britain had really given up nothing by repealing the Stamp Act. It could still impose taxation without representation by its dictatorial demands on local legislatures.

Opposition to the Mutiny Act first occurred in Massachusetts when a storm forced a vessel carrying two companies of English soldiers into Boston. The commander asked for supplies under the law, and the Council ordered them delivered. Boston was in an uproar, and James Otis denounced the seven councillors who voted the supplies as "seven devils" who betrayed their country's liberties. The House of Representatives refused to pay for the supplies, and the English government chose to ignore it, thus establishing a precedent, one upon which Americans relied. Opposition begot no retaliation.

The storm over the Mutiny Act centered on New York, British Army headquarters in America, which would be heavily burdened by the law. Its assembly rejected a request for funds as an unconstitutional tax, but offered to obey a royal requisition, thereby reversing English history by denying parliamentary power and exalting Crown authority. New York's attitude caused America's friends in England serious concern. Chatham suggested that the colonists had lost their senses, while others denounced appeasement and urged stronger action. If Americans nullified the Mutiny Act, they could destroy all parliamentary power. Parliament was pitted against provincial assemblies. One must dominate, for power seemed indivisible, and two loci of power, each capable of nullifying the other, could not exist side by side.

American obstinacy on the Mutiny Act forced Chatham's hand, for even George Grenville began to regain popularity in the Commons. The strong man in Chatham's ministry, Chancellor of the Exchequer Charles Townshend, insisted on coming to grips with the colonists. And the prime minister, suffering from gout and fits of mental illness, left Townshend in virtual command. He promised the gentry no increase in taxes despite the £400,000 annual costs of maintaining and defending the colonies. Seeking popularity, Townshend rashly pledged an American revenue without offending colonials, and he ridiculed the distinction between internal and external taxes as "perfect nonsense."

By inventing a meaningful tax that colonists would accept, Townshend certainly would have won acclaim on both sides of the Atlantic. But he could not, and the opposition gathered strength. Commons voted to cut land taxes by a shilling, pressuring Townshend to keep his pledge. He responded first by proposing to punish New York for its rejection of the Mutiny Act by suspending its assembly if it did not obey the law by a stipulated date. Finally, he introduced his long-awaited revenue measures. Taxes on exports to America of glass, lead, paint, paper, and tea would raise £40,000 a year and be paid to the British Exchequer to establish a civil list for the colonies. The mountain labored and brought forth a mouse, but Parliament hoped this was merely the beginning of a series of brilliant tax measures.

Edmund Burke opposed the Townshend duties as similar in principle to the Stamp Act and liable to the same objections. George Grenville denounced them for damaging English merchants and therefore being both "impolitic and uncommercial." But the measure passed Commons by a two-to-one vote with no one raising the question of Parliament's right to tax trade or to punish New York. Townshend believed his approach infallible, for he thought he had used a distinction between internal and external taxes that Americans understood and accepted. His levies were external and, according to Benjamin Franklin who appeared before Parliament, perfectly proper. Also, by not imposing physical force on New York, he felt he stifled intercolonial unity.

Townshend contributed to the Anglo-American controversy by convincing colonists of the fallacy of the distinction between internal and external taxes. All taxes, regardless of how applied, must be opposed, for Parliament could either tax Americans, or it could not. Moreover, the Townshend duties were even more threatening because they created a civil list, thereby making colonial officials financially independent of their assemblies. Townshend died in the fall of 1767 securely believing that he was a greater financier than George Grenville, but in reality he was a greater bungler.

Suspension of the New York assembly instantly provoked a colonial uproar, for if assemblies were parliaments in miniature, then one could not suspend another. More important, it established the precedent that a parliamentary edict could annihilate any colonial legislature unless it handed over all funds upon demand. Boston's Sons of Liberty began talking of fighting, and New York's radicals wanted to apply to other colonies for aid. However, conservative caution triumphed in New York, and the assembly, just prior to its suspension, agreed to supply the troops by a one-vote margin. No preamble to that act was given, thus avoiding direct mention of both the Mutiny Act and the Suspending Act.

The rest of Townshend's program did not stir immediate concern because Americans still hoped somehow to reconcile colonial liberty and parliamentary authority. The Massachusetts General Court's Circular Letter of 1768 offered one approach. It admitted parliamentary supremacy over the empire, but declared the constitution to be fixed and the ultimate source of legislative power. A legislature that violated the constitution destroyed itself by ripping the fabric of government. The letter then announced that Americans owed allegiance to and should enjoy rights under the English constitution, defining one of those rights as the power to dispose of one's own property, either individually or by collective action. Since Americans had no representation in Parliament, it could not dispose of their property, and thus a parliamentary act to raise a colonial revenue violated the constitution. Only provincial legislatures represented the colonists, and only they could tax Americans. But the Circular Letter had expressed a fistful of heretical political theories, and it added insult to injury by appealing for support to the Crown rather than Parliament.

Much the same view found expression in John Dickinson's *Letters from a Farmer in Pennsylvania* published at the same time. A Philadelphia lawyer, Dickinson looked upon this as a fascinating law case, and he expressed ideas that found general acceptance in America. He accepted Parliament's imperial authority, but insisted that taxation, internal or external, was illegal. He conceded that an incidental duty might arise from regulating trade, but the test was the act's purpose. This effort to reconcile the principle of no taxation without representation and parliamentary authority became an immediate sensation throughout the colonies.

Most colonials considered the Massachusetts Letter and Dickinson's *Letters* as perfectly proper expressions of truth, not as polemics intended to antagonize England. Virginia approved the Massachusetts Circular Letter in April 1768 and urged others to do so. In Pennsylvania, however, conservative Quakers led by Joseph Galloway dominated the legislature, and they deplored Dickinson's arguments and their implications; they preferred to ignore the whole matter. But the English made certain that it would not be ignored.

Grenville referred to the Circular Letter as "an impudent, seditious, infamous libel." Townshend's death and Chatham's illness disorganized the government, but a new muddler appeared — the Earl of Hillsborough. He became Secretary of State for the Colonies, a newly created position designed to develop a coherent colonial policy. High hopes existed for Hillsborough and his new office, as for the first time one man coordinated all colonial policy. He received the task of answering the Massachusetts Circular Letter.

Hillsborough's Circular Letter followed the Stamp Act and Townshend Act in uniting the colonists against English policies. He ordered all governors to ignore the Massachusetts Circular Letter. If any assembly approved it, that body should be immediately prorogued or dissolved; if the Massachusetts General Court did not rescind the offensive document, it should be dissolved. Hillsborough determined to compel submission, but his obstinacy made Americans more aware of the fragility of their rights. Hillsborough made Americans fighting mad, and assemblies, previously lukewarm to the Massachusetts Letter, now enthusiastically adopted it. By a 92 to 17 vote the Massachusetts House refused to rescind its earlier action.

Enforcing the Townshend Duties

As the Hillsborough-Massachusetts argument reached a stalemate, attention focused again on the Townshend duties. Most were innocuous, and only the tea tax had importance for revenue purposes. Taxes on tea imported into England had been removed in 1767, consequently reducing the total tax paid by Americans from one shilling to three pence and making tea cheaper after enactment of the Townshend duties than before. Rather than soothing Americans, this antagonized them even more. Reducing the price of tea made collection of the tax more likely, and it still raised a revenue. Moreover, mercantile grievances remained. The molasses tax of one penny per gallon, the unfavorable balance of trade, scarcity of specie, and Townshend's enforcement policies all alienated colonial merchants.

Townshend's enforcement policies particularly upset Bostonians. He used Writs of Assistance, established four new Vice-Admiralty Courts (one each at Halifax, Boston, Philadelphia, and Charleston), and created a Board of American Customs Commissioners. Bostonians particularly detested the Commissioners because they made enforcement more effective, especially in Boston where they were stationed, while smuggling continued unabated elsewhere. Pennsylvania, for example, continued to smuggle Dutch tea, and the East India Company continued to lose its American market.

Economic reprisals were the order of the day. A boycott of English goods had worked against the Stamp Act, so why would it not work against the Townshend Act? If England actually depended on the American market, any interruption of trade would win immediate results. Boston merchants, most oppressed by taxes, clamored for action. However, James Otis warned that without support from other colonies, Boston would only destroy itself. Philadelphia and New York City, reluctant to take a strong stand, changed attitudes upon receipt of the Earl of Hillsborough's Circular Letter and upon the Customs Commissioners' demand that all duties be paid in specie. Soon even Virginia, not directly engaged in trade and therefore not directly affected by the duties and their enforcement, joined in the quest for effective economic action. A "Buy American" campaign began, Benjamin Franklin urged his compatriots to turn from rum to whiskey, homespun clothing became a sign of patriotism, and the goal became self-sufficiency, not of the empire, but of the colonies. Newspapers played up this theme, and published detailed stories about manufacturing which scared many Englishmen, even though most projects never materialized.

This challenge to English mercantilism cost Americans most of their friends in the mother country, for it struck at England's heart — its countinghouses. Chatham resigned in December 1767 and the Duke of Grafton, who now inherited the problems, succeeded him. Lord North, his Chancellor of the Exchequer, considered the Townshend duties "preposterous," but Americans had made retreat with honor most difficult. The question had narrowed down to parliamentary supremacy, not relief of overburdened English landowners. If Parliament abandoned its colonial tax power, the empire, in any meaningful sense, ceased to exist. Grafton wanted to toss over the Townshend duties and rely exclusively on the Declaratory Act of 1766, but North objected to complete repeal. One tax must remain to remind Americans of Parliament's power. Since English merchants did not pressure the government as they had done in 1766, the cabinet narrowly voted to retain the tea tax.

The Tea Duty

Lord North, strong man in Grafton's cabinet, argued that only the tea tax did not harm English mercantilism because neither England nor the colonies produced tea. Thus Americans had no choice, once smuggling was suppressed, but to buy East India Company tea and pay the duty, providing a revenue of about £11,000 to £12,000 a year for the treasury.

Hillsborough announced to the colonies repeal of all Townshend duties except that on tea, reassuring them that the ministry intended no further colonial taxes for revenue purposes. But repeal again was a concession to English merchants and manufacturers, not to Americans. The radicals rejected Hillsborough's letter and demanded complete repeal, along with removal of the Customs Commissioners, abolition of Admiralty Courts, and abandonment of Writs of Assistance. But a rift had developed between radical Sons of Liberty and conservative colonial merchants because the latter accepted partial repeal.

The radicals based their case on English weakness: force did not support England's sweeping claims of authority. Nonimportation had given the radicals the whiphand, and they saw no reason to yield before winning their point. Those who favored the English position commented that England provided too much hostility for reconciliation and too little force for compulsion. Communication difficulties hampered policy enforcement, and no governor had the strength to insist upon obedience to parliamentary statutes opposed by the colonists. Moreover, radicals controlled the press, a potent factor in stimulating opposition, and there seemed to be no way to curb it. Newspapers kept people constantly excited over their liberties and made the Anglo-American controversy a popular crusade, uniting country and town, frontier and seacoast.

Radical advantages included concrete illustrations of the consequences of English policies. They pointed to Ireland, a once prosperous country transformed into a poverty-stricken appendage of "worn out panderers and whores from England." Now that Ireland had been milked dry, would America be next? And English authorities could not stop these newspaper incitements. In Boston, the Council referred to the *Gazette* as the "Weekly Dung Barge," but the assembly paid the King's Attorney who had no intention of jeopardizing his salary and position by prosecuting the paper. The press had developed over the years a viable theory and attitude of freedom which it now used against England.

THE BOSTON MASSACRE

England's only available resource was military force. In 1768 mobs drove the Customs Commissioners from Boston to Castle William in the harbor, leading to demands in England for military coercion. Grafton finally sent

A BROODING VIGILANCE   163

four regiments to Boston. This threatened to cancel nonimportation's effectiveness, but in 1769 Grafton transferred two regiments to Halifax, leaving not enough troops to maintain the English position, but enough to antagonize the colonials. Newspapers published horrendous tales of brutality by soldiers, and everyone's nerves were on edge. Incidents multiplied; tensions increased.

In March 1770, when a mob moved toward the customs house, the English officer in charge thought they intended to steal the king's revenue and tried to halt them. When he could not, the soldiers finally fired on the crowd. Five Bostonians (among them a black, Crispus Attucks) lay dead, and the town demanded that the culprits be brought to justice and the soldiers be removed. Governor Thomas Hutchinson could not help but comply. The troops left Boston, and a trial was scheduled for the eight soldiers involved in the Massacre. John Adams served as attorney for the accused soldiers. Six were acquitted; two were convicted of

British troops landing in Boston. This engraving by Paul Revere depicts the landing of British soldiers, in response to the Duke of Grafton's orders, in Boston. They were sent to enforce the Townshend Duty on tea and to provide support for the Customs Commissioners. ("Blockade of Boston, 1768," by Paul Revere, Rare Book Department, courtesy of Free Library of Philadelphia)

manslaughter, pleaded their clergy (a medieval means of removing those in holy orders from civil jurisdiction by permitting them to demonstrate their ability to read the Bible), and were branded.

The Boston Massacre, the high point of political resistance, alarmed many moderate Americans. Conservative merchants, now convinced of the dangers of mob rule, abandoned the nonimportation movement. Radical control collapsed, and by the summer of 1770 tension ended. From this point forward radicals no longer trusted merchants and decided that any future campaign against English policy must not rest in their hands. Only those who placed American liberty above their own pocketbooks could be given leadership. Meanwhile, a lethargy set in among the colonists who had been exhausted by tension, hysteria, and idealism from 1763 to 1770.

False Calm

England found reassurance in the immediate aftermath of the Boston Massacre. Bonds of unity dissolved as correspondence between colonies dropped off, and Massachusetts seemed to be left in the lurch. Prosperity returned as English goods flooded the colonies, and an era of good feelings began, although bickering between assemblies and governors continued on traditional issues. No new grievances came from the ministry, however, and radical arguments grew stale.

Indeed, internal dissension again dominated. Connecticut and Pennsylvania controverted ownership of the Wyoming Valley in Pennsylvania, and fighting erupted between partisans of the two colonies. Similarly, New York and New Hampshire contested ownership of a disputed border tract, and Green Mountain Boys ousted Yorkers. In Carolina, the Regulator Movement of 1770 ripped apart the colony's social fabric because aristocratic leaders refused to solve basic grievances. Quarrels on class and sectional lines suggested civil wars within colonies rather than between Americans and Englishmen.

Even the English radical movement, upon which Americans had relied, seemed to fall apart. John Horne Tooke and John Wilkes, leaders of an incipient republican movement in England, fell out over disposition of funds supplied by American sympathizers. Collapse of this alliance hurt American radicalism because Wilkes and Tooke had been spokesmen in England for the colonials. Thus the whirlwind of discontent, in both England and America, seemed to have dissipated. Conservatives rejoiced, and Lord North relaxed. But it was a false calm.

The Gaspée Incident

American concern for liberty quickened in 1772 with the appearance off Rhode Island of an armed English schooner, the *Gaspée*, sent to enforce the Navigation Acts and revenue laws in that colony for the first time. Smugglers, whose way of life had become traditional in Rhode Island, expressed outrage at this intrusion, which they called a piratical act. In March 1772, the *Gaspée* ran aground, and a large number of people gathered, while some went out in small boats and attacked the schooner. The ship was captured and burned, ending interference with smuggling in Rhode Island.

The act's audacity stunned Englishmen and their colonial supporters. Governor Hutchinson of Massachusetts declared that unless England acted swiftly and decisively, the radicals could safely attempt "further measures which are necessary to obtain and secure their independence without any danger of ever being called to account for it." The English ministry quickly appointed a Commission of Inquiry to investigate and to send the culprits to England for trial. Radicals labeled the Commission a Court of Star Chamber, an Inquisition, a "pack of Egyptian tyrants," and it received no cooperation from Rhode Islanders. Even though hundreds witnessed the incident, no one recognized any rioters or admitted culpability, and the Commission concluded that the attack had been led by Americans of property and estate against whom the community refused to inform. Since they could do nothing else, the English authorities closed the case and forgot it.

Security for English officers had ended, radical arrogance now knew no bounds, and the Virginia Burgesses proposed a renewal of intercolonial correspondence. Whatever conciliatory hopes remained were shattered by news that England intended to establish a civil list for Massachusetts with American revenues. Sam Adams responded by organizing a Boston Committee of Correspondence, and by charging his old enemy, Governor Thomas Hutchinson, with full responsibility for this threat to popular government in Massachusetts. A civil list would destroy the legislature's ultimate power over royal officials by making them independent of local appropriations. Governor Hutchinson came from an old colonial family, and his presence in the office blurred the potential danger. Consequently, Sam Adams determined to destroy Hutchinson, so that no one would mistake the civil list's significance.

Benjamin Franklin now entered the scene. While in London as agent for Massachusetts and Pennsylvania, he obtained letters written by Hutchinson and by Lieutenant Governor Andrew Oliver. Franklin, fearing Americans suspected his loyalty, proved his devotion by sending the letters to some Massachusetts radicals with an injunction not to publish them, but only to show them to confidential friends. Hungry men devoured Franklin's feast. The letters were read to the House of Representatives, which directed Sam Adams to edit them for publication.

Hutchinson's letters disapproved of radical activity, and occasionally let slip some impolitic things, but said little that he had not declared in

Boston town meeting. The violence and passion of these sessions is clearly indicated. The town meeting became the focal point for Boston's resistance to British policies, until curbed by the Administration of Government Act in 1774. Then it was replaced by unofficial committees. (Rare Book Division, The New York Public Library, Astor, Lenox and Tilden Foundations)

public messages. However, as editor, Sam Adams made certain that the letters exaggerated the most outrageous statements, and their publication was an Act of Providence to the Sons of Liberty. Franklin saved his position in the colonies, but in England he became *persona non grata*. Hutchinson and Oliver lost the last shred of their influence in Massachusetts, and the General Court voted to impeach them and asked the English government to remove them. Again, colonial vigilance heightened.

Tea and the East India Company

Much of the final controversy between England and its American colonies developed out of problems facing the East India Company, one of England's most important chartered corporations. Sovereign in India, the company drew great wealth from that subcontinent. Most of this went improperly to the pockets of its employees, while the company, without earning profits, continued paying handsome dividends to shareholders. As an integral part of the English economy, the company had to be maintained despite its own corruption and the jealousy of English merchants anxious to break its monopoly.

Chatham and Shelburne in 1767 denounced the "lofty Asiatic plunderers of Leadenhall Street," and urged that the monopoly be broken and trade with India be opened to all Englishmen. The opposition Whigs, led by Charles Townshend and Edmund Burke, proclaimed themselves defenders of the company's charter, a property right. A compromise resulted, with the company retaining its monopoly, and paying a £400,000 a year subsidy to the government. However, this solved neither the company's problem, nor England's. The subsidy represented only a portion of the revenue England could get from independent merchants by ending the monopoly, the company's agents still milked it dry, and India still suffered.

By 1773 the company's treasury was empty, its bills unpaid, and its credit exhausted. It could no longer pay the £400,000 subsidy, and it had several years' supply of tea which it could not sell to Americans. Company directors, fearing a new attempt to break its monopoly, appealed again to the Whigs for support. As before, they received a favorable response. Even American newspapers sympathized with the company's plight and hoped that no one would tamper with its property rights as stipulated in its royal charter. Lord North, to save the company from bankruptcy, decided that its basic problem was loss of its American market. The directors agreed, but did not want to jump into a colonial tax dispute and therefore urged repeal of the tea tax to end colonial boycotting and Dutch smuggling.

Lord North, however, had a better plan. He would not remove the Townshend duty on tea, but instead would permit the company to export directly to the colonies. This eliminated English middlemen to whom tea had been customarily auctioned for resale to colonial merchants. Tea could now be sold in America for less than in England, and the price reduction would destroy smuggled Dutch tea's advantage. Yet, England would keep its tax. Lord North expected to be hailed as thirsty mankind's benefactor.

The East India Company sent its tea to the colonies: nearly 300 chests valued at £11,000 to Boston, 250 chests worth £9,000 to Charleston, and 700 chests worth £25,000 to New York. The cargoes were consigned to company appointees, nominations usually awarded by governors as patronage plums, who would then distribute tea locally. At first the idea of cheap tea delighted Americans, but radicals quickly noted, perhaps whimsically, that much of it had lain in English warehouses for years, and that tea, unlike wine, did not improve with age.

In one stroke Lord North united smugglers, legitimate merchants, and opponents of English taxation by a common grievance. Smugglers saw themselves ruined, for they could not compete with cheaper legal tea. Legitimate merchants dreaded the precedent of monopoly and wondered what commodity would be next. Radicals viewed the Tea Act of 1773 as a subterfuge to force Americans to pay the tax. Suddenly, the East India Company, previously seen as a victim of English tyranny, became in American minds the merciless exploiter of India seeking new worlds to conquer. All colonials agreed that America would not be next.

Although the colonists gave Lord North more credit than he probably deserved, their over-reaction reflected their paranoia. They believed he intended to breach American defenses against taxation by monopolies. His retention of the tea tax reunited merchants and radicals. But unity was now on different terms: radicals controlled the partnership. An intensive campaign began to dissuade Americans from using tea, even suggesting that it caused loss of teeth, upset stomach, spleen, and loss of virility. Since taxed tea could not be distinguished from smuggled tea, all of it would be boycotted. Ironically, the Sons of Liberty now prohibited smuggling in America!

Lord North had anticipated no difficulty in enforcing this Tea Act of 1773. He expected it would be self-executing, for American cupidity would eliminate more expensive smuggled tea from the colonial market and encourage sale of cheaper East India Company tea. Thus responsibility for enforcement belonged to the East India Company alone. Colonial governors, having no special instructions, refused to step in when trouble commenced, but tea consignees, like stampmasters earlier, needed help when Sons of Liberty offered them the alternative of resigning or being mobbed. Most resigned immediately rather than risk their families, homes, and businesses to the mob.

Only in Boston did the situation differ. Governor Hutchinson, bitter over publication of his correspondence, determined to stand up to the radicals. The radicals were equally determined to atone for purchases of taxed tea by Massachusetts from 1768 to 1773, to remove the stain on their patriotism. Two immovable forces now confronted one another. The Boston consignees did not resign, but fled to Castle William in the harbor, and Governor Hutchinson refused to return the tea to England. Unless it were removed by December 17, 1773, it would be seized for nonpayment of customs duties, auctioned, and the tax paid. After several unsuccessful appeals, radicals took matters in their own hands. On the night of December 16, dressed as Mohawk Indians, they boarded the ships and, without opposition, dumped the tea overboard in view of hundreds of spectators.

English officials denounced the Tea Party as treason, but no one came forward as a witness. No one knew for sure who had served as Mohawks, but rumor had it that Sam Adams and John Hancock had participated. Radicals claimed Hutchinson's obstinacy had made dumping necessary, and they justified it as self-defense: "The great law of Nature and reason has possessed every society with a right to defend itself from ruin, without having recourse to books, statutes, or recorded customs." For a moment, it seemed the radicals had gone too far, for the countryside hesitated to support the Tea Party, but British reactions soon won them over.

Tea parties occurred throughout the colonies. Annapolis, Maryland, Greenwich, New Jersey, and Charleston, South Carolina, all flavored their harbors with English tea. Radicals now proscribed all tea, smuggled or otherwise, as the only way to prevent collection of the tax. Leadership had slipped from the merchants to the Sons of Liberty, and the same sabotage that destroyed colonial unity in 1770 would not be permitted again.

English Reactions

The Boston Tea Party shocked Englishmen, who compared its importance to Bonnie Prince Charlie's rebellion of 1745. Lord North, dumbfounded, could not understand why Americans rebelled against a tax that made tea cheaper than before. Even Chatham, America's great defender, thought Boston's action criminal and urged chastisement lest the colonies end up by taxing and controlling England. Boston's primary role strengthened demands for retribution, for the self-righteousness and hypocrisy of "New Englanders" were notorious. If Boston, cause of all England's colonial problems, were subdued, peace might prevail in all the colonies.

Lord North refused demands for bloody reprisals, preferring more subtle approaches; besides, starving Bostonians into submission might even foster disunity among the colonies. Thus he introduced the Boston Port Bill in March 1774 to close the port to all shipping until the town paid for the destroyed tea. By focusing on Boston, Lord North thought other cities would scramble for Boston's trade, England would rise in their esteem for giving them this opportunity, and Boston would find itself isolated. This method also had economy to recommend it, for a few ships could seal the harbor. The Bill passed after heated debate as to whether or not it punished Boston severely enough. The only serious criticism centered on the provision that the king could determine when Boston had complied with its terms and lift the blockade. Some suggested such power should be kept by Parliament, not given to the monarch. The ministry now assumed it could sit back and wait for Boston to be humbled.

However shocking the Tea Party had been to Englishmen, the Port Bill was more so to Americans. Bostonians claimed, with some accuracy, that the Tea Party did not surpass in violence an ordinary English riot. Even Governor Hutchinson was surprised at British severity. When news of the act reached Boston, the townspeople called a meeting in Faneuil Hall. Conservatives urged payment for the tea, but the Sons of Liberty stood their ground. However, they needed support, and they appealed to other provinces, claiming that the frontier of American liberty lay on the Charles River. They also suggested that if Boston succumbed, every other colonial town, one by one, could be brought to heel in the same way.

Many Americans accepted Boston's predicament as their own, agreeing that isolationism offered no security. On June 1, 1774, the Boston Port Act went into effect, and public mourning began in other colonies. In Philadelphia shops closed, church bells rang, and flags flew at half mast. New Yorkers burned effigies of Lord North and Governor Hutchinson. Connecticut ordered the public hangman to burn a copy of the Act. Bostonians suddenly became "innocent, virtuous, religious, loyal people, ever remarkable for their love of order, peace and good government." Lord North had martyred them, and by doing so, he cemented American unity.

Economic Warfare

Sam Adams immediately argued for economic reprisals as America's only hope. He drafted a Solemn League and Covenant, a boycott of English goods and an embargo on exports to England. Merchants opposed this radical scheme and in New York City tried to distract attention by proposing instead an intercolonial congress which merchants could control and which would remove Boston's radicals from leadership. Philadelphia also supported a congress, as did Virginia's burgesses who met in a Williamsburg tavern after the governor dissolved them. Sam Adams and the Boston radicals, needing colonial unity for any action, agreed to the congress as a halfway measure. Boston, Adams knew, could not flout the Port Bill with the same impunity as previous measures.

Meanwhile, Lord North decided to take further steps before the Port Bill became effective. Reform of the Massachusetts constitution, he believed, was long overdue and might free the loyal majority from radical tyranny. To prune crudities from that colony's government, to add a dose of monarchical and aristocratic principles, he introduced into Parliament in May 1774 the Massachusetts Government Act, the Administration of Justice Act, and the Quartering Act. They were referred to in England as the Coercive Acts, but Americans immediately labeled them the Intolerable Acts.

The Massachusetts Government Act eliminated elective councillors, permitting the Crown to appoint them, gave the governor power to appoint and remove judicial officers without legislative approval, and restricted town meetings, which radicals had used so effectively, to one a year and their agenda to local business. The Administration of Justice Act, dubbed the "Murder Act" by colonists, protected royal officials and troops from local prosecution for any offense with which they might

Samuel Adams (1722-1803). Leader of Massachusetts radicals, initiator of the Committee of Correspondence, Adams is represented here as a stern figure, his face set in determination. This portrait was painted by John Singleton Copley during the period of calm from 1770 to 1772. (Museum of Fine Arts, Boston)

be charged if the authorities felt the accused would not receive a fair trial in America. In such instances, the trials would be transferred to England. The Quartering Act required colonial authorities to house troops at the scene of disturbances, not in distant forts.

The Intolerable Acts

Amidst a popular outburst of indignation, royal authority collapsed in Massachusetts. Only Boston, still in the British Army's grasp, remained under royal control. Committees of Correspondence went into immediate action, denying the constitutionality of the Intolerable Acts. "No power on earth," wrote the Boston Committee, "hath a right without the consent of this Province to alter the minutest title of its charter or abrogate any act whatever made in pursuance of it.... We are entitled to life, liberty and the means of sustenance by the grace of heaven and without the King's leave." Throughout Massachusetts, Lord North was denounced and, since he was not within reach, his councillors suffered for him. These hapless officials flocked to join the troops, customs commissioners, and tea consignees in Castle William.

Radicals made effective propaganda use of these laws, as witness their label of "Murder Act" for the Administration of Justice Act. They pointed to England's treatment of the Massachusetts Charter as a scrap of paper and questioned which charter would be next? If charters could be destroyed so easily, then poll taxes, land taxes, and finally confiscation of property would ensue. To Massachusetts, tyranny was no longer a remote possibility, but a present reality. Conservatives argued that radical hysteria was unjustified and the laws not so harsh as imagined, but the British ministry soon destroyed their position.

During these same months, another and totally unrelated British measure further inflamed imperial relations. The Quebec Act recast British policy to solve administrative problems in the Ohio Valley and to relieve the French Canadian population of oppression. The English had introduced the Church of England, common law, and a representative assembly into Canada after 1763. None of these met with approval from the French population accustomed to Roman Catholicism, French law, and an executive form of government. Lord North now attempted to soothe French Canadians by eliminating the assembly, disestablishing the Anglican Church, and restoring French law. For administrative purposes, the act also attached the Ohio country to Quebec, thus subjecting western settlers to the same government as French Canadians. Though this enlightened legislation ultimately prevented Canada from becoming the "fourteenth state," it immediately handed American radicals their best propaganda weapon.

Previous aromas of tyranny now mingled with smells of popery, and English colonists foresaw a horde of papist slaves swarming to destroy American liberty. Suddenly Americans wondered whether the introduction of Catholicism was a premeditated English policy for the colonies. Since Americans had been brought up in an anti-Catholic tradition extending back to the Reformation, this seriously upset them. More immediately, the Quebec Act dashed all hopes for speculative opportunities in the Ohio country because no right-minded Englishman or colonial would venture there without traditional guarantees of English rights, and these had just been wiped out. Virginians and Pennsylvanians alike had the door to the West slammed in their faces.

The parliamentary opposition had denounced the Quebec Act as a "monstrous production of tyranny, injustice, and arbitrary power." News of the act and of opposition to it by Chatham, Charles James Fox, and the Earl of Shelburne reached America as the First Continental Congress assembled in Philadelphia, and it made possible a radical victory in the Congress. Lord North had previously struck only at Massachusetts; now he threatened the religion, property, and liberty of all colonials. American unity became firmer than ever before, and England became a foreign, despotic, papist power in colonial eyes.

First Continental Congress

Philadelphia, America's most conservative town, had purposefully been selected for the First Continental Congress as a means of limiting radical effectiveness. The members attending the meeting were considered "the ablest and wealthiest men in America" by Governor John Penn of Pennsylvania and by Chatham as "the most honorable assembly of statesmen since those of the ancient Greeks and Romans." But the aristocratic nature of the Congress did not guarantee its conservatism, as evidenced by its selection of Carpenter's Hall rather than the State House for its meetings, and by its choice of Charles Thomson, Philadelphia's radical leader, as secretary.

The conservatives expected Bostonians to argue the radical cause, and they prepared accordingly. But Sam Adams and his fellow New Englanders held back and allowed Virginians and South Carolinians to become radical spokesmen. This surprised many because these landowners had the most solid stake of all in society and thus seemed out of character as radicals. Yet Christopher Gadsden of South Carolina urged an attack on British troops in Boston, Richard Henry Lee called for adoption of the Solemn League and Covenant, and Patrick Henry announced that the empire was already dissolved and the colonies were in a state of nature. These southerners, embittered by the Quebec Act which deprived them of land speculation opportunities, insisted that Congress begin its list of grievances with the Proclamation Line of 1763 as the first violation of the old empire's principles. Refusing to recognize Parliament, they urged an appeal to the king to turn from "designing and dangerous men" who perverted his empire.

Joseph Galloway of Pennsylvania best expressed the conservative hope for reconciliation when he insisted that prejudice and misunderstanding

Tryon Palace, described as the most beautiful public building in the thirteen colonies, was completed in 1770. It was the last seat of the Crown government in North Carolina and the meeting place of the first Provincial Convention of North Carolina (1774). (Courtesy of North Carolina Department of Conservation and Development)

could be negotiated away. He urged an American legislature, with delegates elected by local assemblies, to control colonial affairs. This inferior branch of Parliament would have to approve all parliamentary legislation affecting America. A Crown-appointed Governor General with a veto power would act as an overseer. Through this far-sighted "Plan of Union," Galloway hoped to capitalize on American desires to remain within the empire and yet control their own destinies. English sovereignty would then be compatible with colonial liberty.

When Congress tabled Galloway's plan, it cast the die. A rumor then spread throughout Congress that General Gage had begun a "horrid butchery" in Boston and had laid the town in ashes. This "Powder Alarm" proved false, but not until it demonstrated that mobs everywhere were ready to march to Boston's defense. Hostilities in Boston would quickly spread to other colonies and become a general conflagration.

At this critical juncture, Paul Revere, messenger for the Boston radicals, raced into town with the Suffolk Resolves. Drafted by Joseph Warren and ratified by the Suffolk County Convention (i.e., Boston), these resolutions urged disobedience to the Coercive Acts, collection of taxes by a provincial congress, military preparations, and imprisonment of all servants of tyrannical government. On October 8, 1774, Congress approved the resolves, but urged Bostonians to refrain from starting a conflict. Reconciliation was dead, for Congress had now sanctioned a defensive war in Massachusetts and promised intercolonial support.

Congress next approved a Continental Association which imposed nonimportation, nonexportation, and nonconsumption, a stronger proposal than Sam Adams had first suggested. Control had completely slipped from the merchants, for only mob action could enforce nonconsumption of English goods. Nonimportation would begin on December 1, 1774, and nonexportation on September 1, 1775, although South Carolina rice was excluded. These were the strongest measures ever taken against England, and conservatives rightly referred to them as despotic moves to curb individual liberty in behalf of general liberty. Indeed, conservatives complained that Congress had succeeded where England had failed, that assembly powers had now given way to central authority, that one monster had been substituted for another.

Radicals thought the Continental Association an infallible device because England could not survive loss of its colonial markets. They fully expected the West Indies to be bankrupt and starving within six months, and would not have been surprised to see a revolution in England. Tyranny would be destroyed root and branch without a shot being fired. Instead, English troops and Massachusetts farmers would precipitate the last agonies of England's first empire.

LEXINGTON AND CONCORD

Hatred of the English seemed indelible in Boston, and on every March 5, public orations by prominent civic leaders recalled the Massacre of 1770. In 1774 John Hancock was principal orator, and he rekindled Boston's animosity toward redcoats, the "brutal banditti," the "grinning furies gloating o'er their carnage." When 4,000 British troops entered Boston in 1774, the town made it as uncomfortable as possible for them. No barracks were available, and they camped on the Boston Common until November. No carpenters could be found to construct barracks and lumber was unavailable. General Thomas Gage, who had replaced Hutchinson as Governor in May, finally imported carpenters and bricklayers from Nova Scotia to build winter quarters for his men.

Bostonians anticipated the worst from the soldiers, and newspapers reported their crimes in lurid prose. Complaints ranged from barracks-room profanity outside churches on the Sabbath, to new prosperity for bawdy houses, to offering Catholic mass in Puritan Boston. General Gage leaned over backwards to be fair, kept his troops under his civil authority as governor, and quickly and impartially heard complaints of their misconduct. So fair was he that conservatives complained that he was a coddler when they needed a whipper.

By the winter of 1774-1775, radical Bostonians wanted Gage to precipitate a conflict, but how could they force his hand? Outside Boston, militiamen organized, gathered supplies, and listened to clergymen preaching sedition. The winter passed without incident, but tensions increased with news in April 1775 that additional troops were coming from England. English officers wanted to take to the field; they felt humiliated at being cooped up in Boston while rebellion spread through the countryside.

While attitudes hardened in Boston, they softened in other colonies. The Continental Association seemed to have no impact upon English policy, and one colony after another abandoned it. Georgia sent word to the king that it approved parliamentary power over the colonies, and Pennsylvania did almost the same thing. New York underwent a conservative resurgence, and its assembly rejected the Continental Association, though local committees enforced it. In England, Chatham and Burke still hoped for reconciliation. They urged repeal of tax and coercive laws and troop withdrawal, offering in their place a requisition system. Parliament contemptuously ignored their timidity, but Lord North sensed a growing disunity in England and thus proposed his own reconciliation bill. He suggested repeal of colonial taxes and their replacement by a requisition system under parliamentary rather than Crown direction. Parliament, rather than renounce its rights, would simply not use them. This, he felt, would test the honesty of colonial grievances, unite Englishmen, and perhaps disunite Americans. Lord North's scheme barely passed the Commons, which preferred coercion, not conciliation. Americans found North's proposal unappealing because it did not provide an imperial constitution, and because they refused to become parliamentary agents in taxation.

However, the ultimate decision no longer belonged to politicians. Seven hundred English troops moved secretly out of Boston on April 18, 1775, to search for gunpowder stored at Concord and to seize John Hancock

The Battle of Lexington, April 19, 1775. (By Ramberg, The Metropolitan Museum of Art, gift of Charles Allen Munn, 1924)

and Sam Adams. Paul Revere and William Dawes aroused the countryside with their famous ride, and the Lexington militia was ready when the troops appeared. According to Americans the redcoats fired first, while the English told a tale exactly the opposite. Nonetheless, the soldiers moved on to Concord and there met stronger opposition and finally retreated. During the six miles back to Lexington, Americans fired on the English from behind walls, fences, and buildings. A force of 1,200 redcoats from Boston finally arrived and rescued the retreating English. American snipers took a toll of 273 soldiers, while losing 95 casualties themselves. If nothing else, English troops displayed extraordinary discipline and courage on the long march to safety.

American propagandists turned Lexington and Concord to excellent advantage. The English pillaged with the "ferocity of a mad, wild beast," killing men, women, children, geese, hogs, and cattle indiscriminately. Even the Iroquois, according to Joseph Warren, "would blush at such horrid murder and worse than brutal rage." America had its martyrs, and the radicals, controlling the press, distributed their versions. They stopped the mails and removed English accounts so that only the American view would reach other colonies and England.

Lexington and Concord scared the English government, for Americans had stood their ground. General Gage's show of force did not intimidate them. Royal authority in Massachusetts and other colonies, which had been eroding, now collapsed. The English were unprepared to deal with rebellion or sedition, since they had few troops available, and they lacked arms for equipping loyal colonists. King and Parliament now ruled in name only. Committees of Correspondence were replaced by Committees of Safety which ruled with popular support, controlling militia, hounding loyalists, and enforcing the Continental Association. Indeed, the Continental Congress, through local committees, now exercised greater authority than Parliament or the Crown ever could.

Lord North tried to legislate a solution. His plan of reconciliation, passed before Lexington and Concord, basically replaced taxation with parliamentary requisitions. He also sent three major-generals to Boston with troop reinforcements in an effort both to overawe Americans and to encourage them to accept reconciliation. Sir William Howe, who had served under Wolfe at Quebec, led in adopting such new military techniques as light infantry. Sir Henry Clinton, an able officer, could not suffer criticism and relied upon posterity to do him justice. Sir John

Burgoyne, youngest of the three, had a great wit matched by extravagant tastes. These generals, all Whigs, were unhappy about the prospect of war, but eager to win laurels as peacemakers.

If three major-generals were intended to scare Americans, they failed. When Howe, Clinton, and Burgoyne reached Boston, the situation they found scared them. Their army was cooped up in the city by 20,000 militiamen, the fleet lay under American cannon, and Gage continued his cautious attitude. The hills surrounding Boston were a no-man's-land, but if the Americans took Breed's Hill and Bunker Hill, they would command the town's approaches and be in complete control.

SIEGE OF BOSTON

Control of Charlestown Heights, which included Breed's and Bunker hills, was the key to Boston, and Sir William Howe planned to occupy it on June 18, 1775. American spies learned of this, and the militia seized Breed's Hill before the English could do so. Although closer to Boston than Bunker Hill, Breed's Hill was open to English fire. Howe overconfidently permitted Americans to dig in and then foolishly moved without considering the costs. He could have cut them off by moving behind them and taking Bunker Hill, but instead he ordered a frontal assault to show the courage of English soldiers.

Thousands of spectators watched the English assault. The Americans sent a continual sheet of fire down the hill and slaughtered the redcoats. By sheer numbers, the English finally overran the militia positions and triumphantly took Breed's Hill, but one out of three redcoats became casualties to Howe's strategy. One officer reportedly complained that with another such victory there would be no one left to inform England. Howe proved his soldiers courageous and disciplined, but he gave Americans the opportunity to demonstrate their enthusiasm, frenzy, and deadly aim. Most important, the battle illustrated failings on both sides: Howe sacrificed his troops to capture a few acres of land, while the militia were so disorganized that no one knew who commanded on Breed's Hill that day.

Drawn around Boston were four armies, one from each New England colony. Although unanimous in their action, each army was distinct and separate. In June 1775 the Second Continental Congress adopted the army and appointed general officers, picking George Washington as Commander-in-Chief and Charles Lee as second in command. When Wash-

The Battle of Bunker Hill, June 17, 1775. (By Ramberg, The Metropolitan Museum of Art, gift of Charles Allen Munn, 1924)

SIEGE OF BOSTON, 1775

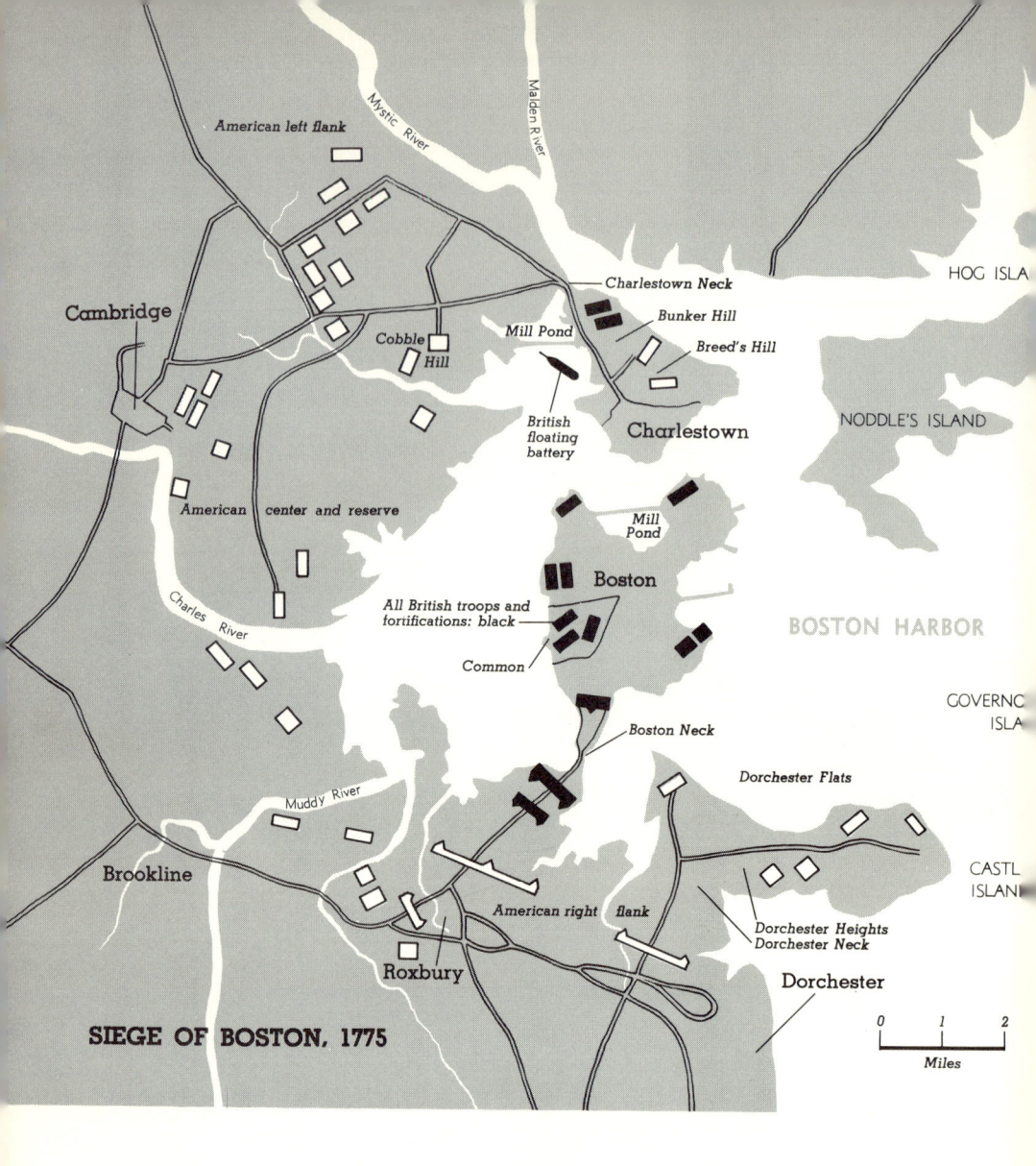

ington arrived outside Boston, he found things in chaos and realized that he had to create a military force out of a democratically-run militia lacking trained officers. While Washington tried to shape his command into an army, the siege of Boston became a stalemate.

By spring 1776, however, Washington felt ready to move against the English in Boston. His army moved into Dorchester Heights, which Howe had failed to seize, gaining control of a vital prominence overlooking Boston. When Howe saw the results of American fortifications, he knew that he had to evacuate Boston or be captured with the town. Washington had been authorized to destroy Boston if necessary, but he preferred to save it by permitting the English to withdraw. Howe sailed with his forces to Halifax, thereby abandoning England's last foothold in the thirteen rebellious colonies.

Second Continental Congress

The First Continental Congress had adjourned after adopting the Continental Association, but it arranged for a new meeting in Philadelphia for May 1775, after provincial congresses instructed their delegates. Most attending the Second Continental Congress were familiar: Sam and John Adams, Benjamin Franklin who had just returned from England, George Washington, Thomas Jefferson, John Dickinson who had led moves for reconciliation, John Hancock, and Richard Henry Lee of Virginia.

Now, after Boston, reconciliation appeared out of the question, and Congress widened the definition of American rights and the gap between England and its colonies. In July 1775 an Olive Branch Petition was sent to George III requesting his protection against parliamentary usurpations.

The Pennsylvania State House, as it appeared in 1774, was the site of the Second Continental Congress and the location of the debate on the Declaration of Independence. This is a rear view. (American Philosophical Society, Philadelphia)

Then a Declaration of the Causes and Necessity of Taking Up Arms announced that Americans had only two choices, submission to tyrannous ministers or resistance by force. They chose the latter.

Gradually Congress took upon itself governmental functions. After Breed's Hill, it adopted the army, appointed general officers, encouraged enlistments, and drafted a military code of justice. Congress also took over the royal postal service under Franklin's control, created a Board of Indian Commissioners, and solved the financial problem by authorizing issuance of paper money, relying upon state contributions for redemption.

Congress also directed committees of safety to arrest all whose freedom might endanger American liberty, and beginning in October 1775, a concerted roundup of loyalists took place. They were forced to take oaths to support American liberty or suffer imprisonment. Royal governors found themselves helpless, and most rushed for safety to the nearest man-of-war or garrison. Lord Dunmore in Virginia could not hold Williamsburg against the militia and fled to a warship near Yorktown, still trying to rule a colony in which he could not step foot.

British Reactions

News of Lexington and Concord threw England into an uproar, for everything, including force, seemed to fail. Reconciliation no longer seemed possible, certainly not on terms agreeable to Parliament. English opinion focused on crushing rebellious colonists. But where could England get the army and navy to do this without bankrupting itself? Perhaps more alarming, however, was England's own disunity. Merchants and manufacturers split on coercion, Irish Catholics applauded the rebels, and others viewed George III as a would-be tyrant.

George III would not tolerate weakness, and he strengthened Lord North's determination by his speech from the throne, condemning Americans as rebels and calling for armed forces to restore them to their allegiance. Accordingly, the Prohibitory Bill, introduced in November 1775, authorized a complete blockade of the colonies and peace commissioners with power to pardon those Americans who confessed their error. Admiral Richard Howe was appointed commander of the British fleet in America, and his brother, Sir William, was named army commander. Both also served as peace commissioners.

These measures met with strong opposition in Parliament. Rockingham Whigs denounced the king's program, and they were joined by Shelburne, Lord Camden, Edmund Burke, and the Duke of Grafton. But theirs was a decided minority, and Burke's bill for reconciliation, renouncing England's right to tax and repealing the Coercive and Tea Acts, failed by a two-to-one vote. The opposition pointed to the impossibility of subduing Americans by force and keeping them permanently cowed, but the majority believed in the loyalty of most Americans and the coercion of the disloyal, vocal, and aggressive minority.

American Acceptance of Independence

The Crown's action had simplified the American decision. By rejecting their plea for royal protection, declaring them rebels, and blockading their harbors, George III told his subjects they were outside the pale. Americans need only accept his decision to complete the break. However, they found it difficult to believe the king, for it meant abandoning a traditional loyalty never before questioned. Most still hoped to remain within the empire and retain their loyalty to the monarch, but on their own terms.

Although Americans totally misunderstood England's climate of opinion, news of the king's speech and the Prohibitory Act, which reached the colonies in January 1776, began sundering ties of loyalty. George III answered pleas for protection by war without restraint. Many Americans turned from the king in disgust, but to win over the majority to independence still required an intensive propaganda campaign. Thomas Paine's *Common Sense*, appearing in January 1776, provided the catalyst.

Paine, an Englishman, had been in the colonies for two years. His previous history was not encouraging, for he had failed in every venture he tried. A deist, devotee of liberty, and despiser of monarchy, he now turned his one gift, a talent for propaganda, to the cause of independence. In *Common Sense* he set forth no new arguments, but restated old ones with a magnificent combination of logic and emotion. He particularly struck hard at Americans' last tie with England — veneration of the monarchical institution — destroying their romantic illusions about monarchy in general and George III in particular. Over 120,000 copies of *Common Sense* were printed in three months, approximately one for every 200 inhabitants.

Paine's writings convinced many of the positive value of separation from the mother country and, when combined with English actions, guaranteed support for independence. The incitement of a slave insurrection by Lord Dunmore, Governor of Virginia, and his burning of Norfolk, a loyalist rising in North Carolina in February 1776, and the

THOMAS PAINE ON THE ENGLISH MONARCHY

ENGLAND, SINCE THE CONQUEST, hath known some few good monarchs, but groaned beneath a much larger number of bad ones; yet no man in his senses can say that their claim under William the Conqueror is a very honorable one. A French bastard landing with an armed banditti, and establishing himself king of England against the consent of the natives, is in plain terms a very paltry rascally original. — It certainly hath no divinity in it. However, it is needless to spend much time in exposing the folly of hereditary right; if there are any so weak as to believe it, let them promiscuously worship the ass and lion, and welcome. I shall neither copy their humility, nor disturb their devotion. (Common Sense [1776], 24-25)

☆☆☆☆☆☆☆☆☆☆☆☆☆☆☆☆☆☆☆☆☆☆☆☆☆☆☆

burning of Falmouth, Maine, convinced Americans that the empire had already cast them out. Deprived of its protection and stripped of their rights, Americans began seeing a positive value in independence. No longer would they be bound by trade and manufacturing restrictions, no longer would they be denied access to the West, but instead they could now achieve their full destiny.

While Americans debated independence, colonies began instructing their delegates to the Second Continental Congress. In January 1776, Massachusetts told its delegates to vote for independence, and in succeeding months South Carolina, Georgia, North Carolina, and Virginia took similar stands. Congress itself took steps tantamount to a declaration, including opening American ports to all shipping except that of England, advising colonies to establish their own governments, and finally, on May 15, urging destruction of every vestige of royal authority within the colonies.

On June 7, 1776, Richard Henry Lee introduced his fateful three-fold resolution calling for independence, an American confederation, and foreign alliances. All three went together, for independence meant nothing without a new central authority to replace the one just destroyed, and without foreign aid Americans could not win against England, Europe's most powerful nation.

Thomas Paine (1737-1809) author of Common Sense, *the influential pamphlet which helped Americans make up their minds for independence, and continual advocate of radical causes. (By John Wesley Jarvis, courtesy of National Gallery of Art, Washington, D.C., gift of Marian B. Maurice, 1950)*

First, Congress debated independence; on June 11 it appointed a committee and charged it with drafting a declaration. This committee, composed of Thomas Jefferson, John Adams, Benjamin Franklin, Roger Sherman, and Robert R. Livingston, had to combine varied sentiments to secure the consent of all, for without unanimity the colonies could never make their independence effective. Some still argued that independence was premature, and so debate was postponed until July 1. By then more states had taken the fateful step. New Jersey imprisoned Governor William Franklin, Maryland ousted Governor Sir Robert Eden, Delaware renounced royal authority, and a new provincial congress in Pennsylvania sanctioned independence. On the initial vote, nine colonies approved the draft, and soon Delaware and Pennsylvania consented. South Carolina and New York abstained but agreed to abide by the majority. John Adams wrote to his wife: "The second day of July 1776 will be the most memorable epocha in the history of America. I am apt to believe that it will be celebrated by succeeding generations as the great anniversary festival. It ought to be commemorated as the Day of Deliverance, by solemn acts of devotion to God Almighty." Although he erred on the

DECLARATION OF INDEPENDENCE, JULY 4, 1776

WHEN IN THE COURSE of human Events, it becomes necessary for one People to dissolve the Political Bands which have connected them with another, and to assume among the Powers of the Earth, the separate and equal Station to which the Laws of Nature and of Nature's God entitle them, a decent Respect to the Opinions of Mankind requires that they should declare the causes which impel them to the Separation.

We hold these Truths to be self-evident, that all Men are created equal, that they are endowed by their Creator with certain unalienable Rights, that among these are Life, Liberty, and the Pursuit of Happiness — That to secure these Rights, Governments are instituted among Men, deriving their just Powers from the Consent of the Governed, that whenever any Form of Government becomes destructive of these Ends, it is the Right of the People to alter or to abolish it, and to institute new Government, laying its Foundation on such Principles, and organizing its Powers in such Form, as to them shall seem most likely to effect their Safety and Happiness. Prudence, indeed, will dictate that Governments long established should not be changed for light and transient Causes; and accordingly all Experience hath shewn, that Mankind are more disposed to suffer, while Evils are sufferable, than to right themselves by abolishing the Forms to which they are accustomed. But when a long Train of Abuses and Usurpations, pursuing invariably the same Object, evinces a Design to reduce them under absolute Despotism, it is their Right, it is their Duty, to throw off such Government, and to provide new Guards for their future Security....

☆☆☆☆☆☆☆☆☆☆☆☆☆☆☆☆☆☆☆☆☆☆☆☆☆☆☆☆☆☆

precise day and method of celebration, Adams correctly predicted the event's importance.

The Declaration of Independence received its formal approval on July 4 (although New York abstained until July 9), and the former colonies published the reasons for their actions to the world. Largely prepared by Jefferson, the Declaration expressed no new ideas, but with eloquence, dignity, and grace put forth America's case. It levelled its allegations against the king rather than Parliament, since Americans had already rejected parliamentary power, and it charged him with violating the compact of government by abuses dating back to 1763. Although it grossly exaggerated George III's crimes, Congress had to prove his tyranny. It could not admit that he and his ministers were little better than fools lacking understanding of the empire they destroyed. Nor could Americans admit that they failed to comprehend the empire they renounced.

Americans rebelled in 1776 against an imperial system which seemed to them corrupt and intolerable. Had they considered British policy on its merits alone, there would have been no need for the Declaration of Independence. British policy, viewed apart from colonial hypersensitivity, seemed too trivial to be the pretext for destroying the ancient connection between mother country and colonies. However, Americans had learned from the English radicals to view all things through the distorting lens of conspiracy, and they persisted in doing so now. Consequently, they had no choice but to break the ties that bound them.

Selected Bibliography

The events leading to the Revolution are discussed in detail in Lawrence Henry Gipson's *The Coming of the Revolution, 1763-1775* (1954), I. R. Christie's *Crisis of Empire: Great Britain and the American Colonies, 1754-1783* (1966), Esmond Wright's *The Fabric of Freedom, 1763-1800* (1961), and Eric Robson's *The American Revolution in Its Political and Military Aspects, 1763-1783* (1955).

The Ambiguity of the American Revolution, edited by Jack P. Greene (1968), provides a convenient collection of essays on the crisis. The ideas underlying the breakup of the British Empire are examined in Clinton Rossiter's *The First American Revolution* (1956), Bernard Bailyn's *The Ideological Origins of the American Revolution* (1967), and an older work of great importance, Charles H. McIlwain's *The American Revolution: A Constitutional Interpretation* (1923). McIlwain's position is challenged in Robert L. Schuyler's *Parliament and the British Empire* (1929).

Specific phases of the American Revolution have been treated in a number of studies. Thomas P. Abernethy's *Western Lands and the American Revolution* (1937) should be read in conjunction with Jack M. Sosin's *The Revolutionary Frontier, 1763-1783* (1967). Carl Bridenbaugh's *Cities in Revolt: Urban Life in America, 1743-1776* (1955) provides the best analysis of the urban element in the revolution. Benjamin W. Labaree's *The Boston Tea Party* (1964) explains the economic role. Carl Ubbelohde, *The Vice Admiralty Courts and the American Revolution* (1960), explores American use of the issue of admiralty jurisdiction. Oliver M. Dickerson's *The Navigation Acts and the American Revolution* (1951) does the same for that issue. Philip Davidson examines *Propa-*

ganda and the American Revolution, 1763-1783 (1941). A classic study is Carl L. Becker's *The Declaration of Independence* (1942). The interrelationship of English politics and the American Revolution is developed in G. H. Guttridge's *English Whiggism and the American Revolution* (1966).

The impact of the Revolution upon American society is considered by such works as Charles S. Sydnor's *American Revolutionaries in the Making: Political Practices in Washington's Virginia* (1952), Robert E. Brown's *Middle-Class Democracy and the Revolution in Massachusetts, 1691-1780* (1955), Daniel J. Boorstin's *The Lost World of Thomas Jefferson* (1948), Dumas Malone's *Jefferson the Virginian* (1948) and his *Jefferson and the Rights of Man* (1951), and Carl and Jessica Bridenbaugh's *Rebels and Gentlemen: Philadelphia in the Age of Franklin* (1942).

Biographical studies of prominent figures are numerous. Among the more valuable ones are Brooke Hindle's *David Rittenhouse* (1964), John R. Alden's *General Gage in America* (1948) and his *John Stuart and the Southern Colonial Frontier* (1944), John C. Miller's *Sam Adams* (1936), Robert D. Meade's *Patrick Henry: Patriot in the Making* (1957) and *Patrick Henry: The Practical Revolutionary* (1969), David J. Mays's *Edmund Pendleton, 1721-1803* (1952), Charles W. Aker's *Called Unto Liberty: A Life of Jonathan Mayhew, 1720-1766* (1964), John H. Cary's *Joseph Warren: Physician, Politician, Patriot* (1961), Gilbert Chinard's *Honest John Adams* (1933), Alfred O. Aldridge's *Benjamin Franklin* (1965), Paul W. Conner's *Poor Richard's Politicks* (1965), Robert A. Rutland's *George Mason* (1961), John C. Miller's *Alexander Hamilton* (1959), George Dangerfield's *Chancellor Robert R. Livingston, 1746-1813* (1960), and Herbert Thomas's *Samuel Seabury: Priest and Physician* (1963).

Studies of individual colonies include a number of very competent works: David S. Lovejoy's *Rhode Island Politics and the American Revolution* (1958); Theodore Thayer's *Pennsylvania Politics and the Growth of Democracy* (1953); David Hawke's *In the Midst of a Revolution* (1961), which also deals with Pennsylvania; Lee N. Newcomer's *The Embattled Farmers: A Massachusetts Countryside in the American Revolution* (1953); Leonard Lundin's *Cockpit of the Revolution* (1940), which deals with New Jersey; Philip A. Crowl's *Maryland During and After the Revolution* (1943); and Kenneth Coleman's *The American Revolution in Georgia, 1763-1789* (1958).

CHAPTER 6

THE WORLD TURNED UPSIDE DOWN, 1776-1783

The Declaration of Independence, proclaimed in Philadelphia on July 8 and announced the next day to the army at Boston, gave the American cause a cloak of nobility and a precise goal. America now had to choose between victory and independence, or surrender and subjugation. More than this, the Declaration sharpened divisions within former colonies because many who had joined in protesting British policies would not cross the line and abjure their fealty to George III. Timidity claimed some, others could not overcome inbred loyalty, and still others found their English connections stronger than their local allegiance. Pro-English sentiment clearly mounted after the fateful decision of July 1776.

Whether one remained loyal to England depended on personal reactions to specific situations. Loyalists (or Tories, as their American

THIS UNFORTUNATE REVOLUTION

> ... *I AM TOLD THAT the great nation, of which we are a part, is just, wise, and free, beyond any other on earth, within its own insular boundaries, but not always so to its distant conquests. I shall not repeat all I have heard, because I cannot believe half of it. As a citizen of a smaller society, I find that any kind of opposition to its now prevailing sentiments, immediately begets hatred: how easily do men pass from loving, to hating and cursing one another! I am a lover of peace; what must I do? I am divided between the respect I feel for the ancient connection and the fear of innovations, with the consequence of which I am not well acquainted, as they are embraced by my own countrymen. I am conscious that I was happy before this unfortunate Revolution. I feel that I am no longer so; therefore I regret the change. This is the only mode of reasoning adapted to persons in my situation. . . .*
>
> *Must I then bid farewell to Britain, to that renowned country? Must I renounce a name so ancient and so venerable? Alas! she herself, that-once indulgent parent, forces me to take up arms against her. She herself first inspired the most unhappy citizens of our remote districts*

☆☆☆☆☆☆☆☆☆☆☆☆☆☆☆☆☆☆☆☆☆☆☆☆☆☆☆

enemies derisively dubbed them) represented every station in life from highest to lowest and reflected every possible motivation. Some were aristocratic and wealthy, others were small farmers and artisans, some were well educated, and others nearly illiterate. Even the clergy split. Virginia Anglicans and Massachusetts Congregationalists led the patriots, but ministers of those sects elsewhere swelled Loyalist ranks. Differences in national origins meant little. New York's Delanceys, of French Huguenot stock, held firm to the Crown, while General Richard Montgomery, a successful English officer, became an American military hero and martyr.

Not only can reasons for loyalism be disputed, but their actual numbers remain conjectural. Some 21,000 fought for the king according to a recent study, and extrapolating from this, Loyalists comprised approximately 16 per cent of the total population or 19.8 per cent of white Americans. At any given moment, they probably numbered about 450,000. Nonetheless, many willing Loyalists could not secure arms, while others sup-

with the thoughts of shedding the blood of those whom they used to call by the name of friends and brethren. That great nation, which now convulses the world; which hardly knows the extent of her Indian kingdoms; which looks toward the universal monarchy of trade, of industry, of riches, of power: why must she strew our poor frontiers with the carcasses of her friends, with the wrecks of our insignificant villages, in which there is no gold? . . .

Restore peace and concord to our poor afflicted country; assuage the fierce storm which has so long ravaged it! Permit, I beseech Thee, O Father of Nature, that our ancient virtues and our industry may not be totally lost: and that, as a reward for the great toils we have made on this new land, we may be restored to our ancient tranquillity, and enabled to fill it with successive generations, that will constantly thank Thee for the ample subsistence Thou hast given them! (From J. Hector St. John de Crèvecoeur, Letters from an American Farmer [London: J. Davies, 1782])

☆☆☆☆☆☆☆☆☆☆☆☆☆☆☆☆☆☆☆☆☆☆☆☆☆☆☆☆

ported king and country up to the point of fighting, and still others served in less obvious ways. In certain areas, Loyalists were the majority or very large minorities — New York City, Philadelphia, New Jersey, Delaware, and Maryland — and the English shaped their policy, at least in part, to take advantage of these pockets of support.

American Unity

The crucible of war forged the American as someone distinct from the Briton, though this process had begun much earlier. Use of the term "American" can be found in the 1720s, but its real meaning emerged in the 1770s. It suggested a community of interest among the thirteen colonies separate and apart from an earlier community of interest they shared with England. As the former colonists realized their loss of involvement with Europe, as their memories of the mother country became distorted by conflict, the novelty of being cast adrift forced their maturity and their whole-hearted "discovery" of America as their nation. The converse of this "discovery" was the rejection by Americans of Europe and of the decadence it represented. Indeed, as a new nationalism took hold of the former colonists, they quickly erected their own pantheon of heroes as a means of escaping from their European past. Nationalism enveloped the Americans as an emotional response to the rending of the imperial fabric which had formerly covered them.

In 1774, de Crèvecoeur first asked: "What then is the American, this new man?" And each succeeding generation has asked this question. Certainly in the 1770s it did not reflect a uniformity, for Carolinians and Virginians diverged from one another as widely as did Philadelphians and Bostonians. Indeed, from the beginning diversity has been American civilization's hallmark, and America has carried that attribute further than any other nation.

So great were differences between provinces (as well as within them) that many seriously questioned the wisdom of unification. Americans' European backgrounds varied widely, their religious experiences differed, their economic and social institutions were obviously unlike, and they suffered from intercolonial conflicts and poor communications. Despite their divisive factors, unifying ones also existed: they all (except for the African) came from Western Europe, and the overwhelming majority shared a common Protestant heritage, spoke a common language (except the Pennsylvania Dutch), participated in the Anglo-American cultural background, were affected by the American environment, and shared past and present common enemies.

On balance, unifying factors tended to outweigh divisive ones. War tipped the scales more than anything else, as Americans everywhere realized that Boston's difficulties were theirs as well. Localism did not disappear; rather it diminished in significance before the greater threat of England. And, once committed to escaping from the empire, Americans intuitively sought to replace British rule with something which would operate properly and protect their liberties. The American Revolution destroyed the empire not for the sake of destruction, but because it malfunctioned and had to be rebuilt in accordance with American needs. They did not oppose unity, but its perversions.

CENTRAL GOVERNMENT

Richard Henry Lee's resolution in June 1776 presented no novel concepts when it called for independence, a *confederation*, and alliances. Most

Americans automatically understood the need for central government, and they only questioned how it should be best constructed to function properly and to guarantee against misuse of power.

Beginning in 1775 Americans created and utilized central government, although its character and organization varied according to their understanding of its functions and of the authority that could safely be committed to it. Even the First Continental Congress had exercised some governmental authority, and the Second Congress actually directed the war effort. It declared American independence, appointed a commander-in-chief, established a navy, founded a diplomatic service, negotiated treaties, set up a postal service, issued currency, and borrowed money. The Second Continental Congress functioned as a government and reflected Americans' deep-rooted impulse toward replacing the empire's unpopular central authority with a more satisfactory one.

The Continental Congress was hampered throughout by its lack of clear organization and by its impermanence, since it had no written definition of its authority and was a temporary agency. Richard Henry Lee's resolution called for its replacement by a permanent, more carefully calculated institution, and Congress appointed a committee of thirteen, one from each colony, to draft a new constitution. They completed their labors within a month, and proposed a central government with a unicameral legislature, one vote per state, no taxing power, and no authority over commerce. It could settle boundary disputes, control western lands, and create new states on an equal basis with the original ones. Its funds would come from state contributions based upon population.

Each stipulation clearly reflected American experiences under the old empire. Taxing power and commercial regulation had precipitated the Anglo-American controversy, and thus any new central government voluntarily established would not possess those contentious powers. Settlement of boundary disputes, on the other hand, was a natural function of central government, as was control of western lands which frequently caused interstate conflicts. Americans even found a solution to the central imperial problem and proposed that new states be given equality with the original ones, a solution England refused to consider.

Some members of Congress quarreled with these proposed Articles of Confederation. States with large populations feared the voting formula would subject them to domination by smaller states, while contributions of money, apportioned on population, would lay the heaviest burden on large states. Moreover, should slaves be counted in population? Further controversies developed over western lands, for seven states had claims, though their validity varied, while six did not. Landless states insisted that all claims be relinquished to the central government, while those possessing such claims refused self-sacrifice. Landless states presented various arguments for a cession of claims, including the common effort of all to win independence and to secure control of the West, and fears that states with western claims would grow too powerful for the safety of smaller states. However, the real motive of landless states was a desire to have their people participate equally with the inhabitants of states with western land claims in speculative possibilities, and they could only do so if all western lands belonged to the union rather than to a few privileged states.

Since the Articles of Confederation required unanimous consent of all thirteen states to become effective, the states had to negotiate these points. Further delays then occurred because of the fortunes of war, and Congress did not seriously consider the matter again until fall 1777. Then potential foreign aid required a semblance of American union, and under this pressure Congress approved a revised set of Articles in November 1777 and sent it to each state for its concurrence. According to these revised Articles, each state would have one vote with no limits placed on western land claims, and contributions to the central government were apportioned on the value of improved lands within each state.

The Continental Congress hoped the new government would be able to assume power by March 1778, but too many obstacles remained. The states qualified their acceptances, and by the summer of 1778 only ten had ratified the document. Maryland, Delaware, and New Jersey held out. These landless states insisted upon transfer of western land claims to the central government. In the winter of 1778-79, New Jersey and Delaware gave in, but Maryland remained adamant until 1781, finally forcing others to accept its position.

State Governments

Many former colonies began organizing permanent state governments before the Declaration of Independence, but the Declaration made such action imperative for those that had not done so. In drafting state constitutions, Americans had a vast reservoir on which to draw. Not only was this the heyday of eighteenth-century liberalism, rationalism, and enlightenment, but Americans had loved liberty and enjoyed more of it than any other people in the world. They rebelled against future threats, not present abuses, and conservatives among the revolutionaries now believed the major problem was one of restraining enthusiasm for liberty so that order could survive. George Washington referred to this as "an epoch when the rights of mankind were better understood and more clearly defined than at any former period."

Early in 1776 the Continental Congress asked states to establish "such governments as shall in the opinion of the representatives of the people best conduce to the happiness and safety of their constituents in particular and Americans in general." Debates immediately ensued in each state over the nature and role of government, and a new radical-conservative dichotomy appeared among those who backed independence. Radicals and conservatives now differed over the relationship between liberty and authority. This was not a new debate. It had continuously existed from the beginning of colonization and had repeated arguments used in seventeenth-century England. In fact, it has been a central issue in politics and political theory throughout modern history.

Conservatives emphasized the need for security, order, and good government, fearing anarchy more than power. They looked upon radicals as devotees of disorder whom they had no intention of joining in a state of nature. Dissolution of the empire, to conservatives, did not require abandonment of colonial governmental forms, property-qualifications for voting and office-holding, or other traditional devices. All that was necessary, they argued, was replacement of the Crown's sovereignty with the people's, together with some minor adjustments to accommodate that change.

The conservative ideal was the English constitution, particularly as it had been described to them by Montesquieu. This French theorist, writing in 1748, totally misunderstood the English constitution, its plan and its operation. He conceived of it as it had been in the early seventeenth century, as a rigid separation of powers which emphasized checks and balances between executive, legislative, and judicial authority, instead of appreciating the interrelationship between the parts which had developed in the eighteenth century. Montesquieu's fallacious, static description of English government had a major influence upon American thought in these critical years. Americans based their state (and later federal) constitutions upon an English pattern as interpreted by a Frenchman who completely misconstrued his subject.

ADAM SMITH QUESTIONS THE CONCEPT OF EMPIRE

THE COUNTRIES WHICH POSSESS the colonies of America, and which trade directly to the East Indies, enjoy, indeed, the whole show and splendour of this great commerce. Other countries, however, notwithstanding all the invidious restraints by which it is meant to exclude them, frequently enjoy a greater share of the real benefit of it. The colonies of Spain and Portugal, for example, give more real encouragement to the industry of other countries than to that of Spain and Portugal. . . .

After all the unjust attempts, therefore, of every country in Europe to engross to itself the whole advantage of the trade of its own colonies, no country has yet been able to engross to itself anything but the expense of supporting in time of peace, and of defending in time of war, the oppressive authority which it assumes over them. The inconveniencies resulting from the possession of its colonies, every country has engrossed to itself completely. The advantages resulting from their trade it has been obliged to share with many other countries.

At first sight, no doubt, the monopoly of the great commerce of America naturally seems to be an acquisition of the highest value. To the undiscerning eye of giddy ambition, it naturally presents itself amidst the confused scramble of politics and war, as a very dazzling object to fight for. The dazzling splendour of the object, however, the immense greatness of the commerce, is the very quality which renders the monopoly of it hurtful, or which makes one employment, in its own nature necessarily less advantageous to the country than the greater part of other employments, absorb a much greater proportion of the capital of the country than what would otherwise have gone to it. . . . (From The Wealth of Nations, *3 vols. [London and New York: G. Bell and Sons, 1896], III, 391-92)*

☆☆☆☆☆☆☆☆☆☆☆☆☆☆☆☆☆☆☆☆☆☆☆☆☆☆

Conservatives wanted to restore old colonial liberties, to avoid the risk of "all the tumult and riot incident to simple democracy," and so they argued for strong governors and councils and independent judiciaries as checks upon popularly elected legislatures. Democracy, they argued, was fit only for angels, and man had too recently fallen from grace to be unselfish, public spirited, and intelligent. They challenged not the people's right to rule, but their ability, and therefore tried to limit the exercise of popular sovereignty. The people, like the Crown, would reign, not rule.

Radicals strongly opposed this conservative position because they regarded revolt against England as a liberating force wiping out old restraints and permitting new experiments with liberty. This, they contended, was the opportunity to make men more free and equal than ever before, and they emphasized the importance of individual liberty. Government was consecrated "not to the emolument of one man or class, but to the safety, liberty, and happiness of each individual." Thus it should be under popular control. The New England town-meeting approach came closest to radical aspirations. Since the town meeting was impractical for a large geographic unit, radicals emphasized representative government under the most direct popular control — universal manhood suffrage, annual elections, rotation in office, and absolute freedom of speech and press.

Radicals did not feel bound by traditional forms of colonial government, but felt the revolution could be meaningful only if they struck out on new paths. No limits should be placed on the people's power, for they believed in the innate goodness of people. This necessitated a weak governor and no upper house of the legislature. Radicals attempted to destroy not only American veneration of the English Crown, but of the English constitution as well. Thomas Paine thus urged a unicameral legislature as the only truly democratic system.

Creation of state constitutions took place amidst continuing controversies between radicals and conservatives. To some extent, radical views secured greater acceptance because of recent experiences with English tyranny. As participants in the empire, Americans had seen power's corruptive effects at work, and thus carefully doled out power to public officials. They also discouraged a career of officeholding because it created a group interested primarily in its own aggrandizement. Americans clearly felt that one-man rule was the greatest menace.

So distasteful had things English become that the colonists now referred to the English language as American, and some even suggested substituting another. Revulsion against the mother country played into radical hands; most state constitutions concentrated power in popularly elected assemblies and provided for weak governors and councils. Even the term "governor" came under suspicion because it connoted both the old colonial situation and excessive authority, and the term "president" began to supplant it. Governors were deprived of veto power, patronage, and the pardoning power, elected for short terms, checked by elective councils, and often prevented from running for reelection for a stipulated time. One complained that he only had power to sign receipts for his own salary.

State constitutions concerned themselves with protecting the individual from governmental oppression. The colonial past made government suspect, and Americans did not emphasize its potential for good, but its ability for evil. This accorded with John Locke's philosophy that the state's sole purpose was a negative one, the protection of property. Americans therefore kept government weak, exalted the individual and his rights, and permitted each person the opportunity to reveal his innate goodness without society's restraints.

Most state constitutions tried to be radical, but few succeeded completely. Radicals agreed that all should possess the franchise, but only Pennsylvania and North Carolina fully applied the revolutionary slogan of no taxation without representation and permitted all taxpayers to vote. Vermont had no requirements for the franchise, but most states retained some form of property qualifications for voting and officeholding. Americans believed that such restrictions were not too important at the end of the eighteenth century because all but a small percentage of Americans were landowning farmers and would qualify as voters. Moreover, the opportunity to acquire land was so great that they could not conceive of anyone being permanently disbarred from voting except by his own failure. Thus property qualifications in America did not carry the same meaning as in England, and once again vast tracts of cheap land modified the impact of traditional English practices.

Other important features of new state constitutions included, as a concession to conservatives, executives and councils elected by assemblies, even though those officials were frequently stripped of any significant powers. Radicals, however, won a redress of the political balance in terms of representation between old seaboard regions and new frontier areas, and some state capitols, originally located in coastal cities, were even transferred to the West. Eight state constitutions had bills of rights, and most provided for annual elections, rotation in office with stipulated periods of ineligibility for reelection, and methods for amendment. All were brief in contrast to modern state constitutions, for they dealt with fundamentals, not legislative details.

The impact of these new state constitutions was twofold. The electorate certainly became broader, a process that had begun with extralegal governments in 1774, and one that dramatically opened the political system for the first time. Those who then exercised the ballot for the first time had no intention of surrendering that power. State legislatures, too, became more broadly based and more truly reflected a cross section of society. However, the second change did not automatically derive from the first.

Men in the 1780s still believed in *noblesse oblige* and still tended to return local squires to assemblies because it was their duty to serve. More important in changing the composition of assemblies than expansion of the electorate was the legislature's increased size, which diluted its previously aristocratic nature, and increased representation from frontier areas which possessed no aristocracy to send to the assembly. In New Hampshire, farmers accounted for about 60 per cent of the representatives in 1785; twenty years before, they totalled somewhere between 20 and 30 per cent. In New York, farmers comprised 42 per cent of the 1785 assembly, but only 25 per cent of the comparable 1769 body. Maryland's farmers increased their control from 18 per cent in 1765 to 28 per cent in 1785. The same pattern occurred in Virginia.

Transfer of power from an aristocracy to a middle class became an evolutionary rather than revolutionary process in America. Factors which aristocrats could in no way control mandated the change for Americans in this era. Some of them, looking back half a century later on what had happened, would bemoan the overthrow of the old order, but it was one of history's gentlest upheavals.

Conduct of the War

Efforts to create state governments meeting American needs were subordinated, of course, to winning the right to do so. Fighting the war dominated men's minds and energies, and state governments and the Continental Congress devoted themselves to it. Americans suffered serious disadvantages in the War for Independence because the English certainly had better equipped and trained forces, naval support, financial strength, and a core of supporters within the former colonies which would today be called a Fifth Column.

Yet not all the advantages were England's. Americans fought on home ground for something in which they believed, and this added immeasureably to their strength. Moreover, adult males were, by and large, acquainted with firearms and formed a reserve force that gave great depth to the American army. Although they lacked officers trained in formal European warfare, many Americans had gained important experience during the French and Indian War, particularly in the type of fighting that prevailed in the New World — a form of guerrilla warfare rather than pitched battles between massed armies as in Europe.

If Washington and his officers could overcome the army's excessive democracy, the complications of short-term enlistments which occasionally caused the army to dissolve at inopportune moments, the inadequacy of supplies, and the need for naval support, America stood a good chance of winning. England, despite its advantages, suffered from poor strategy, lengthy supply lines, and inadequate leadership, and these would have a critical effect upon the war's eventual outcome.

England miscalculated American devotion to independence and overestimated the importance of formal training. Lord Sandwich of the Admiralty commented brashly about the rebels: "They are raw, undisciplined, cowardly men. I wish instead of 40 or 50,000 of these brave fellows, they would produce in the field at least 200,000, the more the better, the easier would be the conquest." Indeed, the ministry assumed that Washington's army would dissolve to avoid winter hardships, and failed to appreciate its ability to reconstitute itself when needed. Conversely, English generals lacked enthusiasm for the conflict. As Whigs, concerned about the expansion of royal power at Parliament's expense and sympathetic to Americans' historical analogies, they reluctantly warred against the colonials and seemed to avoid seizing the initiative. When Chatham heard the names of the English commanders in America, he reportedly commented: "I do not know what effect these names have on the enemy, but I confess they make me tremble." Incompetence of command was perhaps England's most severe handicap throughout the war.

Americans took the offensive before the Declaration of Independence to free Canada from subjugation to British tyranny under the Quebec Act. Americans totally misunderstood the Canadian situation and thought the fourteenth colony held back only because of British troops there. In June 1775, the Continental Congress ordered General Philip Schuyler and General Richard Montgomery to move up Lake Champlain into Canada and capture Montreal and Quebec. Benedict Arnold would lead another force through the Maine woods which would arrive on the south shore of the St. Lawrence across from Quebec.

The Canadian offensive, delayed by recruitment problems, supply difficulties, inadequate Indian support, and Philip Schuyler's illness, did not get under way until the fall. Americans captured Montreal in mid-November, and Montgomery and Arnold joined forces against Quebec. On December 30 the assault took place, and failed. Montgomery died, Arnold lost his leg, and nearly 400 Americans were casualties. The shattered army camped in Canada, beset by starvation, cold, and smallpox, until a relief force arrived in the spring. However, the British fleet arrived at the same time with reinforcements, and the Americans retreated to Montreal. Washington finally convinced Congress that Canada could not be persuaded to join the revolution, but well into the nineteenth century Americans suspected that Canadians would really be happier in the American union than in the British Empire. The dream of continental hegemony was difficult to relinquish. For the moment, however, Americans abandoned Canada for more pressing matters.

The British based their initial strategy upon the existence of pockets of loyalists, especially in New York City. They hoped to capture that city, thereby separating New England from the rest of the colonies and enabling them to seize the others one by one. General Sir Henry Clinton went to strike into the South, then to join Sir William Howe in attacking and seizing New York City. Clinton's southern campaign failed when he could not take Charleston, South Carolina, in June 1776, and Washington anticipated Howe's invasion of New York City and moved his troops down from Boston. Howe, with naval support, landed 32,000 troops on Long Island in August 1776 and proceeded to decimate the American army of 20,000. Washington's battered forces on Long Island fell back to Brooklyn, and then to Manhattan, crossed the Hudson, and made their way through New Jersey and into Pennsylvania with General Charles Cornwallis constantly at their heels. The British captured New York City, New Jersey, and the lower Hudson, but never fully came to grips with Washington's army, and thus never won the real victory.

Washington counterattacked at Trenton in December 1776 and then at Princeton, but despite these efforts even he admitted that all seemed hopeless. At this decisive moment, however, Thomas Paine's *The Crisis* stiffened American spirits. Once again this emigré Englishman stirred Americans by words, this time to sustain them through "the times that try men's souls. The summer soldier and the sunshine patriot will, in this crisis, shrink from the service of their country; but he that stands it *now*,

HUDSON'S BAY
Lake Nipigon
Montgomery, Arnold and Schuyler invade Canada, 1775-1776
QUEBEC
Quebec
Lake Superior
Howe, Carleton and Burgoyne, 1777
Saint Lawrence River
(MAINE)
MASS.
Lake Nipissing
Montreal
Georgian Bay
St. Leger, 1777
Lake Huron
Howe withdraws t
Halifax, N.S., 177
N.H.
Lake Champlain
Lake Ontario
Valcour Island
Mississippi River
Lake Michigan
Fort Schuyler
Saratoga
Boston
MASS.
Detroit
N.Y.
Lake Erie
Hudson R.
CONN.
R.I.
Washington
Hamilton raids Vincennes, 1778
New York
Monmouth Courthouse
Brooklyn Heights
PA.
Wabash River
Trenton-Princeton
Germantown
Howe, 1777
Brandywine
Philadelphia
Washington and Lafayette, 1781
N.J.
Howe capture
New York Cit
(from Halifa
N.S.), 17
Clark, 1779
Vincennes
MD.
Ohio River
DEL.
Cahokia
Charlottesville
Richmond
VA.
Kaskaskia
Williamsburg
Yorktown
Clark captures the Ohio River valley, 1778-1779
Cornwallis invades Virginia, 1781
Fort Massac
Clark, 1778
Greene, 1781
Mississippi River
Clinton (from Charleston), 17
(Guilford Courthouse)
Salem
Kings Mountain
Ferguson, 1780
Cornwallis, 1781
Charlotte
N.C.
Cowpens
Cornwallis, 1780
Tarleton, 1781
ATLANTIC OCEA
Camden
INDIAN RESERVE
Ninety-Six
Winnsboro
Cornwallis and Clinton, 1780
S.C.
Augusta
Savannah R.
Georgetown
Cornwallis and Clinton attack Charleston, 17
Campbell attacks Augusta, 1778
GA.
Charleston
Clinton attacks Charleston, 17
Savannah
WEST FLORIDA
Campbell attacks Savannah, 17
EAST
FLORIDA
REVOLUTIONARY TROOP MOVEMENT
American
British
GULF OF MEXICO

deserves the love and thanks of man and woman. Tyranny, like hell, is not easily conquered; yet we have this consolation with us, that the harder the conflict, the more glorious the triumph. What we obtain too cheap, we esteem too lightly: it is dearness only that gives everything its value." Washington ordered this letter read to every army unit, and American forces held together.

Meanwhile the British devised a new strategy. In February 1777 Generals Howe and Carleton proposed a three-pronged attack to isolate New England by sending one force of 8,000 regulars under Burgoyne southward from Canada to Lake Champlain and the Hudson River, an auxiliary force under Colonel Barry St. Leger through the Mohawk Valley to the Hudson, and a third force under Howe up the Hudson to meet Burgoyne. Lord George Germain, Secretary of State for the Colonies, sanctioned this, but simultaneously approved Howe's plan for an attack upon Philadelphia, seat of rebel government. The Howe-Carleton proposal was thus doomed from the start by Germain's division of forces, by his failure to understand that Howe could not be in two places at once.

Burgoyne moved out from Canada and captured Fort Ticonderoga, but General Benedict Arnold stopped the auxiliary forces coming eastward at Fort Stanwix. Burgoyne then sent a thousand men to raid Bennington, Vermont, for supplies, only to have them nearly destroyed by militia under General John Stark. Sir Henry Clinton reluctantly moved his fleet up the Hudson to Kingston, but felt insecure and withdrew to New York City. Burgoyne, short of supplies, put his men on half rations and pushed southward toward Saratoga, where the Americans were entrenched. General Arnold led a flank attack and stopped Burgoyne's advance. General Horatio Gates surrounded the British by October 12, and five days later Burgoyne surrendered.

The Battle of Saratoga was a vital American victory, for a rebel army stood up against British regulars and won. Moreover, 5,700 picked British troops had surrendered. This shocked everyone, and Lord North asked permission to resign, but George III refused. However, Saratoga caused still another change in British strategy. Since an easy land war seemed unlikely, they now prepared for a long war of attrition based upon a naval blockade.

Meanwhile, Howe was safely settled in Philadelphia, but he had not crushed Washington's army. Americans suffered defeat after defeat — Brandywine Creek, Paoli, and Germantown — and retreated to Valley

Forge, twenty miles from Philadelphia, to wait. But Burgoyne's army was gone while Washington's remained intact. Howe celebrated his pyrrhic victory by resigning.

This was Washington's worst winter. His soldiers suffered from intense cold, inadequate clothing, short supplies, and insufficient food. Rude huts provided their only shelter in mid-winter. In the face of these difficulties Washington, aided by General Nathanael Greene and Baron von Steuben, somehow managed to hold his army together. However, in December 1777 various leaders turned on him, censuring him for his constant defeats and his refusal to engage in general actions. The Commander-in-Chief's reputation suffered from the contrast between his failures and Gates's victory at Saratoga, and rumors developed that Gates would replace Washington. Yet the people idolized him and his popularity with

The defeat of Burgoyne's army, October 17, 1777. (By Ramberg, The Metropolitan Museum of Art, gift of Charles Allen Munn, 1924)

the army halted efforts to supplant him. By the spring of 1778, the crisis ended with Washington in firm command and backed by Congress.

Sir Henry Clinton had now replaced Howe as British army commander. Upon hearing that a French fleet was en route to blockade Delaware Bay, Clinton ordered Philadelphia evacuated. British troops marched overland in mid-June, and Washington left Valley Forge and followed closely on Clinton's heels. Washington planned no major assault, and his one strike at Monmouth Courthouse nearly turned into an American disaster. Clinton's force reached New York City, and Washington's encamped at White Plains. Two years of maneuvering had left the contenders almost exactly where they had begun. Washington would endure still more of this stalemate war before victory came his way.

During this time, raids in the West by irregular British forces in conjunction with Indian allies served to distract Americans from the main theater of war and to challenge their hope of controlling the Mississippi Valley. Colonel Henry Hamilton led a British raiding party from Detroit in 1778 as far south as Kentucky, and soon thereafter Americans under George Rogers Clark raided down the Ohio River. Clark captured Kaskaskia, Cahokia, and Vincennes, breaking British control of the area and causing the Indians to question their alliance with Hamilton. Frontier raids remained a minor aspect of the war, however, dealing as they did with vast areas sparsely settled. Neither side gained dramatic or decisive victories, but the Americans held their own and preserved their claims to the Ohio and Mississippi valleys.

England's main strategy after Clinton's evacuation of Philadelphia centered on the South. Failure of an anticipated French fleet to appear off the coast enabled the British to launch an assault on Georgia. Thirty-five hundred men attacked Savannah, which fell in December 1778, followed shortly by Augusta. Americans temporarily prevented Charleston's fall, but only naval power could cut British supply lines. When Admiral D'Estaing finally brought the French fleet to the Georgia coast, Americans under General Benjamin Lincoln laid siege to Savannah. However, the attack failed, Lincoln retreated to South Carolina, and the fleet returned to France. Now, Clinton decided upon a full-scale invasion of the South, and he moved 8,000 troops to besiege Charleston in January 1780. In May, General Lincoln capitulated, and the British captured 5,000 troops and three generals. Clinton, anticipating an easy victory, left for New York City, putting Charles Cornwallis in command at Charleston.

George Washington (1732-1799). A leader in the independence movement, he was chosen to command the Continental Army surrounding Boston. His most brilliant maneuver led to the important victory at Yorktown. (By Charles Willson Peale, Washington and Lee University)

Cornwallis moved out, attempting to win over loyalists and set up new colonial governments. Congress called General Gates from retirement; he led 5,000 troops against Camden, South Carolina, in August 1780 and suffered a massive defeat. A second major American army surrendered and the British rejoiced. Washington's tribulations came in bunches. His army still suffered from short rations, he had only a thousand men available by mid-summer, the prime fighting time, and in September, General Benedict Arnold deserted to the British with plans for American fortifications at West Point.

However, Cornwallis's southern victories soon dissipated his strength. He marched into North Carolina and in September 1780 took Charlotte with ease, but a thousand-man force under Major Patrick Ferguson was slaughtered at King's Mountain, and Cornwallis retreated to South Carolina. Upon receiving 2,500 reinforcements, he again ventured northward, and now he encountered General Nathanael Greene, who adopted Washington's strategy of harassment. Greene retreated northward and enticed Cornwallis to follow, thereby stretching British supply lines to the breaking point. Two major battles were fought. The Americans won at Cowpens by nearly wiping out Sir Banastre Tarleton's Tory force, but lost at Guilford Courthouse, although the British had greater casualties and

The Surrender of Cornwallis, October 19, 1781. (By Ramberg, The Metropolitan Museum of Art, gift of Charles Allen Munn, 1924)

THE DANCE, 1781

    Cornwallis led a country dance,
        The like was never seen, sir,
    Much retrograde and much advance,
        And all with General Greene, sir.

    They rambled up and rambled down,
        Join'd hands, then off they run, sir,
    Our General Greene to Charlestown,
        The earl to Wilmington, sir.

    Greene, in the South, then danc'd a set,
        And got a mighty name, sir,
    Cornwallis jigg'd with young Fayette,
        But suffer'd in his fame, sir.

    Then down he figur'd to the shore,
        Most like a lordly dancer,
    And on his courtly honor swore,
        He would no more advance, sir.

    Quoth he, my guards are weary grown
        With footing country dances,
    They never at St. James's shone,
        At capers, kicks or prances.

    Though men so gallant ne'er were seen,
        While sauntering on parade, sir,
    Or wriggling o'er the park's smooth green,
        Or at a masquerade, sir.

    Yet are red heels and long-lac'd skirts,
        For stumps and briars meet, sir?
    Or stand they chance with hunting-shirts,
        Or hardy veteran feet, sir?

Now hous'd in York he challeng'd all,
   At minuet or a l'amande,
And lessons for a courtly ball,
   His guards by day and night conn'd.

This challenge known, full soon there came,
   A set who had the bon ton,
De Grasse and Rochambeau, whose fame
   Fut brilliant pour un long tems.

And Washington, Columbia's son,
   Whom easy nature taught, sir,
That grace which can't by pains be won,
   Or Plutus' gold be bought, sir.

Now hand in hand they circle round,
   This ever-dancing peer, sir;
Their gentle movements, soon confound
   The earl, as they draw near, sir.

His music soon forgets to play —
   His feet can no more move, sir,
And all his bands now curse the day,
   They jigg'd to our shore, sir.

Now Tories all, what can ye say?
   Come — is not this a griper,
That while your hopes are danc'd away,
   'Tis you must pay the piper.

Anon.

(From: F. C. Prescott and J. H. Nelson, eds., Prose and Poetry of the Revolution *[New York: Thomas Y. Crowell, 1925], pp. 100-101)*

YORK RIVER **YORK RIVER**

Gloucester

French troops and fortifications: gray

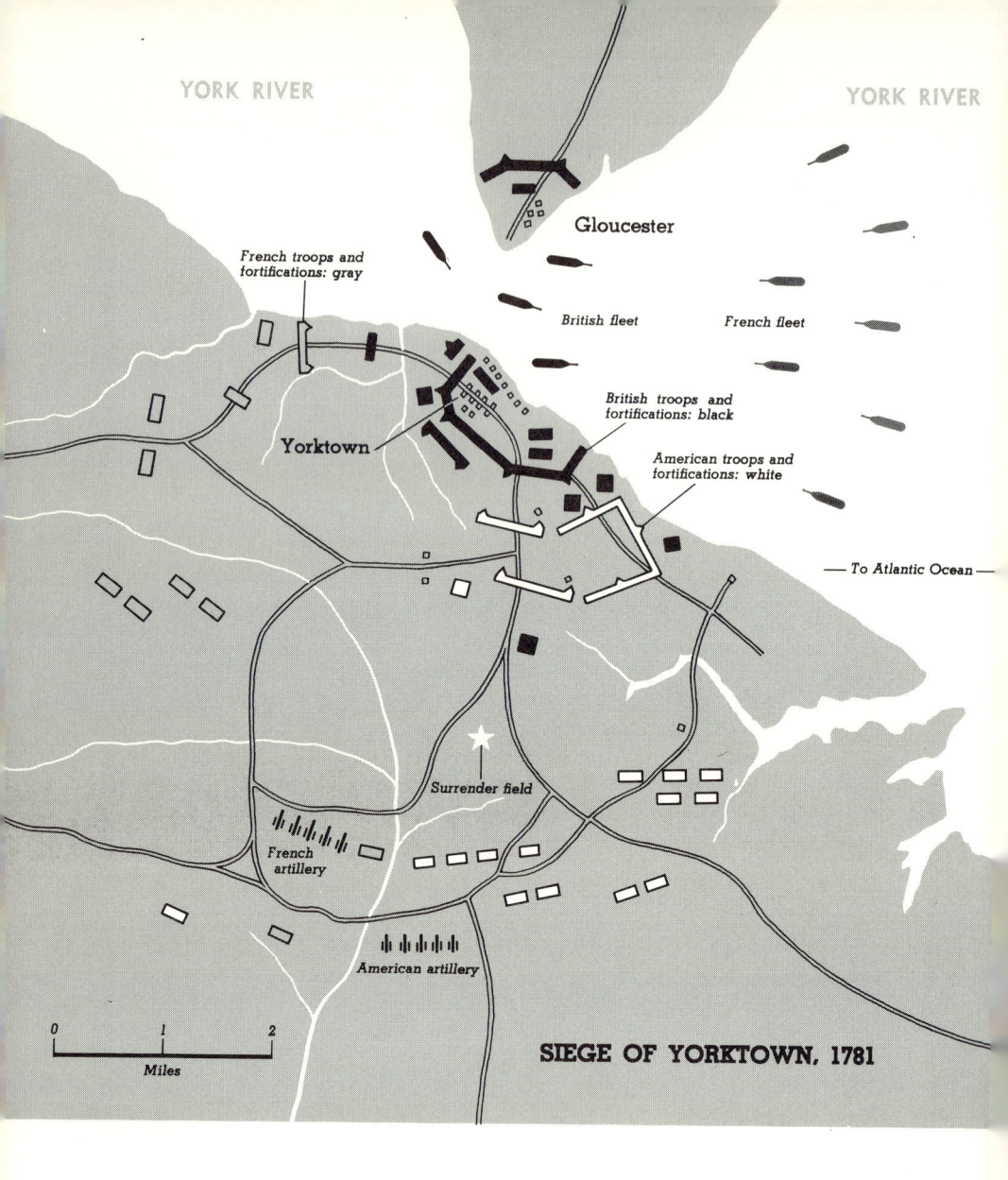

British fleet   French fleet

Yorktown

British troops and fortifications: black

American troops and fortifications: white

— To Atlantic Ocean —

Surrender field

French artillery

American artillery

0 1 2
Miles

SIEGE OF YORKTOWN, 1781

American forces remained intact. By the end of March, Cornwallis moved to the coast at Wilmington, where he could secure supplies by ship. Meanwhile, Greene circled the British and set off to liberate the Carolinas.

In the spring of 1781, Cornwallis decided to invade Virginia, and he rejoined forces with the renegade Benedict Arnold and moved against a small force led by Lafayette. The Frenchman kept his troops just ahead of the English, constantly leading them on. After Lafayette received reinforcements, Cornwallis again retreated to the coast where he received orders to send part of his troops to New York for Clinton's new campaign. Confusion reigned, since the fleet intended to transport the soldiers had sailed after a French convoy, and so Cornwallis waited in a fortified position on Yorktown Peninsula.

Washington, meanwhile, learned that Admiral de Grasse's French West Indies fleet would be in Chesapeake Bay until October 1781, and he saw his opportunity. He force-marched his men and Rochambeau's French troops from New York to Virginia. De Grasse blockaded the Virginia Coast, thus frustrating Cornwallis's hope of reinforcements, while Washington besieged the British by land. Washington launched his attack on the isolated English position and Cornwallis's army capitulated on October 17, 1781. For all practical purposes the fighting war ended. British strategy failed, while Washington's succeeded. Fighting on home terrain, Americans had conducted a war of attrition with far greater success than anyone expected, but they owed much to French aid.

Diplomacy of the Revolution

French aid made possible American victories at Saratoga and Yorktown, the only two major battles won by Washington's forces, and sustained Americans throughout the war. France had joined the rebelling colonials, not out of love for their revolution or its principles, but solely to destroy British power by breaking up its empire. The Comte de Vergennes, Louis XVI's foreign minister, saw America's rebellion as an opportunity to humble England and restore France to its previous position in European politics.

Vergennes had the possibilities presented by the American rebellion brought forcibly to his attention by his secret service agent, Caron de Beaumarchais, who met Arthur Lee, an American, while on a mission in London. Lee had been invited by the Continental Congress's Committee of Secret Correspondence in November 1775 to become its agent to learn the disposition of foreign powers toward Americans. The colonials, venturing into foreign diplomacy, required someone with experience in the field. The Congress chose Lee, despite his relative inexperience, because he was well-connected as a brother of Richard Henry Lee of Virginia and he was loyal to the American cause.

Arthur Lee convinced Beaumarchais that America's quarrel with the mother country was serious, and he talked of securing arms for the rebels.

When Beaumarchais returned to Paris, he convinced Vergennes of France's opportunity. By April 1776 Vergennes, too, had become a firm believer, and he prepared a statement for the king which suggested that, since England and France were natural enemies, and since the colonies supported Britain's manufacturing and naval strength, loss of America would hurt France's enemy, perhaps mortally, and might even benefit France by diverting American trade to it. Moreover, an independent America would give France a colonial empire's advantages with little of its burdens, for Vergennes believed that the former colonies would always remain weak and divided, subject to French control, and offer no threat to the American territories of France's Spanish ally.

Consequently, Louis XVI agreed to transfer munitions from French royal arsenals to a dummy corporation, Rodrique Hortalez and Company, created by Beaumarchais, which would in turn give them to the Americans. Louis XVI then persuaded his uncle, Charles III of Spain, to match this contribution. Thus before the Declaration of Independence, France had agreed to aid in the British Empire's disruption.

The Continental Congress, as yet unaware of French interest, knew only that America needed foreign assistance. Its boycott of 1774 had hurt its own cause by stopping the import of needed goods, including munitions. Americans had little manufacturing ability and had to import most commodities they needed for successful prosecution of war. In April 1776, therefore, Congress opened American ports to all nations except England in the hope of encouraging trade, but few were willing to risk the wrath of the most powerful nation on the high seas.

In March 1776 Congress sent Silas Deane of Connecticut to France to discuss arms purchases. When he arrived in Paris, he was referred to Beaumarchais, for the French government had no intention of granting public recognition to any American agent. Deane showed Beaumarchais his instructions to purchase munitions, and the latter, in possession of several hundred thousand dollars' worth of arms, quickly signed an agreement of sale. Serious complications over Deane's accounts later arose from this manipulation, but these arms arrived in time to supply Americans who surrounded Burgoyne at Saratoga and played an important part in that victory.

After the Declaration of Independence, Congress sent a diplomatic mission consisting of Deane, Lee, and Benjamin Franklin to France. The first two were already in Paris. Franklin soon embarked for France carrying with him a model treaty which became the basis of American diplomacy for more than a century. Realizing they were fighting the nation controlling the high seas, Americans sought to neutralize that naval power by getting other European nations to agree to the model treaty. This treaty expressed fundamental concepts of neutral rights to which Americans adhered until World War I: placing goods on board a neutral vessel neutralized the goods themselves, neutrals had freedom to trade in noncontraband between ports of a belligerent, and all contraband had to be specifically listed, but naval stores and food were not contraband.

British acceptance of these neutral rights as suggested in the model treaty was unthinkable, for it would have destroyed the effectiveness of the British fleet. These rights would mean that American goods on board a neutral vessel could not be seized as enemy property; neutrals could trade with American ports and the British blockade would only prevent the sailing of ships under the American flag; spelling out the precise nature of contraband would hamper British control of trade; and elimination of naval stores and foodstuffs from contraband lists would enable America to supply Europe with materials for ship construction and the foreign West Indies with commodities for their economic survival. America could never convince England to agree to these points, of course, but if other European nations would accept them, they might precipitate serious conflicts with England.

Franklin arrived in France as a goodwill ambassador as well as an official American emissary. Of all Americans he was probably the best known abroad and the most loved. He represented the ideals of the Enlightenment better than any other colonist, and he knew how to play upon his own popularity for his country's benefit. Congress also sent other missions in an attempt to batter down doors to win recognition. Franklin disagreed with this "militia" diplomacy and suggested that "a virgin state should preserve the virgin character and not go about suitoring for alliances, but wait with decent dignity for the application of others." He was right, for missions to Spain, Prussia, Austria, Russia, and Tuscany all proved fruitless.

Franklin worked assiduously on the French, for he understood what they had to gain from war with England. However, he lacked a trump card until news arrived in December 1777 of the Saratoga victory. Lord North immediately proposed reconciliation on the basis of home rule within the empire, a concession which would have stopped the rebellion

Benjamin Franklin (1706-1790), editor and scientist, who became a leading politician in Pennsylvania and then a diplomat and statesman as an agent to London and to Paris. (By David Martin, courtesy of the White House Collection)

even in July 1776, but was now too late. Nonetheless, Franklin, Deane, and Lee conversed with North's agent, Paul Wentworth, while Vergennes sat by and fretted. On December 17, 1777, the French foreign minister promised to recognize American independence and sign a treaty, but the talks continued. Finally, fearing the loss of France's advantages from American rebellion, Vergennes asked what the Americans wanted in order to stop the talks. A treaty and an alliance was Franklin's response. Vergennes agreed.

On February 6, 1778, two Franco-American treaties were signed. The first, a treaty of amity and commerce, recognized American independence and established commercial relations between the two countries. The second, a conditional and defensive alliance, provided that, if Britain declared war on France, neither France nor the United States would sign a separate peace, but both would fight until Britain accepted American independence, and that America would have a free hand with all British possessions on the North American mainland and France with all Britain's island possessions in the Western Hemisphere except Bermuda.

Vergennes sent Lord North a copy of the first treaty, hoping to trigger a war declaration and bring France's defensive alliances into operation, thus arraying most of Europe against England. North, however, already had both treaties through Silas Deane's secretary, Edward Bancroft, a British spy, and North refused to fall into the French trap. Moreover, the English hesitated to escalate the conflict because Lord Carlisle's Peace Commission en route to America would be jeopardized by war with France.

The Franco-American treaties and the Carlisle Commission reached America at about the same time. The Continental Congress now had a choice, and it ratified the French treaties on May 4, 1778, adding insult to injury by celebrating with captured supplies intended for use by the Carlisle Commission when it successfully concluded negotiations with the colonies. France and England drifted into an undeclared war, and French aid eventually culminated in America's most important victory at Yorktown.

Diplomacy of Peace

No sooner had the Franco-American treaties been signed than the emphasis shifted to peace negotiations, usually at the initiative of a European power which saw benefits for itself as negotiator. Most European nations seemed interested in reducing British power without elevating French strength, and they viewed Americans simply as pawns. Congress summed up its attitude toward peace in its instructions for John Adams, whom it appointed peace negotiator. First, Britain must recognize American independence. Then, Adams could negotiate boundary settlements, but these must include the St. John River in the Northeast, the Great Lakes to Lake Nippissing to the Mississippi's source along the North, and the Mississippi River in the West. In all other matters, Louis XVI and his ministers would guide Adams.

John Adams believed in shirt-sleeve diplomacy, in laying his cards on the table without protocol. He first invited the British to talk peace, thereby throwing the onus for continuing war on them. Next he told Vergennes that America was as important to France as France was to America — an obvious fact given Vergennes's ambitions to break up Britain's power, but one which diplomatic niceties precluded mentioning. Vergennes quickly understood that he could not control Adams and urged his replacement. However, Congress, instead of replacing Adams, added Franklin, John Jay, Thomas Jefferson, and Henry Laurens to the mission. Jefferson did not serve, and Laurens was in the Tower of London;

John Adams (1735-1826), one of the outstanding political theorists in America, who served in the Continental Congresses, and became U.S. minister to Britain from 1785 to 1788. He later served as first Vice-President of the United States, and then as the nation's second President. (By Joseph Badger, courtesy of the collection of the Detroit Institute of Arts)

thus Adams, Franklin, and Jay became the three peace commissioners. Congress also modified its instructions to the commission — recognition of independence remained indispensable, but now in all other matters, including boundaries, they were to be guided by the French.

Congress, which desperately needed French aid, had placed itself in an awkward position by becoming a French pawn. This might have had disastrous consequences except for the Yorktown victory, Lord North's overthrow, rivalries within the British government over securing the honor of settling the conflict, and Franklin's astuteness. The British sent Franklin's old acquaintance, Richard Oswald, to conduct informal talks with the American commissioners, and Franklin outlined for him two sets of terms, one necessary and the other desirable. Necessary terms included prior recognition of independence, evacuation of all troops, boundary settlements which would give the Ohio Valley to America, and freedom

PEACE OF 1783

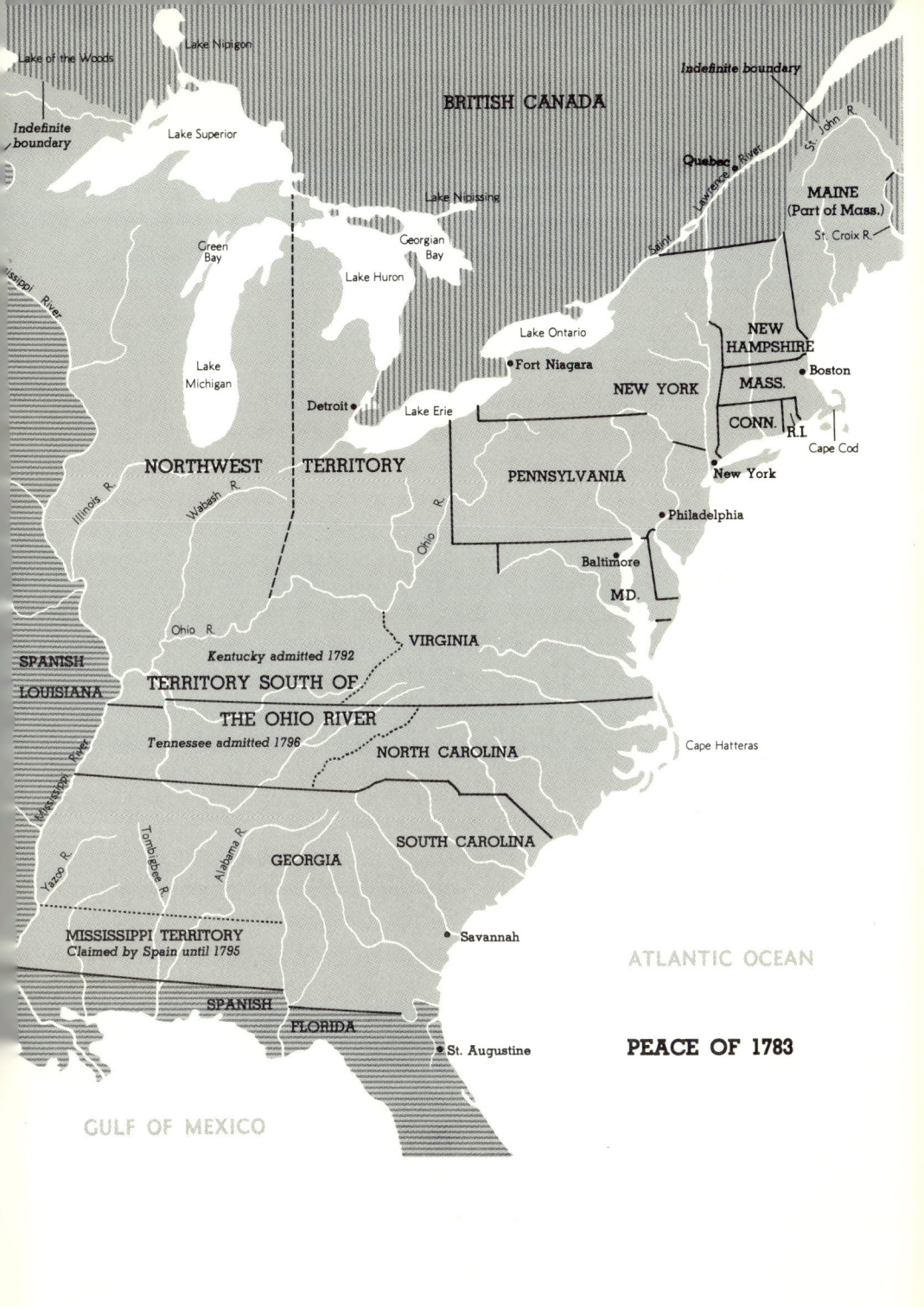

of the Newfoundland fisheries. Full friendship between the two nations could be achieved if Britain conceded the desirable terms: £500,000 indemnity for burning American towns, granting American vessels the same privileges within the empire as British vessels (permitting them the benefits of mercantilism without its restrictions), and the cession of Canada (which would eliminate a potential source of friction).

Oswald received a commission to deal with representatives of the colonies or plantations, and Jay and Franklin told him this was inadequate, that he must be authorized to deal with plenipotentiaries of the United States of America. Meanwhile, Vergennes passed word to the English that he wanted an Indian buffer state created between the Mississippi and the Appalachians to protect Spain's possessions from infection by American republicanism, and that he would not support America's claims to the fisheries, which would give France added competition. Shelburne, then prime minister, seized his opportunity to split the Franco-American alliance and gave Oswald the commission desired by the Americans. Negotiations then proceeded in earnest, and the United States received its necessary terms.

The Peace of Paris gave the United States all the land west to the Mississippi (except Florida, which Britain transferred to Spain instead of giving up Gibraltar) and north to the Great Lakes. (The final northern boundary would not be determined until the Webster-Ashburton Treaty of 1842.) The British agreed to evacuate their western military posts and to give Americans the right to fish off Newfoundland and dry their catches on shore. However, the British demanded repayment of prewar private debts owed British subjects and compensation for confiscated loyalist property. Americans could go no further than to urge each state to place no obstacles in the way of debt collection or loyalist reimbursement.

The preliminary treaty was drafted without Vergennes's knowledge (a direct violation of congressional instructions) and signed two weeks later. It would not become effective until England also signed treaties with France and Spain. Vergennes complained to Franklin, who readily admitted the indiscretion but hoped that it would not mar the great collaboration between France and America. "The English, I just now learn, flatter themselves that they have already divided us," Franklin wrote to Vergennes, "I hope this little misunderstanding will therefore be kept secret, and that they will find themselves totally mistaken." America

Comte de Vergennes (1717-1787), French foreign minister under Louis XVI. Vergennes constantly kept his eye on France's interests and by May, 1781, was willing to end the War of the American Revolution. However, the Yorktown victory upset his plans. (Independence National Historical Park Collection, Philadelphia)

subtly threatened a separate peace, which would leave France at war and deny it any fruits of victory, and Vergennes understood it. When Franklin simultaneously asked for a new loan of $1.2 million the French minister could only agree. When on January 20, 1783, France and Spain signed articles of peace with Britain, the Anglo-American treaty went into effect.

Unresolved Problems

America had its independence, but now had to face problems left unresolved during the crisis of war. For one thing, it had to accept the economic consequences of being outside the empire. Old trade patterns were no longer meaningful, for Americans had relieved themselves not only of restrictions, but also of benefits. England applied its mercantilistic policy with full force, and Americans found the West Indian and Canadian trades closed to their ships. All commerce with British territories had to be in British vessels.

The new nation had also promised to impose no obstacle to collection by Englishmen of prewar debts and to encourage states to compensate loyalists for confiscated property. In return, the British promised in a reasonable time to withdraw their troops from frontier outposts and to compensate Americans for slaves taken away as the British evacuated. These matters continued to plague Anglo-American relations, for the American Congress could not force these agreements on recalcitrant states, and the British retaliated by dragging their heels.

Internal difficulties began even before the war ended. The Continental Congress had kept close control over the army largely because of traditional Anglo-American suspicions of standing armies. Sam Adams, as early as 1776, expressed this feeling: "A standing army, however necessary it may be sometimes, is always dangerous to the liberties of the people. Soldiers are apt to consider themselves as a body distinct from the rest of the citizens. They have their arms always in their hands. Their rules and their discipline is severe. They soon become attached to their officers and disposed to yield implicit obedience to their commands. Such a power should be watched with a jealous eye." And Congress kept such a jealous eye on military affairs that Washington at times was driven to complain of political manipulations.

Part of Washington's difficulties lay in the fact that he dealt with fourteen armies, one from each state plus the Continental Army. State militia received different pay, served varying terms, and presented problems of relative rank between continental and militia officers. Moreover, officers seemed exceptionally conscious of their "honor" which, according to John Adams, was "one of the most putrid corruptions of absolute monarchy." And the shortage of qualified colonial officers led Congress to grant commissions wholesale to foreigners who claimed military experience. Some officers thus obtained proved valuable to Washington's army, but most did not. The French especially flocked to American colors, and even Washington finally denounced most of them as men of "a little plausibility, unbounded pride and ambition, and a perseverance in application not to be resisted but by uncommon firmness."

Officers and men rarely received their full pay, thus reflecting one of Congress's greatest problems, lack of money. Reenlistments dropped. Congress first offered cash bounties, then land bounties, to bolster the army's strength. Of equal importance, soldiers were unaccustomed to discipline. Because they had never known any, it had to be severe when applied, and yet it was not used uniformly. Officers committed the same acts as enlisted men, but only the latter received harsh punishment. Americans may have been fortunate indeed at the end of fighting in 1781, for its prolongation might have led to complete disintegration of their military forces.

The Application of Revolutionary Ideals

By the 1780s American society had undergone basic changes. It still possessed an aristocracy based increasingly on inherited wealth and thus growing more rigid, but the withdrawal of loyalists weakened it at a crucial moment. An estimated twenty-four out of every thousand colonials departed with the British, and their removal eliminated a conservative and tradition-oriented group from society. Many of those who left were not aristocrats, but they provided support for an established hierarchal order, and their absence from the American scene weakened the underpinning for an aristocracy.

Although weakened by the loyalist departure, the aristocracy continued to set the tone in fashion, education, and politics. The degree to which this group dominated in local communities varied according to local conditions. In frontier areas, it was more embryonic than realized. In the North, though less institutionalized and more fluid, it still possessed great influence. In the South, the system of black slavery institutionalized the aristocracy and it controlled much of community life. Americans, like Europeans, respected those who possessed the symbols of success, though the lower classes in America more readily kicked over the traces when conditions became intolerable.

Rising to challenge the aristocracy was a middle class which would have great influence in the near future, especially as national issues emerged and crossed state boundaries. Farmers who possessed their own land and who produced beyond their own needs comprised the bulk of this class. Merchants of moderate means and self-employed urban artisans made up a lesser element of the middle class. Together these groups provided an innovative force in American life.

Revolutionary ideals had meaning to these farmers, merchants, and artisans, and they determined to apply them. More often than not, they had pragmatic motives: as a rising element in society they preferred to shape tax policies to their own benefit, to keep governmental interference with their wishes to a minimum, and to limit judicial procedures which often buttressed the aristocracy's position. To accomplish these objectives, the middle element in American society drew upon doctrines of their own colonial and revolutionary past. They distrusted distant power, an attitude perfectly in keeping with the Anglo-American Whig tradition. Retention of power by the people, preventing its abuse by a favored few to enhance their property holdings, and keeping officeholders responsive by frequent elections and rotation in office — these became the precepts of middle-class political ideology.

In carrying out these ideals, the revolutionary generation began an intensive self-examination of social institutions. The high idealism characteristic of the era unleashed forces for reform that not even conservative aristocrats could withstand. Indeed, some joined in the process with great enthusiasm. The revolution's emphasis upon natural rights gave men incentive to demolish those heritages of the past which contradicted or hampered their rights. They overhauled governmental machinery, created new state constitutions, and initiated a number of significant reforms which they did not always carry to completion, such as new approaches to church-state relations, to the institution of Negro slavery, and to criminal and legal codes.

Religion, an integral part of American life and thought from the very beginning, had not remained static. Although most colonies had state-supported churches by the 1770s, growing opposition to any connection between church and state led to serious questions about the future status of religion. The Great Awakening first introduced doubts about the propriety of state support for any one religion, and as new sects multiplied, Americans increasingly challenged the political wisdom of such establishments. Backcountry farmers, in particular, belonged to new sects and objected to supporting the Church of England or the Congregational church. Often these dissenters were Baptists.

Baptist opposition to state-supported churches found justification during the eighteenth century in the attitude that religion was a matter between the individual and his God, that the state had neither right nor authority in this area and could not prescribe any one variety or force support for it. Thomas Paine, John Adams, Thomas Jefferson, and Benjamin Franklin all shared this attitude and led the assault on establishment of churches. George Mason's Virginia Bill of Rights, adopted in 1776, perfectly expressed their views: "Religion, or the duty which we owe to our Creator, and the manner of discharging it, can be directed only by reason and conviction, not by force and violence; and therefore all men are equally entitled to the free exercise of religion, according to the dictates of conscience; and that it is the mutual duty of all to practice Christian forebearance, love, charity toward each other." However, this only permitted toleration of dissenters from the established Anglican Church.

"Christian forebearance, love, charity" did not completely satisfy men such as Jefferson, who agreed with John Adams when he argued: "When we can enlarge our minds to allow each other an *entire* liberty in religious matters, the human race will be more happy and respectable in this and the future stage of its existence." Jefferson attacked the Anglican Church establishment in Virginia and received support from the backcountry Baptists. (They had initiated the Parson's Cause case in 1760, employing Patrick Henry as their attorney, in an attempt to undermine the Anglican Church establishment.) As the revolution began, the Baptists circulated a petition demanding disestablishment, and many Virginia aristocrats reacted favorably. They shared the same attitude and they needed backcountry support for the revolutionary effort. Thus necessity and idealism combined, and Mason and Jefferson gave dissenters a favorable hearing.

After Virginia's adoption of Mason's Bill of Rights, Jefferson introduced legislation in 1779 to separate church and state, to free men's minds as he put it. Bitter controversy developed as conservatives feared the loss of compulsory support for religion. Patrick Henry suggested the continuance of compulsory support, with each person having the option of designating to which church his money would go. However, Virginia finally adopted Jefferson's statute of religious freedom in 1786. He believed this to be so important that, when he prepared his epitaph in his later years, he listed as his three greatest contributions the Declaration of Independence, the University of Virginia, and the Statute for Religious Freedom. His presidency and its accomplishments paled into insignificance when compared with his efforts to free men's minds.

Disestablishment in Virginia had been hard fought because the Anglican clergy represented a local patriotic influence rather than a distant Loyalist one. In other areas this was not the case. North Carolina had but half a dozen Anglican ministers, all Loyalists, and so it easily accomplished disestablishment in its 1776 constitution. Georgia did the same thing in its 1777 constitution, and South Carolina provided for full equality of all Protestant sects in 1778.

Thomas Jefferson (1743-1826), a Virginia attorney, author of the Declaration of Independence, and advocate of truly republican government. He served as a member of the Continental Congresses, as wartime Governor of Virginia, and as minister to France. (By Rembrandt Peale, courtesy of White House Collection)

In New England, especially Massachusetts, disestablishment created even more difficulty than in Virginia. The established Congregational Church and its ministers had been revolutionary leaders preaching sedition from the earliest days. Thus, while Baptists argued for disestablishment, the Massachusetts constitution of 1780 only modified traditional practices. Individuals could support the church of their choice from among those in their town, but they must support one. Connecticut and New Hampshire followed the same pattern. Although not satisfactory in dissenters' eyes, it remained in effect for half a century.

Most states broke with religious establishment during or immediately after the revolution. This did not suggest any antireligious attitude among Americans, but a realization that religion was a private, not a state, matter. Separation, not destruction, was their goal. Most states retained religious provisions for officeholding and even for the franchise, though usually loosely phrased to include all Protestant denominations.

In large part, this attitude had been inherited from England. English Protestantism differed from that of other European countries because it lacked stability and fragmented easily. Voltaire once explained the consequences of this: "If only one religion were allowed in England, the government would very probably become arbitrary; if there were but two, the people would cut one another's throats; but as there are such a multitude, they all live happily and in peace." Voltaire perfectly summarized English history, but he also projected America's development. By elevating this institutional fragility to a principle, Americans have avoided the kind of religious warfare that has rent almost every other major nation. Religious diversity demands a *modus vivendi,* for the alternative is unending homicide in God's name.

Americans inherited from England not only religious diversity, but also England's religious sects. Most noteworthy and troublesome of these was the Church of England, for America's political break with the king left that institution bereft of leadership. Americans could not deny George III's political authority and yet accept his religious control. Thus the Church of England became the Protestant Episcopal Church, but some means had to be found to establish an American bishop without accepting the king's supremacy. Samuel Seabury, selected as America's first Episcopal bishop, secured ordination from Scotland's nonjuring bishops who never accepted Crown supremacy.

Methodism's strong English ties threatened to become embarrassing to the new nation until John Wesley reorganized what had been an offshoot of the Anglican Church into the independent American Methodist Episcopal Church with an elective bishop. Other churches of English origin presented no such difficulties because they had no connection with the mother country's religious establishment. Neither Congregationalism nor Presbyterianism had legal involvements with English authorities and continued their independent ways, but their intellectual and emotional connections with their English coreligionists remained important.

BLACK SLAVERY

The revolution unleashed a heightened concern over the status of blacks in society. Americans became aware that slavery involved a mental attitude, not only of the black, but of the white as well. Because white Americans viewed the black as inferior, he continued to occupy an inferior position in their economy, society, and laws. However, white

THE TREATMENT OF BLACKS, 1774

I THEN ASKED THE YOUNG MAN what their allowance is? He told me that, excepting some favourites about the table their weekly allowance is a peck of Corn, & a pound of Meat a Head! — And Mr. Carter is allowed by all, & from what I have already seen of others, I make no Doubt at all but he is, by far the most humane to his Slaves of any in these parts! Good God! are these Christians? — When I am on the Subject, I will relate further, what I heard Mr. George Lees Overseer, one Morgan, say the other day that he himself had often done to Negroes, and found it useful; He said that whipping of any kind does them no good, for they will laugh at your greatest Severity; But he told us he had invented two things, and by several experiments had proved their success. — For Sulleness, Obstinacy, or Idleness, says he, Take a Negro, strip him, tie him fast to a post; take then a sharp Curry-Comb, & curry him severely til he is well scraped; & call a Boy with some dry Hay, and

☆☆☆☆☆☆☆☆☆☆☆☆☆☆☆☆☆☆☆☆☆☆☆☆☆

prejudice ran headlong into the revolution's equalitarianism, especially as a consequence of the black's role in the war.

Blacks had served in the armed forces of the new nation, both on land and on sea, and usually in nonsegregated units. The participation increased after the third year of the war, once white fears of arming blacks had given way to the pressing need for troops. The Continental Congress at first had refused to permit enlistment of blacks, either slave or free, but the New England states broke the barrier. South Carolina and Georgia throughout the war refused to utilize Negro troops, even when under direct assault by British forces. They feared the social and economic consequences of arming their slaves, and they worried about the possibility of wholesale desertions to the British. Nonetheless, about 5,000 blacks served in America's armed forces during the revolution, motivated in large part by the movement's idealism and the hope of bettering themselves.

Official American concern with black slavery as an institution had found its initial expression in Jefferson's draft of the Declaration of Independence which indicted George III for, among other things, forcing slavery upon the colonies against their wishes. Although dropped from the final

make the Boy rub him down for several Minutes, then salt him, & unlose him. He will attend to his Business, (said the inhuman Infidel) afterwards! — But savage Cruelty does not exceed His next diabolical invention — To get a Secret from a Negro, says he, take the following Method — Lay upon your Floor a large thick plank, having a peg about eighteen Inches long, of hard wood, & very Sharp, on the upper end, fixed fast in the plank — then strip the Negro, tie the Cord to a staple in the Ceiling, so as that his foot may just rest on the sharpened Peg, then turn him briskly round, and you would laugh (said our informer) at the Dexterity of the Negro, while he was relieving his Feet on the sharpened Peg! — I need say nothing of these seeing there is a righteous God, who will take vengeance on such Inventions!...(From: Philip Vickers Fithian, Journal and Letters, 1767-1774 [Princeton: The University Library, 1900], pp. 68-69)

☆☆☆☆☆☆☆☆☆☆☆☆☆☆☆☆☆☆☆☆☆☆☆☆

version, this reflected a widespread opposition to the institution. Small farmers in the upper South found it impossible to compete with slave labor, Quakers opposed it on religious grounds, and many large planters found it increasingly uneconomical. Yet, how could they solve the problem of slavery? Patrick Henry understood the dilemma: "Is it not amazing that at a time, when the rights of humanity are defined and understood with precision, in a country above all others fond of liberty, that in such an age and in such a country we find men professing a religion the most humane, mild, gentle and generous, adopting a principle as repugnant to humanity as it is inconsistent with the Bible and destructive to liberty?" However, he had no solution and proposed passing the problem on to posterity together with a realization of its incongruity.

America first attacked the slave trade which had been a virtual British monopoly for so many years. Only Georgia and South Carolina, relatively new areas still needing large quantities of manpower, continued the trade after 1783. By then all others had halted the traffic in human beings. But freeing those already enslaved was another, more troublesome matter. Vermont's constitution of 1777 abolished slavery, but that state had few blacks. In 1780, the Massachusetts constitution declared all men free and

JEFFERSON ON DEPRAVITY OF SLAVERY, 1784

THERE MUST DOUBTLESS be an unhappy influence on the manners of our people produced by the existence of slavery among us. The whole commerce between master and slave is a perpetual exercise of the most boisterous passions, the most unremitting despotism, on the one part, and degrading submissions on the other. Our children see this, and learn to imitate it; for man is an imitative animal. This quality is the germ of all education in him. From his cradle to his grave he is learning to do what he sees others do. If a parent could find no motive either in his philanthropy or his self-love, for restraining the intemperance of passion towards his slave, it should always be a sufficient one that his child is present. But generally it is not sufficient. The parent storms, the child looks on, catches the lineaments of wrath, puts on the same airs in the circle of smaller slaves, gives a loose to the worst of passions, and thus nursed, educated, and daily exercised in tyranny, cannot but be stamped by it with odious peculiarities. The man must be a prodigy who can retain his manners and morals undepraved by such circumstances. (From: Notes on Virginia)

☆☆☆☆☆☆☆☆☆☆☆☆☆☆☆☆☆☆☆☆☆☆☆☆☆☆☆

equal, and a few years later the Massachusetts Supreme Court applied this in the Quock Walker Case to blacks as well as whites and abolished slavery. Other states passed gradual emancipation laws, providing freedom for slaves when they reached a stipulated age. Private groups also became active, including the Philadelphia Abolition Society (1774) with Franklin as President, and the Society for the Promotion of the Manumission of Slaves (1785) with John Jay as President and Alexander Hamilton as Secretary. But the revolutionary generation's greatest failure was its inability to match its ideals and its practices in this area, thereby causing much suffering for future Americans and even jeopardizing its other accomplishments.

Legal Reforms

The break with Britain gave Americans an excellent opportunity to recast their legal systems. To begin with, laws were no longer based upon the Crown's sovereignty, but upon the people's. Many English statutes, created for that kingdom's purposes, had only limited validity in America and could now be tossed aside or replaced with laws drawn more closely to American needs.

One example of this was the criminal code. Its brutality was based upon European, not American, problems. England's overpopulation (at least it was then considered overpopulated) placed great emphasis upon protecting property rights from assault by individuals and mobs. Thus English laws provided the death penalty for robbery, forgery, housebreaking, and counterfeiting, but in America these punishments did not coincide with the scarcity of population which had changed the emphasis in the New World from protection of property to individual rights. Americans did not completely overthrow old values; rather, they became aware that human beings were too valuable to be wasted when they might be reformed into useful citizens. Model penal institutions, where convicts could be taught useful trades and contribute to society, replaced capital punishment for most crimes. Pennsylvania, under Quaker guidance, took the lead here and limited the death penalty to willful murder.

Other legal reforms brought civil codes into line with American needs. In Virginia, Jefferson revised the statutes, choosing from English law before and after settlement of the colony in 1603 what was valuable for the state, and selecting from among colonial laws those that fitted more modern needs. He also opposed two feudal practices, primogeniture and entail, as vestigial remnants of an earlier age and different conditions. Primogeniture applied only when a landowner died without a will, and it passed all his property intact to his eldest son. Entail permitted a landowner to require that his property be passed from eldest son to eldest son through all generations in perpetuity. Both served well in land-short Europe where constant subdivision would destroy the aristocracy's economic base, but neither meant much in the New World and had never been seriously applied.

The Nation in 1783

One lesson, clearly an old one, had been reaffirmed by the American Revolution — law is only effective in a consensual society or one ruled by gross fear. When consensus breaks down, so does the law. Until 1763 the British Empire was a consensual society, and colonists accepted most imperial regulation not from fear of British power, but because they

THE INDIAN CONDEMNED, 1782

A WILD INDIAN with his skin painted red, and a feather through his nose, has set his foot on the broad continent of North and South America; a second wild Indian with his ears cut in ringlets, or his nose slit like a swine or a malefactor, also sets his foot on the same extensive tract of soil. Let the first Indian make a talk to his brother, and bid him take his foot off the continent, for he being first upon it, had occupied the whole, to kill buffaloes, and tall elks with long horns. This claim in the reasoning of some men would be just, and the second savage ought to depart in his canoe, and seek a continent where no prior occupant claimed the soil. . . . With regard to forming treaties or making peace with this race, there are many ideas:

They have the shapes of men and may be of the human species, but certainly in their present state they approach nearer the character of Devils; take an Indian, is there any faith in him? Can you bind him by favors? Can you trust his word or confide in his promise? When he makes war upon you, when he takes you prisoner and has you in his

☆☆☆☆☆☆☆☆☆☆☆☆☆☆☆☆☆☆☆☆☆☆☆☆☆☆

consented to the goals sought by that regulation. After 1763 Americans had to form a new consensus. They replaced the English imperial system with one of their own construction, the Articles of Confederation, and they reconstituted local governments to their own liking. They also avoided a basic British mistake. By understanding the cause of their own rebellion, they insisted upon eventually developing the western domain into completely equal states, thereby rejecting British insistence upon perpetual colonial inferiority. Such political experimentation provided but one aspect of the revolution's significance.

Dissolution of the old consensus and disruption of the British Empire resulted in far-reaching changes in American life. Governmental upheaval in the 1770s had enabled frontiersmen to play a part in politics, and they, whether within or beyond the borders of the original states, had no intention of relinquishing their newly found power. British policy no longer hindered settlement of the West, and the outpouring of people into the area between the Appalachians and the Mississippi River became so great that it constantly forced change upon American society. Agrarianism

power will he spare you? In this he departs from the law of nature, by which, according to Baron Montesquieu and every other man who thinks on the subject, it is unjustifiable to take away the life of him who submits; the conqueror in doing otherwise becomes a murderer, who ought to be put to death. On this principle are not the whole Indian nations murderers?

Many of them may have not had an opportunity of putting prisoners to death, but the sentiment which they entertain leads them invariably to this when they have it in their power or judge it expedient; these principles constitute them murderers, and they ought to be prevented from carrying them into execution, as we would prevent a common homicide, who would be mad enough to conceive himself justifiable in killing men. The tortures which they exercise on the bodies of their prisoners, justify extermination. . . . (From: H. H. Brackenridge in Freeman's Journal and North American Intelligencer *[1782])*

☆☆☆☆☆☆☆☆☆☆☆☆☆☆☆☆☆☆☆☆☆☆☆☆☆☆☆☆

would play a forceful role, not only in politics, but in social and economic life as well. Rural values, reinforced for a century by the vast public domain, would dominate America and would conflict with the values of the nation's emerging urban centers. America's economy, so long an appendage of English mercantilism, would change little in the next half-century as the former colonies continued to export raw materials and import finished products from Europe.

The revolution also unsettled established and traditional ways of American life by unleashing unforeseen forces. Americans found not only the opportunity, but also the necessity, to reassess their practices and social institutions and to initiate serious reforms. They brought church-state relations abreast of previous colonial thought, for disestablishment as a concept long antedated its application in America. They revised legal codes and criminal codes, and cast aside British approaches at least partially, although state judiciaries remained very conservative and incorporated English common law in their decisions. Even black slavery, which remained institutionalized in the South, came under sharp scrutiny, and few, even in the South, would deny its incongruity in the new nation though they did not know how to relieve themselves of it.

Despite these advances, Americans still faced serious problems. The Confederation Congress could not secure adequate funds nor enforce its policies on the states. Financial distress created embarrassment because of the heavy debt, foreign and domestic, incurred to fight the war and precipitated a ruinous depreciation of currency. Inability to control commercial relations with other nations led to serious economic trouble, since uniform navigation laws or trade restrictions could not be passed and each state legislated for itself. Commercial treaties consequently became unenforceable, with competition among states becoming the rule. These two weaknesses — inadequate financing and lack of commercial control — prevented maturation of the Confederation Congress into a parliamentary system despite its potential in that direction. Whether these difficulties could have been overcome remains debatable. Certainly proposed solutions all foundered on the reluctance of one or more states to agree, for the Articles could be amended only by unanimous consent of all states.

Selected Bibliography

John R. Alden's *A History of the American Revolution* (1969) summarizes the latest scholarship, as does R. J. White's *The Age of George III* (1968). Russel B. Nye's *The Cultural Life in the New Nation, 1776-1830* (1960) incorporates much material on these years. A most important volume is Jackson Turner Main's *The Social Structure of Revolutionary America* (1965). Benjamin A. Quarles's *The Negro in the American Revolution* (1961) provides a convenient analysis of the black population's participation.

Military aspects of the revolution have been dealt with in great detail. John R. Alden's *The American Revolution* (1954) and John C. Miller's *Triumph of Freedom, 1775-1783* (1948) emphasize the military phase. Lynn Montross's *Rag, Tag, and Bobtail* (1953) is a study of the Continental Army. Howard H. Peckham's *The War for Independence* (1958) provides a standard military history. Hugh F. Rankin's *The American Revolution* (1964) studies the social aspect of warfare. Willard M. Wallace's *Appeal to Arms* (1951) offers a broad approach. Two British views are Pier Mackesy's *The War for America* (1964) and Peter Wells's *The American War of Independence* (1967).

The problem of loyalism has been treated in several recent volumes.

Claude Van Tyne's *Loyalists in the American Revolution* (1929) is an older study with much merit. It should be supplemented by the findings of William H. Nelson's *The American Tory* (1961) and Paul H. Smith's *Loyalists and Redcoats* (1964). Three convenient collections of essays on loyalism are *Allegiance in America: The Case of the Loyalists* (1969), edited by G. N. D. Evans, *Revolutionary vs. Loyalist* (1968), edited by Leslie F. S. Upton, and *The Colonial Legacy: Vol. I: Loyalist Historians* (1971), edited by Lawrence H. Leder.

The diplomatic negotiations of the revolution can be traced in Samuel Flagg Bemis's *The Diplomacy of the American Revolution* (1935) and Richard B. Morris's *The Peacemakers* (1968). The economic side can be found in Robert A. East's important *Business Enterprise in the American Revolutionary Era* (1938), the early chapters of Bray Hammond's *Banks and Politics in America* (1957), and E. James Ferguson's valuable and detailed *The Power of the Purse: A History of American Public Finance, 1776-1790* (1961).

As an era filled with important personalities, the revolution can be traced through biographies of its participants. On the British side are studies such as: William B. Wilcox's *Portrait of a General: Sir Henry Clinton in the War of Independence* (1964), Gerald S. Brown's *The American Secretary: The Colonial Policy of Lord George Germain, 1775-1778* (1963), John R. Alden's *General Gage in America* (1948), Lawrence H. Gipson's *Jared Ingersoll: A Study of American Loyalism* (1920), and two volumes on Benedict Arnold — James T. Flexner's *The Traitor and the Spy* (1953), and Willard M. Wallace's *Traitorous Hero* (1954).

The American side is represented by such studies as Samuel W. Patterson's *Horatio Gates* (1941), Theodore Thayer's *Nathanael Greene* (1960), R. Don Higginbotham's *Daniel Morgan: Revolutionary Rifleman* (1961), John Bakeless's *Background to Glory: The Life of George Rogers Clark* (1957), and *George Washington's Generals* (1964), edited by George Billias.

American political leaders have been examined frequently. Some of the most important studies are: Bernhard Knollenberg's *Washington and the Revolution* (1940), Curtis Nettles's *George Washington and American Independence* (1951), Esmond Wright's *Washington and the American Revolution* (1957). Esther Forbes's *Paul Revere and the World He Lived In* (1942) is an excellent fictionalized biography. Dumas Malone's fine portrait, *Jefferson and the Ordeal of Liberty* (1962), Herbert S. Allan's vivid biography, *John Hancock* (1948), and Verner Crane's *Benjamin Franklin* (1938) are all important works. Finally, mention should be made of a valuable but brief volume by Wesley Frank Craven, *The Legend of the Founding Fathers* (1956), which analyzes the impact of these years and events on American development.

CHAPTER 7

THE CIRCLE TURNED FULL, 1783-1789

Within six years after the revolution, Americans rapidly completed the basic constitutional outline of their new nation. Political experimentation begun in 1776 reached a peak with the adoption of the Articles of Confederation, then lagged for several years, and in a final burst of energy culminated in the federal Constitution. At the same time, Americans accommodated their attitudes and outlooks to the political changes wrought by independence. No longer colonial Englishmen, Americans eagerly accepted their new identity as independent Americans. However, pride in their nationhood was not enough; they had to resolve the critical problem of central government.

A successful national government in the eighteenth century had to regulate and control commerce, conduct foreign relations advantageously, facilitate economic development by a sound currency system, and maintain law and order. Only in creating executive machinery and in handling the western domain did the Confederation Congress demonstrate competence. On all other counts, it failed. Debates still persist as to whether the Confederation Congress, if it had been given additional powers, could have become an effective government, but such arguments are fruitless since no proposal for revision could ever overcome the Articles' requirement of unanimous consent.

Emergence of a Bureaucracy

Having accomplished their political independence from England, Americans had to put flesh upon the skeletal union they created to replace the empire. The Articles of Confederation, first proposed in 1776, were finally adopted by the thirteenth and last state in 1781, and all hoped that a more coherent and effective governmental structure would result. All understood that the Continental Congress had been merely a stopgap, and few had anticipated that it would continue in control during most of the war period. Nevertheless, it did, and experience gained during that time benefited the Confederation Congress.

As originally envisioned, the Confederation Congress would supervise the execution of government policy by committees in much the same way as the Continental Congress had done. However, this had proven cumbersome and time-consuming, as well as ineffective, and secretariats, headed by experts in each field with clerical staffs to assist them, gradually replaced the committee system. In January 1781 a Secretary for Foreign Affairs was appointed, followed by a Secretary at War and a Superintendent of Finance. The Confederation Congress recognized that government's basic problem was not the creation of policy, but its application.

Emergence of a bureaucracy met with hostility from radicals who distrusted all executive authority. But their approach of direct control by committees of congressmen posed such insuperable difficulties and created such confusions in government that establishment of a professional bureaucracy could not be prevented. The committee approach contained within it seeds of a parliamentary form of government, much like the modern British system, and some historians have speculated that if the Confederation Congress had been permitted to develop along these lines, the United States might have shaped its government in much the same way as the English.

Governing the West

One problem facing the Confederation Congress was disposition of the western domain. Maryland's insistence brought about the first cession of land claims by New York and soon other states followed. (Georgia was the last, and it turned over the Yazoo strip, the northern tier of Alabama and Mississippi, only after it became involved in corruption and scandal in the early nineteenth century.) By March 1784 Virginia ceded its vast and legitimate claim, and the Confederation Congress now had to provide for territorial government, a survey, a procedure for land sales, and Indian relations in the area west of the Appalachians, north of the Ohio River, and east of the Mississippi River.

The original idea proposed in the Articles of Confederation promised that new states in the West would be equal with the original thirteen. This would remove the dilemma that had caused the collapse of the first British Empire. It was one thing, however, to make general promises, and another to accomplish them by specific legislation. Congress turned to Thomas Jefferson for guidance, for he had long been interested in the trans-Appalachian region as a workshop for agrarian democracy. He wanted these lands given to settlers, not speculators, and he wanted the greatest possible degree of self-government for them.

Jefferson proposed that actual settlers be given free land and that they establish their own governments immediately using the laws of an existing state as their pattern. This would encourage their loyalty to the union, and they would augment governmental revenues in other ways than payment for lands. He proposed that the western domain be carved into ten states, and that as each reached a population of 20,000 they should elect a convention, adopt a constitution, and send a nonvoting delegate to Congress. When a territory's population equalled that of the smallest state, it would be brought into the union on an equal basis. These new states would be obligated to remain within the union, subject themselves to the Confederation Congress, pay their share of the national debt, maintain a republican form of government, and exclude slavery after 1800. Jefferson's proposals became the Ordinance of 1784 which Congress adopted with only a few modifications. (It deleted the reference to slavery, and it prevented new states from taxing lands still owned by Congress.) Jefferson's Ordinance provided for democratic self-government in the West from the beginning of settlement.

Orderly disposition of the land was prescribed by the Ordinance of

1785 which set rules for survey and sale. It required the division of land into townships of thirty-six square miles, each further subdivided into sections of one square mile (640 acres), with one section in each township reserved for public education. Lands would be sold in 640-acre tracts at public auction at a minimum price of one dollar an acre. The survey would eliminate much quarreling over boundaries, while the sale provisions guaranteed that lands would pass to actual settlers rather than speculators because the minimum price of $640 would require too great an investment for large-scale purchases. (Often, the settler found the cost too great as well.) Moreover, Congress would have an independent income from its one asset — the public domain — and it desperately needed the revenue.

Congress's financial distress actually caused it to ignore some terms of the 1785 Ordinance when presented with an opportunity to sell large tracts to speculators. A group of revolutionary war veterans, organized as the Ohio Associates, petitioned Congress for several million acres on the Ohio River. To win Congressional sanction, these speculators encouraged a number of legislators to set themselves up as the Scioto Associates and apply for a tract on that river. Both companies received authorization to purchase 6.5 million acres at one dollar each in continental currency (worth about twelve cents on the dollar). Soon other speculative groups marched to the Congressional trough.

Before speculators fully committed themselves to purchase lands, however, they insisted upon revising the Ordinance of 1784 and securing more adequate governmental provisions. Speculators in western lands needed law and order, and especially protection of property rights, if they were to make large investments there. Squatters had to be removed, but the absence of strong territorial government left an incipient democracy in its purest sense. Richard Henry Lee argued the necessity "for the security of property among uninformed and perhaps licentious people, as the greater part of those who go there are...a strong-toned government should exist, and the rights of property be clearly defined."

To answer speculators' demands, Congress adopted the more restrictive Ordinance of 1787. This provided three stages of territorial government which recapitulated the transition from colonies to states by the original thirteen. At first, Congress would appoint a governor, secretary, and three judges. After 5,000 males inhabited the territory, the settlers would elect an assembly, which would then nominate ten men from whom Congress would pick five for a council. The appointed governor would have an absolute veto. When 60,000 free adults (including women) lived in the territory, they could apply for equal statehood with the original thirteen. Finally, Congress revived Jefferson's injunction against slavery in the Northwest Territory. This Ordinance set the pattern for disposition of all the public domain by using simple arithmetical standards to determine the stages of development. While modifying Jefferson's original democratic intentions, it successfully brought wilderness areas into political maturity, sometimes with more than necessary speed, and at other times with unconscionable footdragging.

Lack of a Mercantilist System

The Articles of Confederation, which successfully met the problems of administrative organization and land disposition, found greater difficulty in controlling trade. America had won its revolution, but some time elapsed before it understood that it had revolted against a closed economic system. Having freed its merchants, planters, and nascent manufacturers from British economic restrictions, America suddenly became an outsider with all the consequent disadvantages. Trade patterns had changed as a consequence of the Declaration of Independence, but these realignments were temporary. New England shippers, for example, turned to privateering to replace the West Indian trade. Peace ended that profitable occupation, however, and New Englanders suddenly found their capital invested in ships that had nowhere to go and their men unemployed.

New markets could stimulate a renaissance of commerce, but Americans had difficulty opening trade with strange areas. France offered likely prospects, but Americans had few commercial contacts there, did not know the markets, and found long-term credit, the backbone of eighteenth-century trade, unavailable. Yet, they did begin new commercial ventures. In February 1784, the *Empress of China* left New York to sail around South America and enter the China trade at Canton. This took courage, or desperation, for Americans knew very little about this market which had been monopolized by the East India Company and thus closed to British colonials. Independence made it legally possible for Americans to participate in this lucrative and exotic trade, but its dangerous and lengthy voyages proved an inadequate substitute for the less dangerous and more prosaic trips to the West Indies.

Part of America's commercial difficulties stemmed from restrictions imposed by other nations. Americans competed with closed economic systems, especially those of England and France, but did so under the handicap of operating with an open economic system. In 1784 Congress asked for retaliatory power in the form of a fifteen-year navigation law. This would prohibit imports and exports in vessels of nations not having commercial treaties with the United States, and prohibit other countries from bringing to the United States goods of nations other than themselves, from becoming common carriers.

Proposals like this, suggested both in and out of Congress, were supported by several states. New Englanders particularly wanted Congress to have such power, but southerners refused to surrender the competitive advantage they derived from pitting American shipping against foreign shipping. Each time someone proposed giving Congress any power over commerce, at least one state flatly rejected the idea or so hedged its approval as to make it meaningless. Since one negative vote defeated any amendment, revision of the Articles to permit minimal control of commerce seemed hopeless.

Lacking central government action, states created their own closed economic systems. But individual state regulation, wholly uncoordinated, did more damage than good. These regulations were designed not for national purposes, but to give the state involved an advantageous position over its neighbors. For example, New York's tariff revenues from trade with eastern New Jersey and western Connecticut yielded enough to eliminate the need for a land tax. New York's landed proprietors therefore bent every effort to defeat amendments to the Articles which threatened their untaxed status. Local mercantilism, aimed at neighbors not foreigners, produced chaos and competition.

Inability to retaliate against discriminatory trade practices by foreign nations complicated America's economic development. After the war the British dumped goods to stifle new industries in America; this precipitated a steady price decline which further exaggerated economic problems. National wholesale prices fell over 50 per cent from 1781 to 1787. Philadelphia's wholesale price index went from 100.1 in 1784 to 83.3 in 1788, and Charleston prices in the same years dropped from 110 to 97. Inventories whose value constantly declined spelled economic crisis for merchants, but America under the Articles could not protect itself from foreign competition.

Diplomatic Inadequacy

Ineffectiveness in foreign relations challenged the central government's very reason for existence. To conduct diplomacy the nation needed bargaining power, but it could neither offer advantages nor make threats. Its representatives assigned to secure favorable commercial treaties could not promise their enforcement, offer concessions, or threaten to withdraw privileges, for all these powers rested with individual states.

America's most immediate diplomatic problems arose with Spain as westward expansion brought the two nations perilously close to one another on the Gulf coast. Although the Anglo-American peace treaty of 1783 defined both countries' right to free navigation of the Mississippi, Spain controlled the river mouth. Its ministers warned that all foreign vessels entering Spanish territory would be confiscated. Meanwhile its officials intrigued with Indians to make life most unpleasant for American settlers and bribed westerners to revolt either for establishment of an independent nation under Spain's dominance or for merger into the Spanish Empire.

Americans west of the Appalachians depended on the Mississippi for exporting farm products to market, and whoever controlled the river could influence the loyalty of those dependent upon such transportation. Rapid expansion of American population in Kentucky made it imperative to secure free navigation of the Mississippi's mouth. In 1785 John Jay began negotiations with de Gardoqui, Spanish minister to the United States, but accomplished little. Spain owned the area, and Jay could offer no *quid pro quo* for a concession. After a year, he obtained only a limited commercial treaty, for Spain remained adamant about navigation rights and western boundary adjustments. Jay suggested that America take what little it could get in a commercial treaty and abandon, for the time being, its rights to use the river. War, the only alternative, was unthinkable because of the central government's financial plight. However, when Jay asked Congress for authority to conclude a commercial treaty, he could not get the necessary majority of nine votes, and negotiations dragged on into 1787.

Anglo-American relations were in no better shape for much the same reasons. England still held posts in the western territory it had conceded to the United States in 1783, and the English used them to control the fur trade and incite Indians against American settlement in the upper Ohio Valley. John Adams went to England in 1785 to negotiate for England's withdrawal, indemnities for slaves taken by evacuating English forces, and a favorable commercial treaty. Although cordially received, even by George III, Adams found no one rushing to join him at the conference table. By 1786 he finally learned that negotiations would take place only after America paid prewar debts owed Englishmen. The United States had not honored its commitment to prevent imposition of obstacles to debt collections — it could not do so — and England therefore saw no reason to honor its treaty commitments.

America also sought to negotiate with the Barbary pirates of North Africa for commercial treaties and protection of its commerce. Barbary corsairs preyed upon American-flag shipping secure in the knowledge that those vessels enjoyed neither British nor American protection. John Lamb went to Algiers in 1786 to ransom captured Americans at $200 a head, but the pirates demanded six times that sum. Meanwhile John Adams met with the Tripolitan ambassador to London, who suggested that treaties with Tunis and Tripoli would cost about $150,000 each, plus appropriate gifts. The United States signed a treaty with Morocco in 1787 for $30,000, but it left unsettled relations with Algiers, Tripoli, and Tunis, largely because the new nation could afford neither war nor bribes.

Diplomatic failures hurt American trade. England's rejection of a commercial treaty left American merchants some of their traditional markets, but under serious handicaps. Spain's refusal to open its empire to Americans eliminated the once profitable Spanish West Indies trade. Barbary pirates blocked postrevolutionary commerce in flour, fish, and rice to Mediterranean ports. But the depths to which American diplomatic stature had plummeted was suggested by British refusal to send a minister to the new nation. No nation felt it necessary to concede anything to the United States.

Financial Incompetence

Congress's financial difficulties stemmed from its lack of a reliable revenue. Without taxing power or the ability to secure funds by requisition on the states, the central government perpetually verged on bankruptcy. Congress based requisitions on estimated population rather than value of improved lands as required by the Articles because no survey had been made. In its first two years, Congress asked the states for $10 million and received $1 million — not enough to meet operating expenses, let alone principal and interest payments on the national debt.

Before and after adoption of the Articles, Congress had borrowed from private individuals, states, and foreign governments. States owed money to Congress, Congress owed money to states, back pay was due to soldiers and officers, Congressional committees expended funds as did American diplomats abroad — all this had to be rationalized and clarified. Confusion mounted because so many had handled public funds, inadequate records were often kept, and some documentation was lost. Some claims, such as that of Beaumarchais for supplying munitions in the beginning of the revolutionary war, dragged on for more than a quarter century.

Robert Morris, Superintendent of Finance, proposed nationalization of all debts, state and federal, so that all creditors would look to Congress for repayment. Congress needed a source of revenue to do this, and Morris urged an import duty. His idea of strengthening the Confederation Congress in this way antedated Alexander Hamilton's plan for the assumption of state debts by about a decade. Both men dreamed the same dream, but Morris's remained unrealized.

Congress's financial incompetence was not shared by most state governments or private individuals. States usually had adequate taxing powers, and private persons often had specie available to them. England had pumped money into the colonies during eight years of war, and France and The Netherlands had made extensive loans. While much specie returned to Europe to pay for goods flooding into the United States after the war, enough remained to stimulate prosperity for state governments and private businessmen.

However, Gresham's Law operated, and less stable and valuable currencies circulated most freely and drove sound money into hiding, thereby creating further difficulties. Depreciated continental currency (Congress stopped issuing printing press money in 1782), state paper currencies, foreign coins, and even counterfeit money circulated throughout the states. Both the variety of currencies and differences in their values confused businessmen and public officials.

Marginal farmers and artisans were hardest hit by monetary confusion and a continuing deflationary trend. They faced court prosecutions, debtors' prisons, and mortgage foreclosures when they could not meet their obligations, and this led to demands for moratoria and legal tender paper money. Excessive supplies of printing press money, if made legal tender, would rapidly create inflation. Prices of agricultural products and labor would rise sharply, while old debts, stated in fixed dollars or pounds, remained stationary. Thus farmers could reduce their heavy mortgages by forcing repayment on creditors in inflated currency.

In 1785 and 1786, paper money factions in several states demanded this easy solution to deflationary economic trends. Seven states succumbed to this pressure. Georgia, South Carolina, North Carolina, New Jersey, New York, Pennsylvania, and Rhode Island all issued paper currencies, often after intense internal conflict.

Georgia's paper issue of £30,000, guaranteed by state-owned land, did little to inflate the economy, and it aroused little controversy. New Jersey issued bills as loans secured by private real estate holdings, a practice followed by New York. Neither of these issues created undue inflationary trends. The issues of South Carolina, North Carolina, and Pennsylvania, on the other hand, created serious economic problems because they were not handled as cautiously.

In Rhode Island, where the classic example of mismanaged paper money existed, strife dominated. Violent opposition from creditors was finally overcome, but debtors imposed harsh laws as a consequence of the bitterness engendered. Not only did the state make paper legal tender, but the law required a creditor to accept paper or forfeit his claim. Debtors ran after creditors, forcing payment on them. A later law went even further, permitting debt cancellation by payment to a court of record, thereby frustrating the more fleet-footed creditors who eluded their debtors.

Other states managed to resist the paper money panacea altogether. Conservatives in Connecticut, Massachusetts, New Hampshire, Delaware, Maryland, and Virginia defeated cheap money advocates at the polls or in state legislatures. Virginia did permit payment of taxes with warehouse receipts for tobacco, but these had long been used as currency in private transactions and tobacco was the mainstay of the state's economy. Tobacco receipts did not seriously challenge the soundness of Virginia's currency, and their acceptance for tax payments was a minor concession to inflationists.

Inflationist tactics proved more upsetting to conservatives than paper money itself. Rabble-rousers used cheap money as a device to attack the social institution of property rights, and many doubted whether individual states could protect wealth much longer. Rhode Island certainly illustrated what could happen when extreme inflationists gained control. Shops closed down, men were idled, houses became dilapidated, ships remained with sails furled, and misery prevailed. Elsewhere, frustrated paper-money advocates resorted to violence.

Public Disorder

Believing that government should eliminate the evils of a state of nature by protecting life, liberty, and property, conservatives looked upon the

Articles of Confederation as a failure. As postwar economic deflation led to public disorders, conservatives expected the worst. Discontent by small farmers reached a peak in Massachusetts in 1786. High taxes, a large public debt, and a scarcity of currency led to intense deflation and rapidly dropping wages and prices. Those who borrowed earlier at inflated prices found it hard to repay their creditors. Small farmers suffered most, and foreclosures became commonplace. Debtors received little sympathy in Boston, for all power seemed ranged against them. Lawyers, courts, and legislators hooted down all remedial proposals.

Violence began in Massachusetts in August 1786. In one county a convention met and listed grievances. Next, a mob seized a courthouse in Northampton and prevented the judges from sitting. This was repeated in Worcester, Taunton, and Concord. In Great Barrington rioters broke open the jail. Spreading insurrection caused the General Court to promise pardons to those taking an oath of allegiance, but legislators derided the rioters' grievances and took no action to solve them. Once the General Court adjourned, rioting resumed, and Governor James Bowdoin finally called out the militia.

A rebel force under command of a revolutionary war captain, Daniel Shays, gathered at Worcester and threatened to march on Cambridge. General Benjamin Lincoln led more than 4,000 militia against Shays, who retreated to Springfield and attacked the federal arsenal there. Beaten back, the rebels scattered, and Lincoln pursued them. Shays's Rebellion continued in the form of disorganized bands ravaging the countryside. Although Governor Bowdoin gradually suppressed the uprising, his action cost him the next election. John Hancock, the new governor, allowed the rebels to go unpunished, and Shays slipped into obscurity.

More significant than the challenge of Shays's Rebellion to Massachusetts was its threat to the central government. Congress began raising troops to protect its arsenal at Springfield and to quell the rioters, but it camouflaged its purpose by announcing that it intended the soldiers for the frontier. Congress feared adverse reactions if its true intentions became known. Such governmental weakness under relatively minor stress augured badly for the security of property.

Men of wealth feared the consequences of social upheaval, the results of too literal an application of the philosophy expressed in the Declaration of Independence. And their fears became in their minds an overwhelming reality. Paper money, legal or illegal mortgage moratoria, and resistance to taxation seemed to threaten social stability. Conservatives wanted governments of law, not men, but passion ruled Massachusetts, which had one of the most conservative state constitutions. If Massachusetts barely repressed social upheaval, what could then be expected in states whose democratic passions were less bridled? The conservatives' fears ruled their reactions and made them determined to avert the disaster they thought they foresaw.

Conservative Responses

Little Congressional help could be expected to combat anticipated public disorder. Congress's lack of initiative, power, and money had been recognized earlier, and efforts to revise the Articles by means other than those prescribed in the document itself were already under consideration. Washington and Hamilton had understood Congress's ineffectiveness even before the Articles went into effect, and in 1782 Hamilton influenced New York's legislature to call for a revision of the frame of government. James Madison tried to strengthen the Articles by suggesting that Congress coerce recalcitrant states and by urging an amendment to clarify its power to do this. A congressional committee proposed seven amendments, including a tax power. Congress itself ignored most of these recommendations, and men of ability soon abandoned it for positions in state government where something could be accomplished. As Congress lost its most able members, it became increasingly moribund and showed less and less interest in solving its own problems.

Central government, to survive, obviously needed power to tax and to regulate commerce. Continuance of central authority was important, since the alternative, a collection of weak, feuding, independent states, would leave the country prey to every foreign power. Moreover, Americans had a heritage of union which Madison, Washington, Hamilton, and Jay recognized. But how could they revive the dying Congress and instill in it a desire for salvation? How could they overcome the unanimity requirement in the amending process so as to secure changes in the Articles?

Those seeking changes in the Articles realized their only hope lay outside Congress. Washington and Madison for some time had been involved in negotiations between Virginia and Maryland for control of the Potomac River. A meeting in 1785 at Mount Vernon, Washington's home, led to draft proposals which the commissioners of the two states then referred to Pennsylvania and Delaware for their concurrence. From this emerged the idea of a broader interstate compact providing for a central commercial control independent of Congress. Madison finally persuaded the Virginia legislature to call a meeting of all states for September 1786 at Annapolis.

Only five states attended the Annapolis gathering, and Madison's original purpose seemed hopeless. Hamilton prepared a report detailing the nation's critical condition and calling for another meeting to consider the Articles. He again invited all states to send delegates, this time to Philadelphia in May 1787. Hamilton's report, unanimously adopted at Annapolis, went to the states and Congress. After much pressure, Congress hesitantly and with some misgivings issued its own call for the Philadelphia session "for the sole and express purpose of revising the Articles of Confederation."

The Philadelphia Convention

Of seventy-four delegates appointed by twelve states (Rhode Island declined), fifty-five appeared at the Philadelphia Convention at one time or another. Most delegates represented a group in American politics which had been overshadowed from 1763 to 1783 by revolutionary leaders. Some have interpreted the absence of the most fiery revolutionary leaders from the Convention as proof that it was a counterrevolutionary move to overturn the democratic victory embodied in the Articles of Confederation. A simpler, less sinister explanation is that those concerned about the central government's future participated at Philadelphia, while those content with things as they were stayed away. Many of the revolutionary generation sincerely preferred political strength at the state level rather than the national.

Delegates straggled into Philadelphia, delaying official proceedings for about two weeks. When the Convention formally organized on May 25, 1787, the delegates selected George Washington as presiding officer, decided that each state would have one vote, and ordered their deliberations conducted in secrecy so as to permit a free exchange of ideas unhindered by public reactions. Fortunately for future generations, James Madison received permission to record the debates in his own shorthand by promising not to publish them for twenty years. The wisdom of secrecy became evident when Edmund Randolph moved "That a national government ought to be established consisting of a supreme Legislative, Executive and Judiciary." The Virginian's motion to scrap both their instructions and the Articles met with approval from every state but New

York and Connecticut, both of which reluctantly went along with the majority.

Randolph's motion introduced the Virginia Plan for a bicameral legislature with the lower house popularly elected and the upper chosen by the lower. Congress would have all those powers granted to it in the Articles, plus that of legislating "in all cases in which the separate States are incompetent." Congress could also disallow state laws and use force to coerce recalcitrant states. An executive chosen by the federal legislature would sit with the judiciary as a Council of Revision and exercise an absolute veto over all congressional legislation. Federal courts would have limited jurisdiction, including felonies on the high seas, cases involving foreigners and citizens of different states, matters affecting national revenues, impeachment of federal officials, and questions pertaining to national peace and harmony.

Randolph's extremely nationalistic proposals suggested a conservative overreaction to the Articles' deficiencies. Neither Randolph nor his supporters expected full acceptance of the Virginia Plan, for it would return to the old imperial system against which Americans had just rebelled. To permit the federal legislature to determine the limits of its own authority, to disallow state laws, and to coerce states smacked too much of British tyranny to be acceptable to Americans. But Randolph hoped to present the issue dramatically, establish discussion at a high level, and commit the Convention to something more than a rehash of the Articles.

Having agreed to base its discussions on the Virginia Plan, the Convention first considered methods of electing a national legislature and apportioning representation among the states. Debates over details divided the delegates and clouded their initial agreement on the ultimate objective. A number of delegates favored direct popular representation in both houses, while some insisted on equal state representation in one house, and others urged use of one chamber to represent property interests. Madison argued against the latter approach by persuasively demonstrating that no permanent numerical majority would ever form on a national level because, as a combination of special interest factions, the majority's composition would change as issues changed. Special representation for a minority, for men of wealth, was therefore unnecessary. The delegates easily agreed on direct popular election of the lower house, but then ran into difficulty.

Composition of the legislature's upper house divided the delegates.

Roger Sherman of Connecticut proposed equal state representation in the Senate, but the Convention rejected this by a six-to-five vote. Then more delegates arrived, especially from Maryland, Delaware, and New York, throwing the balance in those states to the federalist group. William Paterson of New Jersey tried to reverse the Convention's direction by proposing a modification of the Articles which would give Congress power to tax and to regulate commerce. However, he insisted on retaining state equality and, while conceding that Congress should coerce recalcitrant states, he rejected any veto power over state laws. He suggested instead that federal statutes be the supreme law of the land enforceable in state courts. His idea contained the solution of Federalism's most contentious question: determining limits to state and federal jurisdictions.

The Committee of the Whole rejected the New Jersey Plan by a seven-to-three vote and then favorably reported the Virginia Plan. But the small states insisted on equal Senate representation, and such bitter debates ensued that Benjamin Franklin, by now America's elder statesman, suggested that each session open with prayer to calm heated passions. When proportional representation for the lower house came to a final vote, it barely passed, and nationalists suddenly realized they had to compromise.

After much soul-searching, a committee finally worked out a solution: proportional representation in the lower house and equal representation in the Senate. They added two stipulations. Appropriation and tax measures must originate in the lower house, and Senate voting would be by individuals, not states. Neither side expressed joy over the "Great Compromise," but all understood that the alternative was to break up the Convention.

Some delegates still feared that critical divisions in the legislature would emerge from the large-small state dichotomy. Here again, James Madison's clear vision prevailed. He argued that sectionalism would be far more important, as it already was within the states and as it already operated within the Convention. Only a North-South sectional split would really endanger national stability, he predicted, but other sectional divisions could distract the people from that potentially dangerous one and thus protect national unity. Sectional alignments, except for the North-South one, would constantly shift with changing problems and force compromises on all major decisions.

Having settled the legislative arrangement, happily or otherwise, the Convention next turned to the executive. Although debated extensively,

MADISON ON FACTIONS

BY A FACTION, I understand a number of citizens, whether amounting to a majority or minority of the whole, who are united and actuated by some common impulse of passion, or of interest, adverse to the rights of other citizens, or to the permanent and aggregate interests of the community....

The latent causes of faction are thus sown in the nature of man.... A zeal for different opinions concerning religion, concerning government, and many other points, as well of speculation as of practice; an attachment to different leaders... have, in turn, divided mankind into parties, inflamed them with mutual animosity, and rendered them much more disposed to vex and oppress each other than to cooperate.... But the most common and durable source of factions has been the various and unequal distribution of property. Those who hold and those who are without property have ever formed distinct interests in society.

... A landed interest, a manufacturing interest, a mercantile interest, a moneyed interest, with many lesser interests, grow up of necessity in civilized nations, and divide them into different classes, actuated by different sentiments and views. The regulation of these various and interfering interests forms the principal task of modern legislation, and involves the spirit of party and faction in the necessary and ordinary operations of the government. (The Federalist No. 10)

☆☆☆☆☆☆☆☆☆☆☆☆☆☆☆☆☆☆☆☆☆☆☆☆☆☆☆☆☆☆

organization of the executive branch never threatened the Convention's success in the same way as legislative apportionment. Some wanted a weak executive, still remembering the theoretically all-powerful colonial governors, while others insisted on a strong executive, assuming no danger from him because his power would come from local, not external, sources. Those favoring a strong executive also urged direct popular election as the safest means of choosing a candidate.

A committee considered both the President's power and his selection. It easily agreed on an executive chosen by an Electoral College composed of delegates picked by each state (equal in number to the state's representatives and senators) "in such manner as its legislature may direct." This recognized the states and gave them a role without eliminating the possibility of popular balloting for electors. Everyone simply assumed, since they did not anticipate political parties, that no candidate would ever receive a majority in the Electoral College. Then the House of Representatives, with each state casting one vote, would choose the President from among the three leading candidates. This complicated and detailed mechanism reflected the delegates' lack of strong feelings on the subject. Indeed, explicit detail in the final Constitution suggested general acceptance and agreement on a topic, whereas vagueness meant inability to agree and a decision to transfer the problem to future generations for solution.

More trouble developed over a means of making states abide by federal law. Both the Virginia and New Jersey Plans provided for physical coercion, but many delegates shied away from this as dangerous and unwise. Madison rejected force, noting that its use "would look more like a declaration of war, than an infliction of punishment, and would probably be considered by the party attacked as a dissolution of the union." Yet, how could states be forced to obey federal laws to which they might object?

James Wilson broke the impasse by suggesting a wholly new imperial system. Rather than follow the precedent of the British Empire by imposing the central government's will on states, Wilson proposed that the central government, like the states, should operate directly through the people who would then relate themselves to both central and state authority. This altered man's understanding of the nature and location of sovereignty. To Wilson, the people, not the government, were sovereign, and the people could distribute the exercise of sovereign power as they saw fit, even to different levels of government. By substituting this novel concept for the older, more traditional one, coercion of states became unnecessary.

Luther Martin further amplified Wilson's concept of sovereignty and solved Federalism's final dilemma. Responsibility for determining limits to federal and state authority, he insisted, should be assigned to state courts with the provision that federal law be supreme and binding on all judges. Thus, congressional review and disallowance of state laws became unnecessary. The Convention unanimously resolved that the federal constitution, federal laws, and federal treaties would be supreme law, and all state judges would be bound to uphold them regardless of conflicting provisions in state constitutions or laws. The Convention thought to protect states by making their courts final arbiters of state authority, but vagueness in the Constitution's judiciary clause later permitted a complete reversal of the delegates' intention by transferring ultimate authority to the federal judiciary.

Wilson's and Martin's applications of popular sovereignty removed the last impediment to a quick conclusion of the Convention. Arguments over other matters received speedy disposition. Counting slaves to determine population bothered some delegates. Some argued that slaves, like free persons, represented an aspect of the state's wealth and should be counted, but others contended that they did not have the franchise and should not be equated with those who did. The delegates quickly agreed on the "Three-Fifths Compromise," which permitted each slave to be counted as three-fifths of a person in the federal census and in apportioning the House of Representatives and in levying direct taxes on the states.

Even congressional control of commerce, subject of strong hostilities earlier, presented little difficulty. Southerners opposed navigation acts which, at their expense, benefited New Englanders. South Carolina and Georgia particularly insisted upon no interference with the slave trade, while the upper South called for a halt to the "nefarious traffic." If Congress could stop the slave trade, neither South Carolina nor Georgia would approve the Constitution. New England took an equally dogmatic position in favor of navigation acts. These diverse positions were compromised: Congress could pass navigation acts, but could not levy export duties nor, before 1808, interfere with the slave trade. New England gained its commercial benefits, South Carolina and Georgia could continue importing needed manpower, and southern crops could not be discriminated against by export taxes.

None of the delegates felt wholly satisfied as each viewed the results of months of hard labor. The Constitution was a bundle of compromises, and when compromise failed, vagueness cloaked objections and permitted future generations to find their own answers. Some found the document's flaws greater than its accomplishments and refused to sign it. Franklin urged support for the Constitution, but Luther Martin, George Mason, Edmund Randolph, and Elbridge Gerry all rejected it. Only thirty-nine delegates finally affixed their signatures, and Franklin suggested the phrase "Done in Convention by the unanimous consent of the States assembled" to hide the lack of unanimity among the delegates.

The Constitution specified the procedures for its adoption, and these bore no resemblance to those prescribed for amending the Articles. Special conventions in each state would be elected to consider the document. When nine states approved the Constitution, the new government became effective for them. The delegates purposely bypassed the Articles' procedures, including the unanimity requirement. The Philadelphia Convention had demonstrated the futility of trying to please everyone, and the delegates astutely understood state legislatures' reluctance to diminish their own powers. Special state conventions offered several advantages: their election required popular campaigns on the Constitution's merits, state legislatures with vested interests were ignored, and ratifications, once given, could never be retracted, because the ratifying conventions adjourned *sine die*, forever, upon completing their business.

RATIFICATION

On September 17, 1787, the delegates signed the Constitution and sent it to the Confederation Congress sitting in New York City. Congress gave it a hostile reception, and Richard Henry Lee led the attack. He criticized the Convention for violating its instructions and producing a national, not a federal, government. Some congressmen demanded substantial changes before sending the Constitution to the states, but they finally and reluctantly agreed to forward it without recommendation. They asked each state to hold a special ratifying convention in accord with the Philadelphia Convention's instructions.

Release of the draft Constitution precipitated debates over government's nature and function. Labels emerged which, at first glance, seem confusing. As the Philadelphia Convention ended, the Constitution's proponents realized the tactical disadvantage of describing that document or themselves as "nationalist," for the American people remained provincial and loyal to their locality, not the union. The Constitution's supporters therefore labelled themselves "Federalists" and called their work a "federal" Constitution, even wiping the official journal clean of all references to national government. By seizing the "Federal" label for themselves, they dubbed their opponents "Anti-Federal" and greatly handicapped them. This shrewd propaganda trick, however, confused identities as the Philadelphia Convention's nationalists suddenly became Federalists, and its Federalists suddenly became Anti-Federalists.

Statistical evidence on ratification, although primitive, makes possible some generalizations as to who supported or opposed the Constitution and

JOHN JAY ON THE "SILENT MAJORITY," 1786

THERE DOUBTLESS IS MUCH REASON *to think and to say that we are wofully and, in many instances, wickedly misled. Private rage for property suppresses public considerations, and personal rather than national interests have become the great objects of attention. Representative bodies will ever be faithful copies of their originals, and generally exhibit a checkered assemblage of virtue and vice, of abilities and weakness.*

The mass of men are neither wise nor good, and the virtue like the other resources of a country, can only be drawn to a point and exerted by strong circumstances ably managed, or a strong government ably administered. New governments have not the aid of habit and hereditary respect, and being generally the result of preceding tumult and confusion, do not immediately acquire stability or strength. Besides, in times of commotion, some men will gain confidence and importance, who merit neither, and who, like political mountebanks, are less solicitous

☆☆☆☆☆☆☆☆☆☆☆☆☆☆☆☆☆☆☆☆☆☆☆☆☆☆☆

why. Tidewater areas favored the proposed government, while piedmont and interior regions disliked it. However, local conditions frequently upset such simple generalizations. North Carolina and Rhode Island tidewater areas were Anti-Federalist (in the post-Convention sense), while interior farmers in New Hampshire and Massachusetts were Federalists.

Rhode Island's determination to keep its paper money system foretold its rejection of any central government empowered to regulate currency. North Carolina's coastal area, with its barrier of sand reefs, did not depend on trade as did other seaboard regions, and so found little reason to support the Constitution. Backcountry farmers in New Hampshire and Massachusetts depended on the Connecticut River for transportation, and this involved interstate commerce. To eliminate discriminatory state charges, these farmers preferred a central government with exclusive control of interstate commerce.

Other states and regions within states adopted attitudes based on local circumstances and needs. Virginia's piedmont (now West Virginia) was strongly Federalist because its trade went through the Shenandoah Valley to Philadelphia rather than to the Virginia coast. State interference with commerce was something to be eliminated. Georgia, a frontier region

about the health of the credulous crowd than about making the most of their nostrums and prescriptions. . . .
  What I most fear is, that the better kind of people, by which I mean the people who are orderly and industrious, who are content with their situations and not uneasy in their circumstances, will be led by the insecurity of property, the loss of confidence in their rulers, and the want of public faith and rectitude, to consider the charms of liberty as imaginary and delusive. A state of fluctuation and uncertainty must disgust and alarm such men, and prepare their minds for almost any change that may promise them quiet and security. (From: Jay to Washington, June 27, 1786, H. P. Johnston, ed., Correspondence and Public Papers of John Jay, *4 vols. [New York and London: G. P. Putnam's Sons, 1890-93], III, 203-204)*

☆☆☆☆☆☆☆☆☆☆☆☆☆☆☆☆☆☆☆☆☆☆☆☆☆☆

having difficulties with its Spanish and Indian neighbors, wanted a strong central government's protection.

Economic motives of different groups can also be ascertained with some certainty. Merchants generally favored the new government because it promised sound currency, coherent commercial regulations, and effective diplomatic negotiations. These spelled stability. New York's landowners, on the other hand, opposed the Constitution because the state would have to give up taxation of its neighbors' commerce and rely instead on land taxes for revenue. Some lawyers also opposed the Constitution for fear that a federal judiciary would destroy state courts and cost them their livelihood. Small farmers not dependent on interstate commerce often preferred weak central government so they might maintain inflated currency policies for their own benefit.

Yet, as debates over electing delegates to ratifying conventions proceeded in individual states, economic considerations rarely received mention. As in earlier debates with England, Americans translated their economic problems into legal and constitutional terms. This avoidance of open economic disputation, a habit we still retain, encouraged a fullscale analysis of government's principles and mechanics in 1787 and 1788

JOHN ADAMS'S DREAD OF POPULAR CONTROL

YOU ARE AFRAID OF the one — I, of the few. We agree perfectly that the many should have a full fair and perfect Representation, — You are Apprehensive of Monarchy; I, of Aristocracy. I would therefore have given more Power to the President and less to the Senate. The Nomination and Appointment to all offices I would have given to the President, assisted only by a Privy Council of his own Creation, but not a Vote or Voice would I have given to the Senate or any Senator, unless he were of the Privy Council. Faction and Distraction are the sure and certain Consequence of giving to a Senate a vote in the distribution of offices.

You are apprehensive the President when once chosen, will be chosen again and again as long as he lives. So much the better as it appears to me. — You are apprehensive of foreign Interference, Intrigue, Influence. So am I. — But, as often as Elections happen, the danger of foreign Influence recurs. The less frequently they happen the less danger. — And if the Same Man may be chosen again, it is probable he will be, and the danger of foreign Influence will be less. Foreigners, seeing little Prospect will have less Courage for Enterprize.

Elections, my dear sir, Elections to offices which are great objects of Ambition, I look at with terror. Experiments of this kind have been so often tryed, and so universally found productive of Horrors, that there is great Reason to dread them. (From C. F. Adams, ed., The Works of John Adams, 10 vols. [Boston: C. C. Little and J. Brown, 1850-60], VIII, 464-65)

☆☆☆☆☆☆☆☆☆☆☆☆☆☆☆☆☆☆☆☆☆☆☆☆☆☆☆☆

and produced a literature of political theory whose volume and quality has never since been surpassed by Americans.

Serious criticisms emerged from probing the Constitution's text. Some honestly feared the extensive powers granted to the federal government and faulted the Constitution for not incorporating a Bill of Rights, thereby exposing both state governments and individuals to serious threats. However, the Philadelphia Convention purposely omitted a Bill of Rights for reasons its members believed valid and important. Most states (except Delaware, Connecticut, and Rhode Island) had such lists in their constitutions, and there seemed little point in duplication. Moreover, since the federal government only had delegated powers, it seemed ludicrous to deny it powers it had not been given. Finally, enumerating rights incurred

JEFFERSON'S MISGIVINGS ON THE CONSTITUTION, 1787

HOW DO YOU LIKE our new constitution? I confess there are things in it which stagger all my dispositions to subscribe to what such an assembly has proposed. The house of federal representatives will not be adequate to the management of affairs either foreign or federal. Their President seems a bad edition of a Polish king. He may be reelected from 4. years to 4. years for life. Reason and experience prove to us that a chief magistrate, so continuable, is an officer for life. When one or two generations shall have proved that this is an office for life, it becomes on every succession worthy of intrigue, of bribery, of force, and even of foreign interference. It will be of great consequence to France and England to have America governed by a Galloman or Angloman. Once in office, and possessing the military force of the union, without either the aid or check of a council, he would not be easily dethroned, even if the people could be induced to withdraw their votes from him. I wish that at the end of the 4. years they had made him for ever ineligible a second time. Indeed I think all the good of this new constitution might have been couched in three or four new articles to be added to the good, old, and venerable fabrick, which should have been preserved even as a religious relique. (From: J. P. Boyd, ed. The Papers of Thomas Jefferson, *17 vols + [Princeton: Princeton University Press, 1950], XII, 350-51)*

☆☆☆☆☆☆☆☆☆☆☆☆☆☆☆☆☆☆☆☆☆☆☆☆☆☆☆☆

a greater danger. By implication any rights not so listed could be construed as falling within the central government's authority. This rested on a key eighteenth-century maxim: liberty, derived from a state of nature, was absolute and total, while government, created by specific abridgment of certain liberties, was self-limiting. Liberty never had to prove itself, but governmental power always did. By forcing a definition of liberty, a Bill of Rights violated this maxim.

Other critics of the Constitution noted that it destroyed state sovereignty and autonomy. Luther Martin of Maryland harped on this point, failing to appreciate that James Wilson's concept of sovereignty had completely altered the problem. Martin focused his ire on two constitutional provisions: Article I, section 8, which gave Congress all power necessary and proper to carry out its delegated functions, and Article VI which defined the Constitution, federal laws, and federal treaties as supreme law. Still others argued that federal tax power would lessen state revenues and destroy state authority, harking back to American arguments against British taxation. Madison rebutted all these criticisms by emphasizing the new government's federal nature which guaranteed states direct representation so they might protect themselves.

As election of state ratifying conventions began, the central states leaned toward support of the Constitution, but it seemed doubtful that Massachusetts, New York, and Virginia would ratify it, and without them a successful union was problematical. Pennsylvania's legislature quickly ordered a ratifying convention elected and, when it assembled in November 1787, Federalists like James Wilson and Thomas McKean found themselves pitted against a strong Anti-Federalist group led by William Findley and John Smilie. Wilson, perhaps Philadelphia's ablest constitutional lawyer, bore the brunt of answering the Constitution's critics. He reiterated many points made at the Constitutional Convention on Federalism, advantages of union, and the popular nature of sovereignty. Anti-Federalists emphasized the need for a Bill of Rights and proposed amending the Constitution before ratifying it. Wilson rejected such delaying tactics, insisted on an immediate vote, and Pennsylvania ratified the Constitution by a two-to-one majority on December 12, 1787.

Delaware's ratifying convention, meeting at the same time as Pennsylvania's, unanimously approved the Constitution on December 7. New Jersey also unanimously accepted the new government on December 18. These central states, strongly motivated by prospects of effective commercial power, were joined by Georgia which unanimously ratified on January 2, 1788, as it sought protection from hostile neighbors. A week later, Connecticut added its assent. For these five states, the Constitution offered clear, certain, and immediate benefits.

The issue was not so certain in other states. Four more ratifications were necessary to make the Constitution effective for those states approving it, but they would be more difficult to secure. Massachusetts, a wealthy and important state, could be counted in neither camp. Its electorate was given Richard Henry Lee's *Letters of the Federal Farmer*, the respected George Mason's reasons for not signing at Philadelphia, and Elbridge Gerry's criticisms. Gerry, a Massachusetts man, attacked the representation provisions, vague legislative powers, dangerous executive and judicial authority, and lack of a Bill of Rights. He urged that Massachusetts withhold ratification pending amendment of the Constitution.

These criticisms made many wonder whether the Constitution's faults were greater than its benefits. Massachusetts Anti-Federalists, sharing attitudes which had led to Shays's Rebellion, distrusted the upper classes. As Bostonians, lawyers, clergymen, and merchants joined Federalist ranks, Anti-Federalist suspicions increased. Two men held the key — John Hancock and Sam Adams. They had led in the revolution, and people now looked to them for leadership in making this basic decision.

Hancock's ego gave Federalists a substantial handle with which to work. Dangled before his eyes was the Massachusetts governorship and possibly the Vice-Presidency of the United States. Hancock capitulated. But Sam Adams could not be manipulated, for he had sincere reservations. Federalists breathed a sigh of relief when he decided not to appear at the ratifying convention. Hancock, however, went, accepted the presidency of the meeting, and followed the Federalist line. He called for ratification and consideration of amendments after establishment of the new government. This strategy, used generally by Federalists, won the day, and Massachusetts ratified by a narrow majority of 187 to 168 on February 7, 1788.

Massachusetts, the sixth state, ratified the Constitution and successfully evaded the trap of offering ratification conditioned upon prior acceptance of amendments. Three more acceptances quickly followed. Maryland approved by a wide margin on April 26, as did South Carolina soon thereafter. The ninth and decisive ratification came from New Hampshire in June 1788 by a margin of ten votes. For these nine states, the Constitution became effective upon implementation of its provisions for electing a Congress, President, and Vice-President.

But union without New York and Virginia would start the new government with a severe handicap. Their geographical positions and their wealth made them essential partners in any union. The contest in Virginia was hard fought as Anti-Federalists led by George Mason, Patrick Henry, and Richard Henry Lee found strong support from those fearing destruction of personal liberties without a Bill of Rights, from westerners suspicious of a central government that might abandon navigation of the Mississippi, and from planters afraid of New England's commercial power. However, the Constitution's proponents also had strong leadership, including George Washington, James Madison, Edmund Randolph, and young John Marshall.

Patrick Henry attacked the Constitution by demanding to know why

Alexander Hamilton (1755?-1804). Born a bastard in the West Indies, Hamilton's aggressive search for status soon won him Washington's attention. A strong advocate of central government, he led the move for the Constitutional Convention in 1787. (By John Trumbull, The New-York Historical Society)

it specified "We the People" rather than "We the States." This, he charged, clearly created a consolidated government, not a federal one. Henry then proposed a series of amendments for consideration by a new national convention, but the Federalists insisted on unconditional ratification and submission of proposed amendments to the new Congress. At the end of June 1788, Virginia ratified by a narrow margin.

New York's acceptance of the Constitution seemed less likely than Virginia's, for Governor George Clinton led the Anti-Federalists. To counter his authority and prestige, Alexander Hamilton proposed *The Federalist* papers, a series of essays appearing in various New York City newspapers under the pseudonym "Publius." Hamilton wrote most of them, followed by Madison and then Jay. These eighty-five essays comprise one of the greatest treatises yet written on American constitutional government. Highly partisan and intended to win over doubters, they explained the necessity for each constitutional provision.

Despite *The Federalist*, when the New York Convention met in June 1788 fully two-thirds of its members opposed the Constitution. The minority of Federalists led by Robert R. Livingston, Hamilton, and Jay confronted Governor Clinton, John Lansing, and Melancthon Smith in an uneven battle. Anti-Federalists trotted out time-worn criticisms of the Constitution, but their position weakened with news of New Hampshire's ratification. The new government would go into operation, whether or not New York joined. Word that Virginia had also ratified further sapped Anti-Federal strength. Debates continued, and some urged conditional ratification, but a letter from Madison squelched that last-ditch effort. Madison declared that New York would not be accepted on those terms. When the vote was taken, New York joined the new union by a margin of three votes.

Two recalcitrant states remained. North Carolina refused to act, preferring to wait to see what changes would be made in the Constitution after the new government began operations. Rhode Island's legislature called a popular referendum on the new Constitution, and the people overwhelmingly rejected it, although few Federalists participated. Regardless of decisions by those two states, however, plans proceeded to start the new government.

Successful accomplishment of ratification resulted from the Federalists' positive approach. They offered a remedy for the nation's ills which, while no panacea, seemed the best solution that a diverse group of its leaders could devise. Anti-Federalists, on the other hand, offered only negativism and, if the Constitution were rejected, they would have to bear full responsibility for the debacle predicted by Federalists. Monetary chaos, national bankruptcy, disintegration of the union, civil war, and foreign attack were consequences Americans courted if they rejected the Constitution, or so the Federalists proclaimed.

Federalists enjoyed the further advantage of the method of selecting delegates to state ratifying conventions. In most states, elections were held in the same districts and on the same basis as those for the lower house of the legislature. Since malapportionment still existed, this gave Federalist, tidewater areas greater strength than the Anti-Federalist West. Use of standard suffrage requirements disqualified landless and propertyless persons, some of whom might have opposed the Constitution, although New York used universal white male suffrage in choosing its ratifying convention.

Only 3 per cent of the adult male population, it has been estimated, participated in electing delegates to ratifying conventions. This reflected widespread apathy, refusal by many to participate in what they considered an illegal or improper proceeding, and inadequate notice before ordering elections of conventions. Yet, notwithstanding the electorate's small size, the Constitution was adopted in a more democratic manner than either the Declaration of Independence or the Articles of Confederation. But it was democracy as understood in 1788, not as in 1840 or 1972.

Completing the Constitution

Ratification did not complete the constitution-making process, for much support had come only after promises to amend the Constitution to safeguard states and individuals. Over two hundred suggestions for amendments had been submitted, and this represented a broad public opinion which could not be ignored if the new government wanted maximum support. James Madison understood this and took the promise seriously. As a member of the House of Representatives, he assembled the proposals, coordinated them, and shepherded them through Congress.

Many critics had worried about protecting individual rights. Thomas Jefferson, writing from France, noted the dangers arising from "omission of a bill of rights, providing clearly and without the aid of sophism for freedom of religion, freedom of the press, protection against standing armies, restrictions of monopolies, the eternal and unremitting force of the habeus corpus laws, and trials by jury in all matters of fact triable by the laws of the land." However, others, including his fellow Virginians Richard Henry Lee and George Mason, concerned themselves with safeguarding states against federal power, relying upon state constitutions to protect individual liberties.

Madison undertook to satisfy both demands. He began with a radical departure from tradition by limiting the legislature rather than the executive. Since the seventeenth century England had always imposed restrictions on the Crown to protect the legislature and the people, and American colonies had always curbed gubernatorial power for the same reasons. However, Madison saw the elastic clause, which empowered Congress to make all laws necessary and proper to carry out its delegated powers, as a potential danger to states and individuals alike.

After Madison formally introduced his amendments in the House of Representatives, a committee of one member from each state considered them. Five of its members had served at Philadelphia, thereby providing some continuity. Consideration of the amendments occupied much time

James Madison (1751-1836) participated actively in the call for a federal Convention (1787), had an influential role in the adoption of the Constitution, and wrote a number of The Federalist *Papers. (By Gilbert Stuart, courtesy of Colonial Williamsburg Collection, Williamsburg, Virginia)*

in committee, on the House floor, before the Senate, and finally in a conference committee of both houses. No one knew exactly where the amendments should be placed. Madison urged their incorporation in the text of the Constitution to ensure that they carried the same weight as the original document. Others insisted they be tacked on at the end because the Constitution was the people's work, while amendments were products of state action. Others argued for physical separation of amendments from the Constitution to distinguish the superfluous from the essential.

Congress finally agreed to list amendments separately because insertions proved too awkward. Twelve proposals went to the states for ratification, and by 1791 enough states had approved ten of them to make them part of the Constitution. Two failed to receive ratification. One would have changed apportionment in the House of Representatives by stipulating a minimum and maximum number of members, thereby preventing the House from becoming either too small and easily manipulated, or too large and unwieldy. The second defeated amendment would have prohibited Congressmen from raising their own salaries without an election intervening before the change became effective.

Of the ten amendments approved by the states, eight dealt with individual rights exclusively. These stipulations against legislative action prohibited religious establishments, protected freedom of speech, press, and assembly, guaranteed the right to bear arms, limited the quartering of soldiers, defined procedural rights in criminal and civil trials, and limited criminal punishments. The ninth amendment specified that those rights not otherwise spelled out belonged to the people, thus eliminating the fear that enumeration of some left others subject by implication to federal action. The tenth dealt with state rights by providing that powers not granted to Congress nor prohibited to states are reserved to the states or the people.

Fears of federal interference with state sovereignty received little attention, but dangers to individual rights resulted in an extensive listing of forbidden areas of action. These amendments only limited federal power; their use to restrict state activity emerged later from other constitutional amendments and from Supreme Court interpretations. Adoption of the Bill of Rights completed the constitution-making process and reconciled many Americans to the new government.

End of a Political Experiment

Many viewed the new federal Constitution as an ironic trick of history. Americans had fought against strong central government because of its corruptive power and its ability to destroy local identity and individual liberty. Now Americans adopted a governmental arrangement which mimicked the hated British imperial system against which they had rebelled. Every power which in British hands had violated man's inalienable rights rested in the new federal government. Taxing power, control of commerce, and ability to enforce its decisions had precipitated the revolution against England in 1776. Americans in 1781 replaced the empire with an ideal government, the Articles of Confederation, which possessed none of the dangerous powers. After eight short years, however, they abandoned the Articles.

That abandonment signified the end of an era of political experimentation during which Americans learned the real reason for their unhappiness with the British Empire — they could not control it, and the techniques they had evolved for that purpose all failed after 1763. By reacting so sharply against their own inability to control the empire, they deprived themselves of its many advantages, including a strong central authority. Governmental power presented no danger provided the governed, rather than an external force, controlled it. And the new federal Constitution fulfilled that requirement.

An American Identity and Elan

Creation of a national political structure did not by itself make a nation. Americans needed a sense of unity or identity. Prior to 1763 they identified with and belonged to an Anglo-American community and gloried in being Englishmen. This came into question beginning in 1763, and thirteen years later they repudiated it. Yet, Americans needed to belong to something greater than an individual colony or state; their whole history involved participation in a broad and unified community. They therefore substituted an American identity for the discarded Anglo-American one, and war's exigencies accelerated this development.

Many years later, when the Constitution of 1787 and the concept of union faced its most serious challenge, Abraham Lincoln precisely defined the origin and meaning of American unity. "The Union is older than any of the States; and in fact, it created them as States. Originally, some dependent colonies made the Union; and, in turn, the Union threw off their old dependence for them, and made them States.... Not one of them ever had a State Constitution independent of the Union." No matter how weak or how much other loyalties dominated, an American identity did exist before the Stamp Act Congress, Continental Congress, Articles of Confederation, the Philadelphia Convention, and the Constitution. All were simply emanations of a national consciousness whose mode of expression changed from time to time, but whose existence began before men fully realized it.

Soon, the new nation became aware of its distinctiveness and its uniqueness. Americans looked about them and saw the broad Atlantic as a buffer, the vast and relatively unpopulated West as an experimental laboratory, and a population growth rate that far exceeded Europe's. Americans prided themselves on these things because they suggested the nation's difference and superiority. Jefferson, writing in his *Notes on the State of Virginia*, exemplified this spirit as he itemized how much bigger

THE SCIENCE OF LIBERTY

... IN THE UNITED STATES OF AMERICA, the science of liberty is universally understood, felt, and practiced.... Their deep-rooted and inveterate habit of thinking is, that all men are equal in their rights, that it is impossible to make them otherwise.... This point once settled, everything is settled. Many operations, which [result] ... are but the infallible consequences of this great principle. The first of these operations is the business of election, which, with that people, is carried on with as much gravity as their daily labor.... Any man in society may attain to any place in the government, and may exercise its functions. They believe that there is nothing more difficult in the management of the affairs of a nation, than the affairs of a family; that it only requires more hands.... Banish the mysticism of inequality, and you banish almost all the evils attendant on human nature.

The people, being habituated to the election of all kinds of officers, the magnitude of the office makes no difficulty in the case. The president of the United States, who has more power while in office than some of the kings of Europe, is chosen with as little commotion as a churchwarden.... The servant feels honored with the confidence reposed in him, and generally expresses his gratitude by a faithful performance. Another of these operations is making every citizen a soldier, and every soldier a citizen; not only permitting every man to arm, but obliging him to arm.... It is because the people are civilized, that they are with safety armed. It is an effect of their conscious dignity, as citizens enjoying equal rights, that they wish not to invade the rights of others. The

☆☆☆☆☆☆☆☆☆☆☆☆☆☆☆☆☆☆☆☆☆☆☆☆☆☆☆

and better were all things American. Even our prehistoric animals, he commented with visible pride, were larger than any discovered in Europe.

Americans also believed that they had a better grasp of political essentials than any Europeans, and the new Constitution with its innovations gave ample proof. Andrew Burnaby foresaw a great destiny: "Every one is looking forward with eager and impatient expectation to that destined moment when America is to give the law to the rest of the world." Intoxicated with the American experiment's seeming success, Joel Barlow prepared his *Advice to the Privileged Orders in the Several States of Europe Resulting from the Necessity and Propriety of a General Revolution in the Principle of Government.*

danger (where there is any) from armed citizens, is only to the government, not to the society; and as long as they have nothing to revenge in the government (which they cannot have while it is in their own hands) there are many advantages in their ... use of arms, and no possible disadvantages.

Power, habitually in the hands of a whole community, loses all the ordinary associated ideas of power. The exercise of power is a relative term; it supposes an opposition.... Where the government is not in the hands of the people, there you find opposition, you perceive two contending interests. ... And whether this power be in the hands of the government or of the people, or whether it change from side to side, it is always to be dreaded. But the word people, in America ... means the whole community, and comprehends every human creature....*

Another consequence of the habitual idea of equality, is the facility of changing the structure of their government, whenever, and as often as the society shall think there is anything in it to amend. As Mr. Burke has written no "reflections on the revolution" in America, the people there have never yet been told that they have no right "to frame a government for themselves"; they have therefore done much in this business, without ever affixing to it the idea of "sacrilege" or "usurpation," or any other term of rant, to be found in that gentleman's vocabulary. (From Joel Barlow, Advice to the Privileged Orders *[London: J. Johnson, 1792])*

☆☆☆☆☆☆☆☆☆☆☆☆☆☆☆☆☆☆☆☆☆☆☆☆☆☆☆☆☆☆☆

Enthusiasm for America led many to question the traditional practice of sending children to Europe for an education. John Jay feared that they might be aliens in their own land upon their return. Some warned they should only be sent to Protestant countries after they received a basic education at home. Jefferson also questioned the advisability of sending youngsters abroad and warned that the only safe places were Geneva, Rome, or Edinburgh, the centers of European republicanism.

Having made a conscious effort to divest themselves of British trappings, having rejected much of Europe, Americans in 1789 turned inward to find themselves. Never could they fully separate from their Old World past, and continuing waves of immigrants would constantly remind them of it, but an American élan developed as the nation embarked on social and economic experimentation on a heretofore unknown scale.

SELECTED BIBLIOGRAPHY

Construction of America's basic frame of government has led to a vast controversial literature. Interpretations have swung from one extreme to another. Before the student becomes a partisan of any one viewpoint, he should examine some standard accounts such as: A. C. McLaughlin's *The Confederation and the Constitution, 1783-1789* (1907), Max Farrand's *The Framing of the Constitution of the United States* (1913), Charles Warren's *The Making of the Constitution* (1937) and Carl Van Doren's *The Great Rehearsal* (1948).

Much of the controversy surrounding the Constitution began with Charles Beard's *An Economic Interpretation of the Constitution* (1913). A number of scholars have controverted Beard's findings; among the important ones are: Forrest McDonald's *We The People: The Economic Origins of the Constitution* (1958) and his *E Pluribus Unum: The Formation of the American Republic, 1776-1790* (1965), Merrill Jensen's *The Articles of Confederation* (1940) and his *The New Nation* (1950), Jackson Turner Main's *The Antifederalists: Critics of the Constitution 1781-1788* (1961), Robert A. Rutland's *The Ordeal of the Constitution: The Antifederalists and the Ratification Struggle of 1787-1788* (1966), and Robert E. Brown's *Charles Beard and the Constitution* (1956).

Other studies of the Constitution, less directly related to the Beard controversy, are: Catherine Drinker Bowen's *Miracle at Philadelphia, The Story of the Constitutional Convention* (1966), Clinton Rossiter's *1787: The Grand Convention* (1966), Benjamin Wright's brief but significant *Consensus and Continuity 1776-1787* (1958), and Elisha P. Douglass's perceptive *Rebels and Democrats: The Struggle for Equal Political Rights and Majority Rule During the American Revolution* (1955).

Other aspects of the Revolution are discussed in J. Franklin Jameson's *The American Revolution Considered as a Social Movement* (1926), Curtis Nettles's *The Emergence of a National Economy 1775-1815* (1962), and Allan Nevin's *American States During and After the Revolution* (1924).

Biographies, once again, offer valuable insights. Many of those cited for Chapter 6 are useful here as well. In addition, Charles Page Smith's *James Wilson, Founding Father* (1956), Robert A. Davidson's *Isaac*

Hicks: New York Merchant and Quaker 1767-1820 (1964), W. H. Masterson's *William Blount* (1954), and Carl S. Driver's *John Sevier: Pioneer of the Old Southwest* (1932) are all worth examination. Perhaps the most important biography for this period is Irving Brant's *James Madison: The Nationalist 1780-1787* (1948).

EPILOGUE:
THE THRESHOLD OF NATIONALITY

Changes in America between 1600 and 1789 proved momentous. A raw wilderness discovered by first settlers had become a burgeoning nation. The domain of scattered migratory Indians was now home for three million transplanted Europeans and Africans. Their reasons for migration to the New World ranged from political to social and economic or, in the case of Africans, physical coercion. The European groups developed a society which sought as best it could to imitate life in Old England, while the Africans found themselves, whether free or slave, subjugated as a servile class.

Settlement initially centered on the Atlantic seaboard, especially in the tidewater area sheltered by the Appalachian mountain range. As population pressure developed in older settlements, people moved westward into river valleys that led to the interior. The Connecticut and Hudson rivers provided the only access to fertile lands in the interior of New England and New York. Similarly, the Delaware and Schuylkill opened into Pennsylvania's backcountry. To the South, the Potomac, Rappahannock, and James rivers did the same for Virginia's piedmont area. As the tidewater region broadened out further south, rivers played a less important role in distributing population, though they still influenced settlement by providing cheap transportation.

Availability of great quantities of fertile lands also shaped the colonies' economic development. In the South, where a broad tidewater facilitated agricultural expansion, cash crops dominated. Tobacco, rice, indigo, naval stores, and some cotton became the economic underpinning of southern society, utilizing large numbers of black slaves to exploit the rich soil. Further north, as the tidewater narrowed, agriculture changed. The Middle Colonies became noted for grain crops and became the "breadbasket" of English America. New England, on the other hand, ill-favored in the quality and quantity of arable land, farmed its timber resources and its fisheries, and from this developed a preoccupation with trade.

This pattern of economic development also had its impact upon Anglo-American relations throughout the colonial period. The mother country looked with favor upon the South, which produced cash crops that did not conflict with English agriculture. The Middle Colonies exported surplus grains and other products to the West Indies, but found no market in England. The northernmost area, New England, competed directly with the mother country and almost immediately conflicted sharply with English mercantile policies.

Conflict between England and its colonies, until 1763, remained obscured by the overriding hostility between England and its commercial rivals — Spain first, The Netherlands next, and finally France. Though basically international conflicts over raw materials and markets, much hostility centered about the North American colonies. Indeed, the final battles for empire would be fought between England and France for control of the Ohio Valley, the Great Lakes, and eventually Canada. Many colonists believed an Anglo-American victory would solve all problems by permitting unhindered expansion into the West. However, resolution of the imperial wars created more problems than it settled.

For nearly a century England and its colonies had moved apart without fully realizing it. Mainland colonies became self-conscious entities interested in loosening the restrictive bonds of empire without renouncing their dependency. By 1763 a few in England understood that the empire had become more than a series of Crown appendages valued primarily for their raw materials. However, it proved impossible to convert that view into practical policies in time to forestall imperial disruption. England's acceptance of colonies as population centers and markets for its manufactures would not come until after the colonies had won their independence. Indeed, Adam Smith did not enunciate this idea until 1776, almost simultaneously with America's Declaration of Independence.

American independence came as a consequence of Britain's inability to adjust to its changing relationship with the mainland colonies. Most Americans found themselves unwilling revolutionaries, stirred on by radicals in their midst who played upon ideas and themes that struck responsive chords. American radicals used England's own traditions against the mother country, and Englishmen found themselves unable to answer the virtuous slogans. Americans thus fought Englishmen, not for new freedoms, but because the mother country had postulated the virtues and then seemingly abandoned their practice. No one realized, and certainly not the Americans, that they had more freedom than any other colonial people as a consequence of their English heritage, frontier circumstances, and English indifference.

Once Americans determined upon independence in 1776, they quickly discovered the difficulty of putting ideals into practice. The slogan "All men are created equal" applied to whites only, not to blacks, Indians, and certainly not to women. Central government, odious to colonials, suddenly became essential to win freedom from England. And the difficulties of applying their ideals increased after victory. Trade regulation, root of all Anglo-American problems, had to be instituted to prevent chaos. Taxation, source of America's most famous slogan, could not be avoided if a central government was to have strength.

Americans went through a period of experimentation and adjustment. From the Continental Congress to the Articles of Confederation, and finally to the Constitution, they searched for and debated the most effective and least damaging form of unity and authority. Imprecision, they suddenly discovered, was perhaps the best answer of all, and the Philadelphia Convention of 1787-88 postponed more decisions than it made. As delegates found it impossible to agree upon details, they utilized vague statements which future generations could freely interpret.

Shunting aside troublesome issues at the Philadelphia Convention proved temporary indeed, for the new government under the federal Constitution quickly faced postponed problems and had to come up with substantial answers. Included in areas of disagreement had been such matters as organization of the executive and judiciary, and even the extent of Congressional authority. Very quickly the new government would have to answer these questions in a specific way.

Less easily resolved, but of even greater import, was the necessity of instilling in the people a sense of national identity. To some degree, the revolutionary war had begun this process, but Americans still thought of themselves as members of a local community first, and then as members of the larger whole. This task would take another three quarters of a century, and localism would not be overcome until after a second bitter war with Britain (1812-15), a controversial conflict with Mexico (1846-48), and finally a violent, internal bloodbath (1861-65). From these critical moments would emerge a new nationalism.

Involved in developing national identity was economic maturation. British mercantilist restraints ended with the Treaty of Paris in 1783, and America faced the world on its own. However, America suddenly discovered the disadvantages of its situation — its traders found the West Indies closed to them, they could trade with the rest of Britain's empire only as outsiders, and their commerce with other nations faced insurmountable tariff barriers.

Yet Americans had great economic potential within their own borders. Not only did they have vast reserves of raw materials, but, with rapid population growth as a consequence of large-scale immigration, America became one of the world's major markets. By the early nineteenth century there began a pattern of industrialism which would grow over the years with increasing rapidity. However, not all parts of the country participated in this pattern. While New England shifted its investments from shipping to manufacturing, the South maintained and strengthened its agrarian outlook.

Southern agriculture, utilizing the plantation to produce cash crops of tobacco at first and later cotton, reemphasized the area's dependence on black slavery. Failure by the revolutionary generation to resolve this question, to apply broadly its own ideals, presented later generations with serious economic and moral dilemmas. When combined with increasing westward expansion, southern sensitivity about its "peculiar institution," and moral aggressiveness of northern reformers and agitators, slavery loomed so large that the question of its future could only be answered by what some called the "Second American Revolution" of 1861-65.

Societal development during the years following the Declaration of Independence from Great Britain changed little from the pattern of the preceding two centuries. Despite increasing industrialization of America, much of life remained agrarian in orientation, and even emergence of vital urban areas did little to disturb patterns of social thought. A certain wistfulness began to appear in literature, art, and architecture as intellectuals celebrated rural values and nature. This romanticism perhaps heralded the changes taking place, but it also reflected the distaste of those sensitive enough to understand them.

America in the decades following 1789 became increasingly a restless country. It strove to exploit its abundant resources, it worked hard to establish itself as a nation, and it argued mightily over the meaning of its experience. In doing all this, it created a viable existence for itself.

INDEX

Abernethy, Thomas P., 189
Acadia; *see* Nova Scotia
Acadians, 127, 133
Adams, John: attorney for British troops, 163-64; and Barbary Pirates, 244; on church establishment, 224; and Declaration of Independence, 187; on elections, 258; on honor of officers, 222; as minister to England, 243-44; as peace negotiator, 217; portrait of, 218; on purpose of government, 126; on religious liberty, 225; at Second Continental Congress, 183
Adams, Samuel: and Boston Committee of Correspondence, 165; and Boston Tea Party, 169; English try to seize, 179; in First Continental Congress, 174; and Hutchinson's Letters, 166; portrait of, 172; and ratification of Constitution, 261; at Second Continental Congress, 183; and Solemn League and Covenant, 171; on standing armies, 222; and Sugar Act, 149
Administration of Justice Act, 171-73
Admiralty, 98
Admiralty Courts, 147, 162; *see also* Navigation Acts, Vice-Admiralty Courts

Africa: and Portuguese, 21; and slavery, 104-7
African Company, 18; *see also* Guinea Coast, Royal African Company, slavery
Agrarianism, 232-33
Agriculture: in eighteenth-century colonies, 116; in England, 15; in Virginia, 71; *see also* farmers, indigo, rice, sugar, tobacco
Aix-la-Chapelle, Treaty of, 135
Aker, Charles W., 190
Albany Conference of 1754, 135
Albany Plan of Union, 135
Albemarle, Duke of, 68, 86
Albemarle Sound, 34
Alden, John R., 190, 234, 235
Aldridge, Alfred O., 190
Algiers, 244
Algonquins: and French alliance, 28; and Iroquois, 31; and Queen Anne's War, 132
Allan, Herbert S., 236
Allegheny River, 135
Allen, William, 153
Alliances: Americans need, 186; requires American unity, 196; Second Continental Congress seeks, 213-14; tied to independ-

ence and confederation, 194-95; between United States and France, 216-17
America: English loss of and French benefits, 214; Spanish discover, 22
American: army defeated at Camden, 208; peace terms in 1782, 219-21; problems after 1783, 221-23; victory at Yorktown, 213
American Methodist Episcopal Church, 227
American Philosophical Society, 116
American Revolution: purpose of, 194
Americanization, 101, 130
Americans: advantages of in revolution, 201-2; attitude toward England, 143-44; and central government, 194-96; definition of, 194; identity of, 193-94, 237, 267; imitate English ways, 111-16, 139-40
Anarchy, 197-98
Andrews, Charles McLean, 65
Andros, Sir Edmund, 92, 95-96
Anglo-American relations, 243-44, 274
Anglo-Dutch Wars, 70, 74, 81
Angola, 32
Annapolis Convention, 249
Annapolis (Md.), 169
Anne, Queen, 97, 133
Anti-Federalist: defined, 255; in Massachusetts, 261; negativism of, 263
Appalachian Mountains, 23
Aragon, 26
Aristocracy: economic base of, 231; in English society, 14; and Loyalism, 192; and revolution, 223; and Sons of Liberty, 153; in southern colonies, 45; in Virginia, 152, 225; weakened, 201
Armada, 7, 34, 37
Army: American adopted by Congress, 184; blacks serve in, 228; Congress suspicious of, 222; difficulties of in 1780, 208; problems of, 202, 206; Washington popular with, 206-7; see also troops
Army, standing, 146, 150
Arnold, Benedict, 202-3, 205, 208, 212
Articles of Confederation: assessment of, 238-48; difficulty of amending, 242; enforcement powers lacking, 222; and foreign relations, 242-44; as ideal government, 266; as imperial union, 232; and land speculators, 240; moribund nature of, 248; and Philadelphia Convention, 249; as political experiment, 237; problems of, 234; proposals for, 195-96; and ratification of federal Constitution, 255; and Shays's Rebellion, 247

Artisans: and deflation, 245; and Loyalism, 192; as middle class, 223; see also labor
Asiento, 132-33
Assembly: civil list and power of, 165; and colonial governors, 129-30; in colonies limited, 127; and Dominion of New England, 92; farmers gain increased role in, 201; in Georgia, 111; limit colonial governors, 129; in Massachusetts, 94-95; in New York, 82; in New York under Leisler, 96; in Pennsylvania, 86; in Quebec, 173; radicals attitude toward in revolution, 199; revolution expands base of, 201; in state government, 199; Townshend threatens power of, 158-59; see also Burgesses, General Court, representation
Astronomy, 117-18
Attucks, Crispus, 163
Augusta (Ga.), 207
Austria, 135, 215
Authority: exercise of in colonies, 143-44; and liberty, 197-99
Aztecs, 26

Bacon, Sir Francis, 90
Bacon, Nathaniel, 87-91
Bacon, Nathaniel Sr., 90
Bacon's Rebellion, 87-91
Baer, Elizabeth, 65
Bailyn, Bernard, 99, 141, 189
Bainton, Roland, 24
Bakeless, John, 235
Balboa, Vasco Nuñez de, 26
Baltimore, Lord; see Calvert
Bancroft, Edward, 217
Baptists: in Massachusetts, 76; in New England, 226; and state supported religion, 224-25; support Jefferson in Virginia, 225
Barbados, 86
Barbary Pirates, 244
Barbour, Philip L., 65
Barlow, Joel, 268-69
Barnes, Viola F., 99
Bartram, John, 118
Beard, Charles, 270
Beaumarchais, Caron de, 213, 214, 245
Becker, Carl L., 190
Bemis, Samuel F., 235
Benezet, Anthony, 107
Bennett, Lerone Jr., 64
Bennington (Vt.), 205
Berkeley, Lord John, 82-84, 86
Berkeley, Sir William: apologia of, 91; in Bacon's Rebellion, 90-91; and Carolina, 86;

INDEX

and Interregnum, 71; as Virginia's governor, 70
Bermuda Islands, 39, 80, 216
Bible Commonwealth, 57; *see also* Massachusetts
Bill of Rights, 258-61, 264-66
Billias, George, 235
Bishop of Durham Clause, 86
Black Hills (Dakotas), 29
Blacks; *see* Negroes, slavery, slaves
Blackwell, John, 86
Board of Trade: and Albany Conference, 135; and colonial control, 10; and colonial manufacturing, 114-16; power of in colonies, 97-98
Book of Common Prayer, 49
Boorstin, Daniel, 64, 190
Boston (Mass.): American troops at, 203; Andros captured in, 94; British besieged in, 180; British troops occupy, 174; and Committee of Correspondence, 165; Customs Commissioners driven from, 162; and English enforcement policies, 160; First Continental Congress cautions, 176; hatred of English in, 176-77; illustration of in 1722, 103; map of siege of, 182; and Powder Alarm, 175-76; as radical center, 171; rioting in, 152; siege of, 180-83; and social mobility, 144; and Sugar Act, 149; and tea controversy, 169-70; town house of illustrated, 75; and Townshend Duties, 161; Vice Admiralty Court in, 160
Boston Gazette, 162
Boston Massacre, 163-64, 176
Boston Port Bill, 170
Boston Tea Party, 169-70
Bostonians, 171
Boundary disputes, 195
Bounties, 155; *see also* subsidies
Bowdoin, Governor James, 247
Bowen, Catherine Drinker, 270
Boycott, 171; *see also* nonimportation
Braddock, General Edward, 135
Bradford, William, 53
Brandywine Creek, Battle of, 205
Brant, Irving, 271
Brattle, Thomas, 120
Brattle, William, 120
Brazil, 31-32
Breed's Hill, Battle of, 180
Bridenbaugh, Carl, 23, 99, 141, 189, 190
Bridenbaugh, Jessica, 190
Bristol (Eng.), 32
Brooklyn (N.Y.), 203

Brown, Gerald S., 235
Brown, Robert E., 190, 270
Bullion: attracts Spaniards, 26; problem of aggravated by Stamp Act, 153, supplied by West Indies trade, 148-49; *see also* currency, gold, money, silver
Bunker Hill, Battle of, 180-81
Bureaucracy, 238
Burgesses, House of: authority of increased, 71; free trade policy of, 70; and Henry's Resolves, 151-53; and intercolonial correspondence, 165; origin of, 43
Burgh, James, 147
Burgoyne, General Sir John, 179-80, 205, 206, 214
Burke, Edmund, 167, 177, 184-85
Burnaby, Andrew, 268
Byles, Reverend Mather, 118

Cabinet, 98
Cabot, John, 32
Cabot, Sebastian, 32
Cahokia, 207
Calvert, Cecilius, 44-45
Calvert, Charles, 97
Calvert, Sir George, 43
Calvert, Leonard, 72
Calvert family, 96
Calvin, John, 5, 7, 24, 51
Calvinism: in Church of England, 7, 49; in eighteenth century, 120; inheritance of in America, 118-19; in The Netherlands, 5; *see also* Congregational Church, Dutch Reformed Church, Presbyterian Church, Protestantism, Puritanism, Separatists
Cambridge University, 19-21
Camden, Lord, 184
Camden (S.C.), Battle of, 208
Canada: and American Revolution, 202-3; Americans ask cession of, 220; and Iroquois, 132; Leisler's assault on, 96; and Quebec Act, 173; and Seven Years War, 137; trade with closed to United States, 221
Canterbury, Archbishop of, 49
Canton (China), 241; *see also* China, trade
Cape Anne (Mass.), 53
Cape Breton Island, 133
Cape Cod, 52
Cape of Good Hope, 31
Caribbean Islands, 26
Carleton, General Sir Guy, 205
Carlisle, Lord, 217
Carolinas: Carteret and Berkeley interested

in, 82; development of, 86-87; founding of, 101; Regulator Movement in, 164; *see also* North Carolina, South Carolina
Carpenters' Hall (Phila.), 174
Cartaret, Sir George, 82-84, 86
Cartier, Jacques, 28
Cary, John H., 190
Castile, 26
Castle William (Boston), 162
Champlain, Samuel de, 28-29
Charles, Archduke of Austria, 131
Charles I (Eng.), 54, 68, 70
Charles II (Eng.): and charter revocations, 80; and colonial government, 78; and France, 131; and religious repression in Massachusetts, 76; restoration of, 68, 71
Charles III (Sp.), 214
Charleston (S.C.): Clinton attacks, 203; English besiege, 207; prices in, 242; and social mobility, 144-46; and Tea Party, 169; Vice Admiralty Court in, 160
Charlestown Heights (Mass.), 180
Charlotte (N.C.), 208
Charters: attempts to revoke, 78-80; fragility of, 173; of Massachusetts forfeited, 92; of Massachusetts revamped, 95; Massachusetts seeks restoration of, 94-95; of New York, 81-82; as property right, 79; *see also* Connecticut, Pennsylvania
Chatham, Earl of; *see* Pitt, William
Chauncy, Reverend Charles, 118
Chesapeake, 36, 37, 38, 48, 213
Chibchas, 26
Children, 12-13
China trade: opened to Americans, 241; and War of Austrian Succession, 133; *see also* Canton
Chinard, Gilbert, 190
Christianity: heritage of, 3; and slavery, 106-7; *see also* Presbyterian Church, Protestantism, Puritanism, Roman Catholic Church, Separatists
Christie, I. R., 189
Church of England: dissent from in Virginia, 225; and education, 20-21; under Elizabeth, 49; hostility toward, 224; and Loyalism, 192; in Massachusetts, 94; modifications of, 121; and Parson's Cause, 140; in Pennsylvania, 85; and Puritanism, 58, 68; in Quebec, 173; status of after Revolution, 227; in Virginia during Civil War, 70
Churches: and conversion experience, 50; covenant in, 55; in English society, 14; Separatists define true, 51-52; and tie to state, 224; *see also* Church of England, Presbyterian Church, Protestantism, Puritanism, Separatists
Cider tax, 155
Circular Letter of 1768, 159
Civil List, 129-30, 149
Civil service, 19
Civil War and Interregnum, 45, 63, 68-77, 80
Clarendon, Earl of, 86
Clark, G. N., 24
Clark, George Rogers, 207
Classics, 21
Clergy, 57, 192
Clinton, Governor George, 262-63
Clinton, General Sir Henry, 179, 203, 207, 213
Cloth weaving, 17-18
Coddington, William, 61-62
Coercive Acts; *see* Intolerable Acts
Colbert, Jean Baptiste, 28
Colbourn, Trevor, 141
Coleman, Kenneth, 190
Colleton, John, 86
Colonialism, 232, 239
Colonies: English motives for acquisition of, 37; planting successful, 42; problems of private, 78-79; relationship to England, 124; supervision of, 77-80
Columbus, Christopher, 1, 26, 27
Columbus, Ferdinand, 1
Commerce: and English policy, 16-18; and Mississippi River, 243; problems of under Articles of Confederation, 234; and Queen Anne's War, 132; and ratification of Constitution, 256-57; regulation of, 237-38; regulation of under Articles of Confederation, 195, 248; regulation of under Constitution, 254; regulation of under New Jersey Plan, 251; treaties of under Articles of Confederation, 243-44; treaty with England for, 243
Committee system, 238
Common law: in Quebec, 173; in Stuart era, 68; U.S. courts retain, 233
Common Sense, 185
Commons, House of: and class system, 125; colonists identify with, 97, 129; role of, 10
Concord (Mass.), 178-79, 247
Confederation, 186, 194-95
Congregational Church: definition of, 76; and disestablishment, 226; and English ties, 227; hostility toward, 224; and Loyalism, 192; membership requirements of, 120
Connecticut: and Anglo-Dutch rivalry, 73; and Boston Port Bill, 171; characterized in 1640s, 73; charter of, 79; and disestablish-

ment of Congregational Church, 226; and Dominion of New England, 80; as Federalist area, 256; founding of, 62-63; and fur trade, 62; government of, 63, 97; in New England Confederation, 74; and paper money controversy, 246; and ratification of Constitution, 260; and settlement, 73; trade of, 242; and Wyoming Valley dispute, 164
Conner, Paul W., 190
Consensual society, 231
Conservatives, 197-98, 246-47
Conspiracy, attitude of, 189
Constitution: Americans want clarification of imperial, 140; British view of, 127; imperial defined, 124-26; of states, 196-201, 224
Constitution, United States: and Bill of Rights, 264-66; Jefferson on, 259; as political experiment, 237; ratification of, 255-64; as supreme law, 253-54
Continental Association, 176-79
Continental currency, 245; *see also* finances, money, taxation
Contraband, 215
Convention; *see* Philadelphia Convention, ratifying conventions
Conversion experience, 50
Coode, John, 96
Cooper, Anthony; *see* Shaftesbury, Earl of
Cornwallis, General Charles: at Charleston, 207; follows American retreat, 203; satirized, 210-11; southern strategy of, 208; surrender of illustrated, 209
Correspondence, Committees of: in Boston, 165; after Intolerable Acts, 172-73; replaced by Committees of Safety, 179
Cortes, Hernando, 1
Cotton, Reverend John, 76, 121
Council for New England, 44, 53
Councils, 199; *see also* governors councils, Privy Council
County government, 71-72
Cowpens, Battle of, 209
Craddock, Matthew, 53
Crane, Verner, 98, 236
Craven, Wesley Frank, 64, 98, 236
Craven, Lord William, 86
Credit, 241; *see also* commerce, trade
Crèvecoeur, Michel de J. Hector St. John, 194
Crime, 117
Criminal law, 231, 233
Crisis, The, 203-5
Cromwell, Oliver: attitude toward colonies, 72-73; controls England, 68; and Dutch treaty, 74; and imperial policy, 77; and religious repression in Massachusetts, 76; and Virginia trade, 70-77
Cromwell, Richard, 68
Crowl, Philip A., 190
Crown, English: Americans appeal to in 1768, 159; authority of collapses in Massachusetts, 172; authority of in colonies collapses, 179; and empire after 1763, 144; First Continental Congress appeals to, 174; and House of Lords, 10; limits assembly power, 129-30; power of in Massachusetts increased, 171; radicals destroy veneration of, 199; restrictions on by Parliament, 264; role of in England, 9; simplifies American decision for independence, 185; sovereignty of and law, 230; *see also* monarchy
Crown Point (N.Y.), 136
Crusades, 3
Curaçao, 31
Currency, 238
Customs Board, 98
Customs Commissioners, Board of American: Americans demand removal of, 162; in Boston, 160; demands duties in specie, 161; driven out of Boston, 162
Customs Service, 147, 149

Dale, Sir Thomas, 40
Dangerfield, George, 190
Dare, Virginia, 37
Davidson, Philip, 189
Davidson, Robert A., 270
Dawes, William, 179
Deane, Silas, 214, 216, 217
Debt: colonial public, 148; English after 1763, 146-48; repayment of pre-war private, 220, 222
Declaration of Causes and Necessity of Taking Up Arms, 184
Declaration of Independence: and American offensive, 202; Jefferson and, 225; purpose of, 191; quoted, 188; and Shays's Rebellion, 247-48; and slavery, 228-29; and state governments, 196
Declaratory Act: defines empire, 126; and parliamentary supremacy, 161; quoted, 154; and Stamp Act, 154
Deflation, 245
Deism, 121-22
Delancey family, 192
Delaware: and Loyalists, 193; paper money rejected, 246; ratifies Constitution, 260; refuses ratification of Articles of Confed-

eration, 196; renounces royal authority, 187; settlement of, 103
Delaware River, 73, 82
De la Warr, Lord, 39
Democracy: conservatives deprecate, 198; and Great Awakening, 124; Paine advocates, 199; in West, 239, 240; *see also* politics, representation
Denmark, 5
Descartes, Rene, 116-17
Detroit, 207
Dickerson, Oliver M., 189
Dickinson, John, 159, 183
Dinwiddie, Governor Robert, 135
Diplomacy: of American Revolution, 213-17; and Articles of Confederation, 242-44; conduct of by government, 237-38; *see also* treaties
Discipline: in army, 222-23; in English family, 12, 13
Disease, 15
Disestablishment, 233; *see also* religion
Dissenters, 58
Dominion of New England: establishment of, 80; James II proposes, 87; Massachusetts in, 92; New York in, 82; organization and collapse of, 92-94
Dorchester Heights (Boston), 182-83
Douglass, Elisha P., 270
Douglass, Dr. William, 119
Drake, Sir Francis, 33
Driver, Carl S., 27
Driver, Harold E., 64
Dudley, Joseph, 92
Dudley, Thomas, 56-57
Dulany, Daniel, 151
Dunmore, John Murray, Earl of, 184-85
Durham, Bishop of, 44
Dutch: English conquer, 130; on Hudson River, 31; Lisbon closed to, 31; nationalism of, 30; settlements of, 103; smuggling by, 148; and tobacco trade, 46; *see also* Netherlands
Dutch East India Company, 31
Dutch Reformed Church, 122
Dutch West India Company, 31-32

East, Robert A., 235
East India Company (Eng.): and American tea market, 160-61; and China trade, 241; controversy over, 167-70; and English trade, 33, 42; and tea trade, 162
East Indies, 31
Eastland Company, 33
Economy: and Anglo-American relations, 274; in Georgia, 110-11; in Maryland, 45, 96; in New Jersey, 83; in Plymouth, 53; ratification controversy involves, 257; revised approach to, 42-43; in Rhode Island, 61; in Virginia, 41; in Virginia and Bacon's Rebellion, 87-90; in Virginia during Civil War, 68-71; of Virginia and slavery, 47; *see also* agriculture, commerce, manufacturing, mercantilism, trade
Economy, American: government role in, 238; inflation of, 246; potential of, 276; and public disorder, 247; restrictions on ended, 241; unchanged by the revolution, 233
Economy, colonial: depression of, 150; development of, 111-16; in eighteenth century, 116; immigration stimulates, 108-110; map of, 112-13; self-sufficiency in, 114-16; and slavery, 107; and Townshend Acts, 161
Economy, English: and East India Company, 167; and family, 12-13; not affected by Continental Association, 177
Eden, Governor Sir Robert, 187
Edict of Nantes, 104
Education, 19-21, 269
Edwards, Reverend Jonathan, 122
Elections: frequency of, 199, 224; John Adams on, 258; *see also* assemblies, politics
Electoral College, 252-53
Elizabeth I (Eng.): church settlement of, 48-49; description of, 8-9; portrait of, 33; government of, 34-35; reshapes church, 7; selects successor, 51
Elizabethan Settlement, 7
Empire, British: after 1763 (map), 134; American experience with, 199; Americans attitudes toward, 124-26; Americans misunderstand, 188-89; Americans outside of, 221; attitude toward after 1763, 144; break with begins, 186; central government of replaced, 195; and coercion of colonies, 253; compared to United States, 266-67; concept of questioned by Adam Smith, 198; as consensual society, 231-32; Dickinson defines, 159; difficult to break with, 185; dilemma of and Articles of Confederation, 239; France seeks benefits of, 214; future of questioned, 150-51; Galloway's proposal for, 175; government of, 127; Massachusetts Circular Letter defines, 159; nature of, 67, 126, 161, 274-75; physical expansion of, 101-3; problems of after 1763, 137-41; replacement of, 194; success of, 139; Virginia's place in, 128; Virginia Plan reflects, 250
Empress of China, 241

INDEX   285

Enclosure movement, 15-17
England: and Acadians, 133; advantages of in the revolution, 201; Americans change attitude toward, 174; and Armada, 7; army encourages blacks to desert, 228; and Canada during the revolution, 202-3; capitulates at Yorktown, 213; and colonial manufacturing, 115-16; colonial sentiment favors, 191-93; colonial weakness of, 162; colonization process misunderstood, 42; Crown of and colonization, 37; defeated at Saratoga, 205; and Dutch rivalry, 73, 80-82; economic system of, 241-42; empire of, 23, 32-34; and finances of United States, 245; France as natural enemy, 214; French rivalry, 67-68, 131-37; French seek to break power of, 213; gains of in 1714, 133; goods of dumped in United States, 242; and Hundred Years War, 7; imperial problems after 1763, 137-41; and Loyalists, 203; merchants of and New World, 37; as nation-state, 6; national church of, 5; navy of and American policy, 215; navy of sent to Canada in 1711, 132; and New Netherland, 32; and Ohio Valley, 135-36; and peace with United States, 217; policies of after 1763, 146-48; policy of reviewed, 189; political system of, 8-12; power of, 8; problems of in the revolution, 202; radicals destroy veneration of, 199; and relief of Quebec siege, 203; religion in, 227; and religious toleration, 74-75; and the revolution in West, 207; rivalries within government of, 218; and Seven Years War, 135-37; slave trade monopolized by, 229; and Spanish rivalry, 33-34, 133; statutes of reviewed by Americans, 230-31; strategy of after Philadelphia evacuation, 207; tobacco purchased from Spain, 41; trade with Asia, 3; troops to crush rebellion, 184; and War of Austrian Succession, 133-35; withdraws from colonies, 183
English: as common language of Americans, 194; constitution as model for Americans, 197; prejudice of against blacks, 47-48; society of, 12-14
Englishmen, rights of, 97
Enlightenment, 117-18, 196-97, 215
Entail, 231
Enumeration, 148; see also commerce, Navigation Acts, Trade
Estaing, Admiral Comte d', 207
Europe: and American peace, 217; Americans reject, 194; Catholicism in, 5; expansion of, 3; and New World, 25-26
Evans, G. N. D., 235

Executive, chief, 250-52
Explorations, 1, 22

Factions, 252
Falmouth (Me.), 186
Family, 12-13, 23
Farmers: and Constitution, 256; difficulties of in Massachusetts, 247; and franchise, 200; and Loyalism, 192; as middle class, 223; and Mississippi navigation, 243; and postwar deflation, 245; power of in assemblies, 201; and slave competition, 229; tenant in England, 15; yeoman in Virginia and Maryland, 45-46; *see also* agriculture, economy
Farrand, Max, 270
Federalism, 251, 253
Federalist, The, 262
Federalists, 251, 255, 261, 263
Ferdinand of Aragon, 1, 26
Ferguson, E. James, 235
Ferguson, Major Patrick, 208
Feudalism: in Carolina, 87; in England, 3, 7, 8-9; in Maryland, 43-44; nation-states supplant, 6
Finances: of Articles of Confederation, 234, 244-46; of Continental Congress, 184; English conflict over in seventeenth century, 68; of states under Articles of Confederation, 245; *see also* money, taxation
Findley, William, 260
First Continental Congress: as central government, 195; power of described, 179; and preparation for war, 174-76; Second Congress called by, 183
Fisheries, 52-53, 133, 220
Fitzhugh, William, 114-15
Flag-of-truce, 147
Flax, 116
Flemings, 17
Flexner, James T., 235
Florida, 101-3, 220
Forbes, Esther, 235
Foreign aid, 196
Foreign relations; *see* diplomacy, treaties
Fort Duquesne, 135, 136
Fort Frontenac, 136
Fort Louisbourg, 133, 135, 136
Fort Orange, 82
Fort Stanwix, Battle of, 205
Fort Ticonderoga, 205
Fox, Charles James, 174
France: and American aid, 213-17; Catholicism in, 5; economic rivalry with England, 131; economic system of closed, 241-42; England rival of, 8, 94, 133, 146, 214;

and exploration of North America, 29; fleet of to Delaware Bay, 207; imperial growth of hindered, 28; and Indians, 28; and King William's War, 131; in Louisiana, 110; as market for Americans, 241; as nation-state, 6; and Ohio Valley, 135-36; and Peace of 1763, 137; and Peace of 1783, 217; settlers of, 104; and Seven Years War, 135-37; and Sugar trade, 148-49; United States borrows from, 245; and Yorktown victory, 212-13
Franchise, 200-1; *see also* assemblies, elections, politics
Franco-American alliance, 216
Franklin, Benjamin: and Albany Plan of Union, 135; American delegate to France, 214-17; on American society, 116; and Buy American Campaign, 161; as colonial scientist, 118; and Constitution, 254; and Declaration of Independence, 187; and deism, 122; as elder statesman, 251; on external taxes, 154; "On Felons and Rattlesnakes," 119; and Governor Hutchinson, 165-66; and Great Awakening, 123-24; and peace negotiations, 217-21; and Philadelphia Abolition Society, 230; portrait of, 216; and postal service, 184; and religious establishment, 224; at Second Continental Congress, 183; "Silence Dogood" essays, 119; on slavery, 107; on social mobility, 144-46; on taxation, 158
Franklin, Governor William, 187
Frelinghuysen, Reverend Theodore, 122
French Guinea Company, 132
French and Indian War, 135-37, 146-47, 202
Frontenac, Comte de, 131
Frontier, 200-1, 223; *see also* West
Fundamental Orders of Connecticut, 63
Fur trade: and Anglo-French rivalry, 131; and Bacon's Rebellion, 87-90; and colonization, 23; in Connecticut River Valley, 62; and Dutch, 31; and English in the West, 243; and French Empire, 28; importance of, 80-81; and King William's War, 131; and Proclamation of 1763, 146; and Queen Anne's War, 132; and Seven Years War, 137; *see also* commerce, trade

Gadsden, Christopher, 153, 174
Gage, General Thomas, 175-77, 179, 180
Galloway, Joseph, 159, 174-75
Garden, Alexander, 118
Gardoqui, Don Diego de, 243
Gaspée Incident, 165
Gates, General Horatio, 205, 206, 208
Gates, Sir Thomas, 38
Gaustad, Edwin S., 141
General Court (Mass.), 55-57; *see also* assembly in Massachusetts
Geneva, 5
Gentry, 14
George I (Eng.), 133
George II (Eng.), 110, 140
George III (Eng.): and John Adams, 243; and American decision for independence, 185; Americans seek his aid against Parliament, 183-84; and Church of England, 227; in Declaration of Independence as villain, 188-89; declares Americans to be rebels, 184; Grenville irritates, 150; and Lord North, 205; and Pitt, 136-37; Rockingham replaced by Pitt, 155; slavery blamed on, 228; and Stamp Act repeal, 154; and Writs of Assistance, 140
Georgia: blacks rejected for army, 228; as buffer area, 103; Church of England in, 121; Constitution ratified by, 260; and disestablishment of religion, 225; English forces attack, 207; as Federalist area, 256-57; on independence, 186; and paper money, 246; parliamentary power accepted by, 177; settlement of, 110-11; slave trade supported by, 254; slaves needed for manpower, 229; and western land claims, 239
Germain, Lord George, 205
German princes, 4
Germantown (Pa.), Battle of, 205
Germany: Catholicism in, 5; Lutheranism in, 5; settlers from, 103-4
Gerry, Elbridge, 254, 260
Gilbert, Sir Humphrey, 34, 37
Gipson, Lawrence H., 141, 189, 235
Glorious Revolution, 91-97, 124
Gold, 1; *see also* bullion, money
Gorton, Samuel, 62
Government: American attitude toward, 266-67; Americans view as suspect, 200; central, 194-96, 200; colonial under Dominion of New England, 80; colonial form stable, 97; English and local institutions, 11-12; functions of in eighteenth century, 237-38; in Massachusetts revamped, 94-95; and middle class, 223; Paine defines, 144; power of limited, 259; radical view of, 199; reform of, 224; and representation, 97; of Rhode Island, 61; state, 196-201; state broadened, 232-33; in West, 239-40, 240-41.
Governor, colonial: power of in Virginia,

INDEX

71; practical power of, 129; retreat from colonies, 184; role of, 127; theoretical power of, 128
Governor, state: conservatives want strong, 198; elected by assemblies, 200; radicals want weak, 199
Governor's Council, 86, 129
Grafton, Augustus Henry Fitzroy, Duke of, 161-63, 184
Granada, 26
Grasse, Admiral Comte François de, 213
Great Awakening, 122-24, 224
Great Barrington (Mass.), 247
Great Compromise, 251
Great Lakes, 131, 217
Great Salt River (R.I.), 61
Green Mountain Boys, 164
Greene, Jack P., 141, 189
Greene, General Nathanael, 206, 208-210, 212
Greenwich (N.J.), 169
Grenville, George: and fiscal policy, 147-48; and Massachusetts Circular Letter, 159; regains popularity, 157; and Stamp Act, 149-50; tightens trade patterns, 148
Grenville, Richard, 35.
Gresham's Law, 245
Grimm, Harold J., 24
Guadeloupe, 137
Guild system, 18
Guilford Courthouse (N.C.), Battle of, 209
Guinea Coast, 23
Guttridge, G. H., 190

Hakluyt, Richard, 21, 34-35
Halfway Covenant, 120
Halifax (Nova Scotia), 160, 163, 183
Hall, Michael G., 98, 99
Haller, William, 24
Hamilton, Alexander: and Articles of Confederation, 248-49; and federal funding, 245; and *The Federalist*, 263; as a Federalist, 263; portrait of, 262; and slavery, 230
Hamilton, Colonel Henry, 207
Hammond, Bray, 235
Hancock, John: and Boston Tea Party, 169; English try to seize, 178; as Massacre Day Orator, 176; and ratification of Constitution, 261; at Second Continental Congress, 183; and Shays's Rebellion, 247; and Sons of Liberty, 153
Hanoverian succession, 67
Hanoverians, 104, 133
Hanseatic League, 16-17
Hanseatic Merchants, 18

Hansen, Marcus Lee, 64
Hapsburg Empire, 7
Harbison, E. H., 24
Hariot, Thomas, 35
Hartford (Conn.), 62, 74
Hartford, Treaty of, 74
Harvard University, 118
Havana, 137
Hawke, David, 190
Headrights, 40, 86
Heaton, Herbert, 24
Hemp, 116
Henry VII (Eng.), 7, 18, 32
Henry VIII (Eng.), 7, 32, 48
Henry, Patrick: and Baptists, 225; and Constitution, 261-62; and empire's dissolution, 174; and Parson's Cause, 140; portrait of, 152; on slavery, 229; and Stamp Tax, 151-52
Higginbotham, R. Don, 235
Highland Scots, 104
Hillsborough, Wills Hill, Earl of, 160, 162
Hillsborough's Circular Letter, 160-61
Hindle, Brooke, 141, 190
History in colonies, 118-19
Hooker, Reverend Thomas, 92
Howe, Admiral Richard, 184
Howe, General Sir William: Boston evacuated by, 182-83; and Charlestown Heights, 180; commander and peace commissioner, 184; assaults New York City, 203; Lord North sends to Boston, 179; resigns, 206; strategy of, 205
Hudson, Henry, 31
Hudson River, 23, 31-32, 73-74, 80
Hudson's Bay, 132
Huguenots, 29, 104
Humanism, 3
Hundred Years War, 6, 7, 17
Hunter, Governor Robert, 96
Hutchinson, Anne, 59, 61-62, 76, 120
Hutchinson, Governor Thomas: and Boston Port Bill, 170; effigy of burned, 171; and Gaspée Incident, 165; letters of, 166-67; removes troops from Boston, 163; replaced by Gage, 177; and tea controversy, 169

Iberian Peninsula, 5
Idealism of the revolution, 223-30
Ideology, 139
Immigration: to colonies, 104-7; and colonial economy, 108-10; of slaves to colonies, 104
Imperial controls, 67
Imperial policy: in Penn's charter, 85; in

seventeenth century, 87; in 1680s, 80; *see also* empire
Imperialism of Stuarts, 77-80
Incas, 26
Independence: as idea, 275; French recognition of, 216, movement for, 185-89; and peace negotiations, 217-18; resolution for by Lee, 186; Second Continental Congress declares, 195; tied to confederation and alliances, 194-95; *see also* Declaration of Independence
India, 23, 167-68
Indian Commissioners, Board of, 184
Indians: and Articles of Confederation, 239; in Bacon's Rebellion, 87-90; conquest of, 22; conversion of, 37; and Dominion of New England, 94; and English frontier posts, 243; extermination of advocated, 232-33; and Franco English conflict, 82; and French and Indian War, 135; in King William's War, 131; map of distribution of, 40; menace of suppressed in Virginia, 71; and New England, 73; Pennsylvania's relations with, 109; position of after 1763, 137-38; and Proclamation of 1763, 146; and the revolution in West, 207; and slavery, 48; in Spanish America, 26-27; and Spanish territory, 243; Spanish urge buffer state of, 220; Virginia attacked by in 1622, 41; *see also* Algonquins, Iroquois
Indigo, 87, 111, 116
Industrial development, 114-16, 242
Influence, role of, 98
Interregnum, 68, 72-77
Intolerable Acts, 171-74, 176
Ireland, 103-4, 162
Irish, 184
Iroquois: and Dominion of New England, 94; and Dutch fur trade, 31; and French, 28; in King William's War, 131; neutrality of, 132; redcoats compared to, 179
Isabella of Castile, 1, 26
Italy, 5

Jacobs, Wilbur R., 141
Jacobsen, Gertrude Ann, 98
Jamaica, 147
James I (Eng.), 32, 41, 50-51, 67-68
James II (Eng.): abdicates, 94; and colonial government, 78; and Dominion of New England, 80; and France, 131; in Glorious Revolution, 91; imperial policies of, 82; imperial unification proposed by, 87
James, Sidney V., 141
James River, 38, 90
Jameson, J. Franklin, 270

Jamestown (Va.), 38, 41, 43, 48, 71, 90
Jay, John: and Articles of Confederation, 248; on education, 269; as Federalist, 263; and *The Federalist*, 262; on peace commission, 217; and peace negotiations, 220; on silent majority, 256-57; on slavery, 230; and Spanish negotiations, 243
Jefferson, Thomas: on American superiority, 267-68; on Bill of Rights, 264; on Constitution, 259; Declaration of Independence drafted by, 187-88; on education, 269; and land ordinances, 239-40; and legal reforms, 231; on peace commission, 217; portrait of, 226; and religious establishment, 224-25; at Second Continental Congress, 183; on slavery, 230; slavery blamed on George III by, 228
Jenkins, Captain Robert, 133
Jensen, Merrill, 270
Jernegan, Marcus W., 65
Jesuit Order, 28, 44-45
Johnson, Isaac, 53
Joint-stock companies, 18; *see also* commerce, mercantilism
Jones, Howard Mumford, 64
Judiciary: conservatives want independent, 198; middle class view of, 223; under Virginia Plan, 250
Justices of Peace, 12

Kammen, Michael, 99, 141
Kaskaskia, 207
Katz, Stanley N., 141
Keith, Sir William, 126
Kentucky, 207, 243
Kieft, Willem, 74
King William's War, 131
King's Mountain, Battle of, 208
Kingston (N.Y.), 205
Knollenberg, Bernhard, 235
Knox, Reverend John, 5, 51

Labaree, Benjamin W., 189
Labaree, Leonard W., 141
Labor: attitude toward, 42-43; convict sent to colonies, 110-11; productivity of in England, 15; in Virginia, 39
Lake Champlain, 202, 205
Lake Nippissing, 217
Lamb, John, 244
Lancastrian dynasty, 7
Land: attitude toward, 43; distribution of in Virginia, 39-40; and legal code, 231; policies, 139; and social system, 144; use of in Maryland, 45
Land speculation: in New Jersey, 82-83; in

INDEX

Ohio Valley, 135; by Penn, 85; and Quebec Act, 173-74; role of, 111; settlement influenced by, 274; in western domain, 240
Land tax, 242
Landless states, 196
Landowners, English, 155
Lands, western: and Articles of Confederation, 195; claims to, 196
Language, 199
Lansing, John, 263
Lafayette, Marquis de, 212-13
LaSalle, Sieur de, 29
Laslett, Peter, 23
Latin America, 23
Laurens, Henry, 217
Law, 224, 230-31, 233, 238
Lawyers, 257
Leach, Douglas, 98, 141
Leder, Lawrence H., 99, 141
Lee, Arthur, 213-16
Lee, Charles, 180
Lee, Richard Henry: on Bill of Rights, 264; brother of Arthur, 213; central government proposed by, 195; on Constitution, 255, 260-61; on law and democracy in West, 240; resolutions of, 186-87, 194; at Second Continental Congress, 183; and Solemn League and Covenant, 174
Legislature, 250, 264; *see also* assembly, politics
Leisler, Jacob, 95-96, 131
Letters from a Farmer in Pennsylvania, 159
Levant, 2
Levant Company, 33
Lexington (Mass.), Battle of, 178-79
Lexington and Concord, 184
Leyden (The Netherlands), 41, 52
Liberty: American attitude toward, 143-44; and American situation in empire, 196-97; and authority debated, 197-99; Barlow defines, 268-69; and Bill of Rights, 264-66; conservatives seek to restore, 198; definition not needed, 259; frontiers of, 170; Mutiny Act challenges, 155-56; Parliament challenges, 151; and Quebec Act, 173; radicals argue for greater, 199; and the revolution, 275; and slavery, 229; standing army threatens, 222; Williams defines, 60-61; Winthrop defines, 58
Lincoln, General Benjamin, 207, 247
Linnaeus, Carolus, 118
Lisbon, 3, 31
Livingston, Robert R., 187, 263
Livingston, William, 153
Livy, 21
Localism, 194

Locke, John: Americans apply philosophy of, 200; political theory of, 124; portrait of, 125; tradition of, 125-26
Logwood, 148
London: in English economy, 16; entrepot for Virginia, 70; illustration of, 20; as tobacco market, 46; urban center for Virginia and Maryland, 48; as urban complex, 19-20
London, Bishop of, 121
Long Island (N.Y.), 74
Long Island (N.Y.), Battle of, 203
Long Island Sound, 63
Long Parliament, 68
Lords, House of, 10, 125
Lords of Trade: and charters, 80; and colonies, 78; created, 10; and Pennsylvania charter, 85; under Privy Council, 77
Lotteries, 41
Louis XIV (Fr.), 28-29, 30, 104, 131
Louis XV (Fr.), 133
Louis XVI (Fr.), 213-14, 217
Louisiana, 137
Lovejoy, David S., 190
Loyalism: and Church of England, 225; origins of, 191-93
Loyalists: Committees of Safety hound, 179; confiscated property of, 220; Congress authorizes arrest of, 184; Cornwallis seeks support of, 208; English strategy based on, 203; number of, 192-93; rising of in North Carolina, 185; withdrawal of, 223
Lumber, 116
Lundin, Leonard, 190
Luther, Martin, 3-4, 7, 24
Lutheranism, 5

McDonald, Forrest, 270
McIlwain, Charles H., 189
McKean, Thomas, 260
McLaughlin, A. C., 270
Mackesy, Pier, 234
Madison, James: and Articles of Confederation, 248-49; and Bill of Rights, 264-66; and conditional ratification, 263; on Constitution, 261; on factions, 252; and *The Federalist*, 262; and notes on Philadelphia Convention, 249; on numerical majorities, 250; on physical coercion of states, 253; portrait of, 265; on sectionalism, 251; states protected by Constitution, 260
Madras (India), 135
Main, Jackson Turner, 234, 270
Maine, 73, 74, 82
Malone, Dumas, 190, 235
Manhattan Island, 31, 203

Manila (Philippine Islands), 137
Manorial system, 45
Manors, English, 15
Manufacturing: in colonies, 114-16; and private colonies, 78-79; restrictions on ended, 186; see also commerce, economy, Navigation Acts, trade
Marlowe, Christopher, 21
Marquette, Père Jacques, 29
Marriage, 12-13, 23
Marshall, John, 261
Martha's Vineyard, 82
Martin, Luther, 253-54, 259
Martinique, 137
Martyr, Peter, 21, 34
Mary (Eng.), 94
Maryland: agriculture in, 116; Articles of Confederation rejected by, 196; Church of England in, 121; farmers' power in, 201; and Glorious Revolution, 96-97; and Interregnum, 71-72; and Loyalists, 193; manufacturing in, 115; origins of, 43-45; and paper money, 246; and Potomac negotiations, 248-49; proprietary power in, 72; ratifies Constitution, 261; royal governor ousted, 187; urban center of in London, 48; western claims of ceded, 239
Mason, George: as Anti-Federalist, 261; on Bill of Rights, 264; and Constitution, 254, 260; and Virginia Bill of Rights, 224-25
Massachusetts: and Boston Massacre, 164; challenges to, 58-59; charter of, 95; Circular Letter of, 159; civil list for, 165; and Civil War, 72-73; and Connecticut, 63; constitution of reformed, 171; and Constitution of United States, 260-61; and disestablishment of religion, 226; and dissenters, 75-77; in Dominion of New England, 80; Federalism in, 256; founding of, 54; and Glorious Revolution, 91-95; government of, 55-57; government of in eighteenth century, 97; Hillsborough threatens, 160; Hutchinson and Oliver impeached, 167; on independence, 186; and Lords of Trade, 78-80; and Mutiny Act, 157; in New England Confederation, 74; paper money scheme rejected by, 246; population of, 73; public disorder in, 247; and self-government, 130; settlement of, 53-54; slaves in freed, 229-30; social structure of, 91-92; and Sugar Act, 149; and tea controversy, 169-70; and Writs of Assistance, 140
Massachusetts Government Act, 171
Masterson, W. H., 271

Mather, Reverend Increase, 95
Maury, Reverend James, 140
Mayflower, 52
Mayflower Compact, 53
Mayhew, Reverend Jonathan, 121
Mays, David J., 190
Meade, Robert D., 190
Mercantilism: American economy controlled by, 233; America seeks benefits of without restrictions, 220; Articles of Confederation lack, 241-42; colonial self-sufficiency challenges, 161; colonies affected by, 116; English and Americans conflict over, 221, 274-75; English defined, 116; and independence, 276; New England marginal to English, 73; rivalry of English and French, 131-37; in seventeenth century, 87; and tea tax, 161-62; see also commerce, economy, Navigation Acts, trade
Merchant Adventurers, 18
Merchants: and Boston Massacre, 164; and British economic policies, 160; English bypassed in tea sales, 168; and Solemn League and Covenant, 171; and Sons of Liberty, 162, 169-70
Merchants of the Staple, 18
Merchants, United States: under Articles of Confederation, 242; as Federalists, 257, as middle class, 223
Methodism, 122, 227
Mexico, Gulf of, 26
Middle class: in England, 19; power of increases, 201; in United States, 223; see also artisans, farmers, merchants
Migration, 273
Militia diplomacy, 215
Miller, John C., 190, 234
Miller, Perry, 24
Milton, John, 21
Mississippi River, 217, 243
Mississippi Valley, 207
Mohawk Indians, 169
Mohawk River, 80, 205
Molasses; see sugar
Molasses Act; see Sugar Act
Monarchy, 185, 186
Money, 246; see also currency, finances, taxation
Monk, General George, 68
Monmouth Courthouse, Battle of, 207
Monongahela River, 135
Monopoly, 167-68
Montesquieu, Charles-Louis de Secondat, Baron de, 197
Montgomery, General Richard, 192, 202-3

INDEX

Montreal, 136, 203
Montross, Lynn, 234
Moors, 6, 26
Morgan, Edmund S., 64
Morison, Samuel Eliot, 64
Morocco, 244
Morris, Richard B., 235
Morris, Robert, 245
Mortgage moratoria, 247-48
Morton, Richard L., 99
Mt. Vernon (Va.), 248
Munitions, 213-14
Murder Act, 171
Muscovy Company, 18, 33
Mutiny Act, 155-58

Nantes, Edict of, 28-29
Nantucket Island, 82
Napoleon, 8
Narragansett Indians, 73
Nationalism: Americans develop, 193-94, 237, 276; and Constitution, 255; and religion, 6; of Virginia Plan, 250
Natural Rights, 224
Nature, State of: and Bill of Rights, 259; evils of, 246
Naval power, English, 215
Naval stores, 116
Navigation Acts: adoption of, 46, 70; of Cromwell, 77; Dutch violate, 81; limit colonial economy, 111-14; Massachusetts disobeys, 79; in Pennsylvania, 85; in Rhode Island, 165; of 1696, 147
Navigation laws, United States, 242, 254
Navy, British, 201
Near East, 3
Nef, John U., 24
Negroes: and Great Awakening, 124; military service by, 228; in New England, 63; in New Netherland, 32; treatment of described, 228-29; in Virginia, 46-48; *see also* labor, slave trade, slavery, slaves
Nelson, William H., 235
Netherlands, The: Calvinism in, 5; as English ally, 131; English rivalry with, 8, 73, 80-82; English Separatists in, 51; imperial policy of, 30-32; independence of, 7; loans money to United States, 245; as nation-state, 6; Spanish war with, 52; trade of, 3; trade with Virginia, 70; and War of Austrian Succession, 135
Nettles, Curtis, 235, 270
Neutral rights, 215
Nevins, Allan, 270
New Amsterdam, 82

New England: agriculture in, 116; blacks in army of, 228; discrimination wanted against foreign ships, 242; and disestablishment of religion, 226; Dutch grievances of, 81; Howe tries to isolate, 205; illegal trade of to West Indies, 147; immigration to, 109-10; and Interregnum, 72-77; manufacturing in, 114; and navigation laws by United States, 254; and Pilgrims, 53; population of, 73; privateering in, 241; and Queen Anne's War, 132; religious toleration in, 75; town meeting of as radical ideal, 199; and trade with foreign West Indies, 111; unity of, 74; West Indies rivalry with, 148
New England Company, 53-54
New England Confederation, 74
New England Courant, 119
New England Primer, 93
New England Way, 76
New France, 28, 82, 131; *see also* Canada
New Hampshire: as Crown colony, 80; development of, 73; disestablishment of religion in, 226; and Dominion of New England, 80; farmers power in, 201; Federalism in, 256; manufacturing in, 115; and New England Confederation, 74; and New York border conflict, 164; paper money scheme rejected by, 246; ratification by, 261, 263
New Haven (Conn.), 74
New Jersey: and Articles of Confederation, 196; in Dominion of New England, 92; and Loyalists, 193; and paper money, 246; problems of, 82-84; ratifies Constitution, 260; royal governor of imprisoned, 187; settlement of, 103; trade of taxed by New York, 242
New Jersey Plan, 251, 253
New Lights, 122
New Netherland: advantages of, 81; and Connecticut Valley, 63; desirability of, 80-82; economy and population of, 31-32; English conquer, 82, 103; and New England Confederation, 74; surrender of, 81
New Orleans (La.), 29
New York: assembly of supplies troops, 158-59; assembly of suspended, 158; Canton trade opened by, 241; Church of England in, 121; Continental Association rejected by, 177; as Crown possession, 80; and Dominion of New England, 80, 92; Glorious Revolution in, 95-96; immigrants not attracted to, 110; and independence, 187; Iroquois treaty with, 132; and King Wil-

liam's War, 131; landowners in Anti-Federalist, 257; manufacturing in, 114; Mutiny Act centers on, 157; New Hampshire border conflict with, 164; New Jersey land title conflict with, 83; and paper money, 246; power of farmers in, 201; ratifies Constitution, 262-63; slave uprisings in, 106; social mobility in, 144-46; tariff replaces land tax in, 242; western lands ceded by, 239

New York City: burns effigy of North and Hutchinson, 171; Clinton located in, 207; East Jersey dominated by, 83; English capture, 203; English strategy based on, 203; and Loyalists, 193; merchants of and intercolonial congress, 171; and Stamp Act Congress, 153; and Townshend Duties, 161

New World, 25 26

Newcomer, Lee, 190

Newfoundland, 34, 44, 131, 220

Newport, Christopher, 38

Newport (R.I.), 62

Newspapers: attack British troops, 163; and British troops in Boston, 177; in colonies, 119-20; as controversialists, 162; and East India Company, 167; economic reprisals urged by, 161; Lexington and Concord reported by, 179

Newtonian science, 118

Newtonianism, 116-18, 121, 122

Niagara (N.Y.), 136

Nicholson, General Francis, 132

Nicolls, Governor Richard, 82

Ninety-Five Theses, 4

"No taxation Without Representation," 152, 153, 159

Nobility, English, 14

Noblesse oblige, 71, 201

Nonconsumption, 176; *see also* Continental Association, Solemn League and Covenant

Nonexportation, 176; *see also* Continental Association, Solemn League and Covenant

Nonimportation: Boston Massacre ends, 164; as colonial economic policy, 162; and First Continental Congress, 176; troops threaten effectiveness of, 163; *see also* Boycott, Continental Association, Solemn League and Covenant, Stamp Act, Tea Act

Norfolk (Va.), 70, 185

North, Lord Frederick: American liberty threatened by, 174; and Boston Massacre, 164; as Chancellor of Exchequer, 161; and East India Company, 167-68; effigy of burned, 171; and Franco-American treaties, 216; French provocation ignored by, 217; government of falls, 218; home rule offered by, 215-16; king strengthens hand of, 184; and reconciliation plan, 179; and requisition system, 177-78; Saratoga defeat prompts resignation offer by, 205; and Tea Act's implications, 168-69; Tea Party reactions of, 170

North, 223

North Africa, 244

North Carolina: Anti-Federalism in, 256; Church of England in, 121; and disestablishment of religion, 225; on independence, 186; Loyalist rising in, 185; and paper money, 246; rejects ratification, 263; taxpayer franchise in, 200; Tryon Palace illustrated, 175

Northampton (Mass.), 247

Northern Ireland, 104

Northwest Territory, 240-41

Notestein, Wallace, 23

Nova Scotia, 127, 132-33, 177

Nowell, Charles E., 64

Nye, Russel B., 234

Officers, army, 222

Oglethorpe, General James, 110

Ohio Associates, 240

Ohio Valley: and Anglo-French rivalry, 135-36; English control of, 243; Iroquois and fur trade in, 31; and Proclamation of 1763, 146; and Quebec Act, 173; and Seven Years War, 137

Old Lights, 122

Olive Branch Petition, 183-84

Oliver, Lieutenant-Governor Andrew, 166-67

Ordinance of 1784, 239

Ordinance of 1785, 239-40

Ordinance of 1787, 240-41

Osgood, Herbert Levi, 65

Oswald, Richard, 218, 220

Otis, James: and economic reprisal policy, 161; on Henry's Resolves, 152; on Stamp Act Congress, 153; on supplying British troops, 157; and Writs of Assistance, 140

Oxford University, 19-21

Packard, Lawrence B., 24

Paine, Thomas: *Common Sense* written by, 185; *The Crisis* written by, 203-5; on democracy, 199; and disestablishment of religion, 224; on English monarchy, 186; government defined by, 144; portrait of, 187

INDEX

Panama, Isthmus of, 26
Paoli (Pa.), Battle of, 205
Paper money, 245-46; *see also* currency, finances, money, taxation
Paranoia, American, 151, 168
Pardoning power, 199
Parliament: and Americans after 1763, 144; Americans try to limit power of, 151; and Boston Port Bill, 170; Burke's reconciliation bill rejected by, 185; conciliation policy rejected by, 177; colonists identify with, 97, 129; Declaration of Independence ignores, 188; described, 10-11; empire defined by, 126; First Continental Congress rejects authority of, 174; and indirect taxation, 157; land taxes cut by, 158; measures of feared by Americans, 146; and Navigation Acts, 70; Otis challenges power of, 140; power of accepted in some colonies, 177; power of challenged by assemblies, 157; power of defined by Circular Letter, 159; power of defined by Dickinson, 159; power of really lacking in colonies, 179; and Rhode Island, 62; Scotch-Irish economy restricted by, 104; slave trade monopoly broken by, 104-5;. and Stamp Act, 150; Stamp Act Congress accepts power of, 153; and succession to throne, 67; and Sugar Act, 149; supremacy of as issue, 161; and tax power, 148, 158; tax power unused by, 127, 154; and trade and navigation laws, 77
Parliamentary system, and Articles of Confederation, 238
Parson's Cause, 140, 225
Paterson, William, 251
Patronage, 199
Patterson, Samuel W., 235
Pauperism, 12-13
Peace: British overture for, 217; British send commissioners for in 1775, 184; negotiations for in the revolution, 217-21; United States terms for, 218-19
Peace of Paris, 220-21
Peace of 1763, 138, 143-46
Peare, Catherine O., 99
Peckham, Howard H., 234
Penal institutions, 231
Penn, Governor John, 174
Penn, Admiral Sir William, 84
Penn, William: as land promoter, 85, 108-9; portrait of, 83; as proprietor, 84-86
Pennsylvania: anti-English position abandoned by, 177; founding of, 84-86; immigrants attracted to, 108-9; and independence, 187; manufacturing in, 114; and Massachusetts Circular Letter, 159; and paper money, 246; penal reform in, 231; ratifies Constitution, 260; settlement of, 103; smuggling tea into, 160-61; taxpayer franchise in, 200; Wyoming Valley dispute with Connecticut, 164
Pennsylvania Dutch, 194
Pennsylvania State House, 183
Pepperell, William, 135
Pequot Indians, 73
Pequot War, 73
Peter, Reverend Hugh, 53
Philadelphia: and Boston Port Bill, 171; Clinton evacuates, 207; and First Continental Congress, 174; founded, 85; growth of, 108; Howe occupies, 205; intercolonial congress meets in, 171; and Loyalists, 193; map of in 1702, 84; prices in, 242; social mobility in, 144-46; and Townshend duties, 161; Vice Admiralty Court in, 160; West Jersey trade with, 83; Whitefield's visit to, 123
Philadelphia Abolition Society, 230
Philadelphia Convention, 249-55, 275
Philanthropy and Georgia, 110-11
Philip of Anjou, 131
Philip II (Sp.), 34
Philip V (Sp.), 132
Philippines, 23
Piedmont, 256
Pietists, 85, 109
Pilgrims; *see* Separatists
Piracy, 244
Pitt, William: and East India Company, 167; on English commanders, 202; and New York's rejection of Mutiny Act, 157; and Quebec Act, 174; reconciliation proposed by, 177; and requisition system, 147; resigns as Prime Minister, 161; Rockingham replaced by, 155; and Seven Years War, 136; and Stamp Act, 154; and Tea Party, 170; on virtual representation, 151
Plains of Abraham, 136
Plan of Union of Galloway, 175
Plantation Office, 77
Plymouth Colony, 53, 73-74, 95
Political theory, 257-58
Politics: American understanding of, 268; broadened base of in the revolution, 200-1; characterized after 1763, 139; instability of colonial, 130; religion in, 6
Poor Richard, 144; *see also* Benjamin Franklin
Popular rule, 198

Population: Appalachians limits expansion of, 146; of Carolina, 86-87; colonial expands rapidly, 144; distribution of as problem in Articles of Confederation Congress, 195-96; of England and Wales changes, 15; in English settlements, 23; ethnic character of, 103-7; and law, 231; map of in 1660, 69; map of in 1700, 102; map of in 1760, 145; in New England affected by Civil War, 72; New England's pattern of, 73; in New York, 82; in Pennsylvania, 85; settlement patterns, 273-74; surplus, 110-11; survey of needed to implement Articles of Confederation, 244; value of in New World, 43; in Virginia, 41, 71; in West and statehood determination, 239
Port Royal (Nova Scotia), 132
Portsmouth (Rhode Island), 62
Portugal: empire of described, 22-23; expansion of, 3; explorations by, 21-23; as nation-state, 6; trade with under Spanish control, 31
Postal service, 184
Potomac River, 248
Poverty, 12-13, 19, 21
Powder Alarm, 176
Powell, Sumner Chilton, 64
Power: federal government had only delegated, 258; indivisible nature of, 157; limits on, 125-26; location of according to middle class, 224; locus of, 266-67; separation of in English constitution, 197
Prejudice and slavery, 47-48, 227-28
Prerogative power, 97
Presbyterian Church: and English ties, 227; and Great Awakening, 122; in New England, 120; in Scotland, 5
Price index, 242
Primogeniture, 231
Prince, Reverend Thomas, 119
Princeton (N.J.), Battle of, 203
Prisons, debtor, 110-11
Privateering, 241
Privy Council: and assemblies, 127; functions of in England, 9; and Leislerian Rebellion, 96; in local government of England, 11; Lords of Trade created by, 77; and Parson's Cause, 140; and Pennsylvania Charter, 85; power of in colonies and England compared, 97-98
Proclamation Line, 146, 150, 174
Prohibitory Act, 184-85
Property, protection of, 200, 250-51
Property qualifications, 200; see also, elections, politics

Property rights: Dominion of New England affects, 92-94; in English law, 79; and Intolerable Acts, 173; and population pressure, 231; in West, 240
Proprietors, 44, 127
Protestant Episcopal Church, 227; see also Church of England
Protestant reformers, 50
Protestantism: breeds dissension, 59; common American heritage of, 194; in England during Interregnum, 74-75; nature of in United States, 226-27; status of in Maryland, 72
Providence (R.I.), 61
Prussia: American recognition efforts rebuffed by, 215; England abandons, 146; Lutheranism in, 5; and Seven Years War, 135
Public disorder, 246-48
Puritanism: and Church of England, 58; challenges to, 59; change feared by, 77; conflict of with Stuarts, 68; defensiveness of, 76-77; English authorities offended by, 79; and Great Awakening, 124; modifications of, 91-92, 120-21; New World impact on, 59; Quakerism compared with, 85; in Virginia during Civil War, 70; victorious in Old England, 72; zenith of, 75-76
Puritans: and Church of England in Massachusetts, 94; and James I, 50-51; in Massachusetts, 55; persecution of, 49; and Quakers, 76

Quadruple Alliance, 133
Quakers: in New Jersey, 83; and penal reform 231; and William Penn, 84-85; in Pennsylvania, 85-86; in Pennsylvania reject Massachusetts Circular Letter, 159; and Pietists, 109; and Puritanism, 76; and slavery, 107, 229; in Virginia, 70
Quarles, Benjamin A., 234
Quartering Act, 171-72
Quebec, 28, 29, 136, 202-3
Quebec Act, 173-74, 202-3
Queen Anne's War, 131-32
Quinn, David B., 65
Quintuple Alliance, 133
Quo Warranto, 42
Quock Walker Case, 230

Radicals: attitude toward bureaucracy, 238; in England, 164; and Intolerable Acts, 173; oppose limits on popular power, 199; on state governments, 197

INDEX

Raleigh, Sir Walter, 34-35, 37, 103
Randolph, Edmund, 249, 254, 261
Rankin, Hugh F., 234
Ratification of Constitution, 254-64
Ratifying conventions, 263
Rationalism, 3, 118-19, 196-97
Reconciliation, 183, 184, 215-16
Redcoats, hatred of, 176; *see also* army, troops
Reform impulse, 224
Reformation, 4, 48
Regulator Movement, 164
Religion: in Carolina, 86-87; disestablishment of, 224-27; and education, 20-21; in eighteenth-century America, 120-24; in English life, 14; and exploration impulse, 22; heritage of, 3; in Massachusetts, 57-58; in Massachusetts as franchise requirement, 95; persecution of dissenting, 76-77; and politics, 6; and slavery, 106-7; state connection with, 224-27; toleration of in England, 74-75; toleration of in Maryland, 72; Voltaire on, 227
Renaissance, 3, 21
Representation: Anglo-American conflict over, 151; definitions of, 124-25; expansion of under states, 200-1; in federal Congress, 250-51; virtual, 151
Representative government, 199
Representatives, House of, 253
Republicanism, 239, 269
Requisition system: Americans propose in lieu of stamp duty, 150; in French and Indian War, 147; Pitt and Burke propose, 177
Restoration, 68, 72, 80
Revenue, 147-48, 240
Revere, Paul, 176, 179
Revolution, 192-93, 223-30, 249
Revolutionary war, 201-13
Rhineland, 131
Rhode Island: Anti-Federalism in, 256; and Baptists, 76; characterized in 1640s, 73; charter of, 79; Constitution rejected by, 263; and Dominion of New England, 80; founded, 60-62; and Gaspée Incident, 165; and Glorious Revolution, 95; government of, 97; manufacturing in, 115; New England colonies challenge, 62; New England Confederation excludes, 74; and paper money, 246; and Philadelphia Convention, 249
Rice, 87, 116
Rights: Americans claim, 141; Circular Letter defines, 159; English, 130; Henry defines, 151-52; state constitutions protect, 200
Rioting, 153
Rivers, influence of, 274
Roanoke Island, 34, 35, 37
Robinson, John, 152
Robson, Eric, 189
Rochambeau, Comte de, 213
Rockingham, Charles Watson-Wentworth, Marquis of: Americans appeased by, 154-55; Grenville replaces, 150; King's program denounced by, 184; and Stamp Act, 153-54
Rodrigue Hortalez and Company, 214
Rolfe, John, 40
Roman Catholic Church: in Boston, 177; in Canada, 28-29; challenges to, 4; and Charles II, 131; and English colonies, 94; in Germany, 104; hegemony of, 3, 6; Henry VIII breaks with, 7; and James I, 50-51; James II favors, 91, 131; Luther challenges, 4; in Maryland, 44-45, 72, 96; and Quebec Act, 173; reform of, 3; in Southern Europe, 5; and Church of England, 49
Rossiter, Clinton, 189, 270
Rotation in office, 199, 224
Rowse, A. L., 24
Royal African Company, 81, 104, 132; *see also* slave trade
Rum industry, 149; *see also* molasses, sugar
Rupert, Prince, 86
Rush, Benjamin, 107
Russia, 135, 215
Russian Company, 18; *see also* Muscovy Company
Rutland, Robert A., 190, 270
Rutman, Darrett B., 24, 64
Ryswick, Peace of, 131

Safety, Committee of, 179, 184
St. Eustatius, 31
St. John River, 217
St. Lawrence River, 23, 28, 132, 202-3
St. Leger, Colonel Barry, 205
Saltonstall, Sir Richard, 53
Sandwich, Earl of, 202
Sandys, Sir Edwin, 41
Saratoga (N.Y.), Battle of: depicted, 206; described, 205; Franklin aided by, 215-16; French aid makes victory possible at, 213; Gates victorious at, 206
Savannah (Ga.), siege of, 207
Savelle, Max, 141
Saxony, 135

Schutz, John A., 141
Schuyler, General Philip, 202-3
Schuyler, Robert L., 189
Science, 3, 116-18
Scioto Associates, 240
Scotch-Irish, 104
Scotland: Knox's church reforms in, 5; nonjuring bishops of, 227; Presbyterianism in, 5; source of settlers, 103-4
Scott, John Morin, 153
Seabury, Reverend Samuel, 227
Second Continental Congress: blacks rejected by for army, 228; as central government, 195; and Committee of Secret Correspondence, 213; English peace overture rejected by, 217; and foreign aid, 214; Gates recalled from retirement by, 208; George III attacked by, 188-89; and independence, 183-84, 186-87; meeting place of depicted, 183; money lacking to support, 222; peace commission of, 217-18; peace commission instructions, 217, 218; and standing armies, 222; states asked by to create new governments, 197; trade with foreign ships opened by, 186; war effort of, 201-13; Washington criticized by, 206; Washington named commander of army by, 180-82
Secretary for Foreign Affairs (U.S.), 238
Secretary of State for Colonies, 196
Secretary of State for Southern Department, 98
Secretary at War (U.S.), 238
Sectionalism, 251
Self-government, 43, 90-91
Senate, 251
Separatists: and Church of England, 50; in Leyden, 52; and The Netherlands, 51; and Virginia Company plans, 52; Virginia as refuge for, 41; and Weston agreement, 52
Servants, 12, 46-47; *see also* labor, Negroes, slavery, slaves
Settlement patterns, 273-74; *see also* population
Seven Years War, 135-37
Shaftesbury, Anthony Cooper, Earl of, 86-87
Shakespeare, William, 21
Shays, Captain Daniel, 247
Shays's Rebellion, 247, 261
Sheep grazing, 15
Shelburne, William Petty, Earl of, 146, 167, 174, 184, 220
Shenandoah River, 108-9
Shenandoah Valley, 256

Shepherd, Reverend Thomas, 92
Sheriffs, 11
Sherman, Roger, 187, 251
Shipping, 73, 111; *see also* commerce, trade
"Silence Dogood" essays, 119
Silver, 133; *see also* bullion, money
Slave ship illustrated, 106
Slave trade, 32, 132, 229
Slave uprisings, 106
Slavery: and aristocracy, 223; in Carolina, 87; challenged, 233-34; description of, 108-9; development of in colonies, 104-7; and English indemnities, 243; failure to resolve issue of, 276-77; George III blamed for, 228; and Great Awakening, 124; Jefferson quoted on, 230; in New England, 63; in Northwest Territory, 241; and the revolution, 227-30; in Virginia, 105; in Virginia and Maryland, 47-48; in West, 239
Slaves: and census under Constitution, 254; description of treatment of, 228-29; Dutch import into Virginia, 70; English fail to compensate for, 222; and population count under Articles of Confederation, 196; taxation of imports of proposed, 150
Smilie, John, 260
Smith, Abbot E., 65
Smith, Adam, 198, 275
Smith, Charles Page, 270
Smith, Captain John, 38-39
Smith, Melancthon, 263
Smith, Paul H., 235
Smuggling: by Americans, 147; of Dutch tea, 168; by English into Spanish America, 133; of tea, 160-61; of tea proscribed by Sons of Liberty, 169-70; and tea tax, 161-62; and Writs of Assistance, 140
Social conflict, 144-46
Social institutions, 224-30
Social upheaval, 248
Society: cleavages in, 164; development after the revolution, 277; mobility in colonies, 144-46; reform of, 233-34; stability of challenged by Great Awakening, 124; stability of in England, 15; structure of in colonies, 125, 144-46; structure of in New England, 63; structure of in Virginia and Maryland, 45-46
Society for Promoting Christian Knowledge, 21
Society for the Promotion of the Manumission of Slaves, 230
Solemn League and Covenant, 171, 174
Sons of Liberty, 153, 158, 162, 167

INDEX

Sosin, Jack M., 189
South: aristocracy in, 223; opposes federal navigation laws, 254; wants unrestricted export trade, 242
South Carolina: agriculture in, 116; blacks rejected for army of, 228; Church of England in, 121; and disestablishment of religion in, 225; and First Continental Congress, 174; Georgia created to protect, 110; on Independence, 186-87; manufacturing in, 115; paper money in, 246; ratifies Constitution, 261; rice of exempted from nonexportation, 176; and slave trade, 254; slaves needed for manpower in, 229; slave uprisings in, 106
South Seas Company, 133
Southampton (Eng.), 17
Spain: American no threat to, 214; American recognition efforts rebuffed by, 215; and Articles of Confederation government, 243; and Dutch independence, 30; and Dutch War, 52; empire of, 22-23, 27, 131-32; and English conflict, 33-34, 133; English and Dutch defeat, 8; expansion of, 3; explorations by, 21-23; imperial advantages of, 26, 28; Lisbon closed by, 31; as nation-state, 6; republicanism feared by, 220; and Seven Years War, 135; tobacco trade of, 41; trade of colonies of, 132; and War of Austrian Succession, 133-35
Spaniards, 1
Speculation in western lands, 196
Speech and press, 199
Speedwell, 52
Spenser, Edmund, 21
Springfield (Mass.), 247
Stamp Act, 114-16, 126, 149-53, 160
Stamp Act Congress, 153-54
Stamp Tax, 149
Star Chamber, Court of, 165
Stark, General John, 205
State capitols, 200
State sovereignty, 259, 266
States: individual mercantilism of, 242; western equal with original, 195, 239
Statute for Religious Freedom (Va.), 225
Steuben, "Baron" von, 206
Stiles, Ezra, 155
Stoddard, Reverend Solomon, 120
Stone, Lawrence, 24
Straits of Magellan, 31
Stuart dynasty: imperialism of, 77-80; monarchs of characterized, 9; problems of, 68; throne claimed by exiled, 133; uprisings of against Hanoverians, 104

Stuyvesant, Peter, 74, 81, 82
Subsidies, 116
Subsistence crisis, 13
Suffolk (Mass.) Resolves, 176
Suffrage, 199; *see also* assemblies, constitutions, elections, politics
Sugar: in Barbados, 86; in Bermuda, 39; and illegal trade, 147; and Seven Years War, 137; trade for, 148; in West Indies, 131
Sugar Act of 1733, 148-49
Sugar Act of 1764, 148, 155
Superintendent of Finance (U.S.), 238, 245
Supremacy, Act of, 49
Supreme Court (U.S.), 266
Sweden, 5, 103
Sydnor, Charles S., 190

Tacitus, 21
Tarleton, Sir Banastre, 209
Taunton (Mass.), 247
Tawney, R. H., 24
Taxation: Articles of Confederation government needs power of, 195, 244, 248; and central government, 275; of commerce by New York, 242; under Constitution, 266-67; Dickinson on British power of, 159; in Dominion of New England, 94; by Duke of York in New York, 82; English ability to use in colonies, 151; importance of, 129; middle class attitude toward, 223; New Jersey Plan proposal for, 251; Parliament's power of, 150; Parliament's power of partially accepted by Americans, 154; Penn threatened by, 86; policies of Townshend, 157-58; power of, 127; and public disorder, 247; repeal of English urged by Pitt and Burke, 177; resistance to, 247-48; and Sugar Act, 149; of tea challenged, 168-69; of tea important, 160; in Virginia and Bacon's Rebellion, 90
Tea: controversy over, 167-70; exported directly to colonies, 168; smuggling of, 160-61; tax on, 161-62
Tea Act of 1773, 168-69
Tea consignees, 168-69
Tennent, Reverend William, 122
TePaske, John J., 64
Territorial government, 240-41; *see also* West
Thayer, Theodore, 190, 235
Thirty-Nine Articles, 49
Thirty Years War, 104
Thomas, Herbert, 190
Thomson, Charles, 174
Three-Fifths Compromise, 254

Thucydides, 21
Ticonderoga, 136
Tobacco: and Bacon's Rebellion, 87-90; dominates Maryland, 43; in eighteenth century, 116; expansion of, 111; and Parson's Cause, 140; prices of and enumeration, 46; receipts for as tax payments, 246; and rise of slavery, 47-48; trade in between England and Spain, 41; in Virginia, 40-41; in Virginia during Civil War, 70; in West Indies, 131
Tolles, Frederick B., 141
Tooke, John Horne, 164
Tories; see Loyalists
Town meeting: ideal of radicals, 199; illustrated, 166
Townshend Act, 160
Townshend, Charles, 157-58, 167
Townshend Duties, 158, 160-61, 168
Trade: Articles of Confederation cannot regulate, 241-42; and central government control, 275; with colonies after 1763, 139; in England, 16-19; First Continental Congress's measures on, 176; with foreign West Indies, 155; illegal during French and Indian War, 147; with Levant, 2; map of, 112-13; and neutral rights, 215; of New England during Interregnum, 73; of New Jersey, 83; oriental, 2-3; and parliamentary tax power, 149; patterns of after the revolution, 221; patterns of under Articles of Confederation, 241; and private colonies, 78-79; regulation of according to Dickinson, 159; restrictions on ended, 186; Second Continental Congress opens to foreigners, 186, 214; in slaves, 229-30; and Stamp Act, 153; and Townshend Duties, 161; and War of Austrian Succession, 133; with West Indies, 148
Treasury Board, 98
Treaty of Peace (1783), 219, 243-44
Trenton (N.J.), Battle of, 203
Trevelyan, George M., 24
Triple Alliance, 133
Tripoli, 244
Troops, American, 180-82
Troops, British: in Boston, 162-63, 177; and Boston Massacre, 163-64; in colonies after 1763, 146; at Concord, 178-79; conquer Breed's Hill, 180; evacuate United States, 218; evacuation of from Northwest delayed, 222; and Mutiny Act, 155-57; not available to suppress rebellion, 179; satirized in cartoon, 156; source of, 156
Troops, movement of: map, 204
Tryon Palace, 175

Tudor, Henry, 7; see also Henry VII, Henry VIII
Tudor dynasty, 9
Tunis, 244
Tuscany, 215
Tuscarora Indians, 87
Two Penny Act (1758), 140

Ubbelohde, Carl, 64, 189
Union: Americans try to recreate, 231-32; concept of, 193-94; nature of, 267; western lands and, 239
Unity: Americans search for, 275; factors encouraging, 194
Universities, 19-21
Upton, Leslie F. S., 235
Urban areas, 144-46
Urbanism, 233
Utrecht, Treaty of, 132-33

Valley Forge (Pa.), 205-7
Van Doren, Carl, 270
Van Tyne, Claude, 235
Vane, Harry, 59
Venetian merchants, 16-18
Venice, 3
Venus, transit of, 118
Vergennes, Charles Gravier, Comte de, 213-14, 216-17, 220-21
Vermont, 200, 229
Verrazano, Giovanni de, 28
Ver Steeg, Clarence, 64
Veto power, 199
Vice-Admiralty Courts, 160; see also Admiralty Courts, Navigation Acts
Vincennes (Ind.), 207
Violence, 247-48
Virginia: agriculture in, 116; and Annapolis Convention, 249; Bill of Rights of, 224-25; black and white servants in, 47; buffer area needed by, 101; Church of England in, 121; as Crown colony, 42; economic diversification proposed for, 41; economy of, 39; estate in described, 114-15; farmers power in, 201; Federalism in, 256; in First Continental Congress, 174; founded, 34-35; and French and Indian War, 135; and Gaspée Incident, 165; goals of first settlers of, 38; government of, 38; on independence, 186; and inter-colonial congress in 1774, 171; legal codes of reformed, 231; manufacturing in, 115; and Maryland in Interregnum, 72; and Massachusetts Circular Letter, 159; Parson's Cause in, 140; population of, 39, 86; and Potomac River negotiations, 248-49; problems of in 1670's,

INDEX

87-91; ratifies Constitution, 261-63; royalism in, 68-71; self-government in, 130; Separatists attracted to, 52; slave uprisings in, 106; slavery in, 105; and Stamp Act, 151-52; "Starving Time" in, 38-39; tobacco culture in, 41, 246; and Townshend duties, 161; University of, 225; urban center of, 48; and Virginia Company of London, 70; western land claims ceded by, 239
Virginia Company of London: agrees with Separatists, 52; chartered, 32; charter of 1624, 42; feared in Virginia, 70; plans of for Bermuda, 39; lotteries used by, 39; second charter of, 38; encourages settlement, 41; settlers sent out by, 38; territorial limits of, 37; third charter of, 39
Virginia Company of Plymouth, 32, 37, 44
Virginia Plan, 249-50, 253
Voltaire, François-Marie Arouet, 227

Wainwright, Nicholas B., 141
Wallace, Willard M., 234, 235
Waller, G. M., 99
Walloons, 32
War of the Austrian Succession, 133-35
War of Jenkin's Ear, 133-35
War of League of Augsburg, 104
War of Spanish Succession, 104, 131-32
War Office, 98
Warren, Charles, 270
Warren, Joseph, 176, 179
Warren, Sir Peter, 135
Wars, imperial, 130-31
Wars of the Roses, 7
Warwick (R.I.), 62
Warwick, Robert Rich, Earl of, 53, 54, 62
Washburn, Wilcomb, 99
Washington, George: and Articles of Confederation Congress, 248; Canadian conquest abandoned by, 203; and Clinton's retreat to New York City, 207; Congress tries to manipulate, 222; on Constitution, 261; as Continental Army commander, 180-82; and *The Crisis*; English in Boston besieged by, 182; in French and Indian War, 135; on liberty, 197; military problems of, 202; New York City's defenses, 203; and Philadelphia Convention, 249; portrait of, 208; at Second Continental Congress, 183; and winter of 1777-78, 206-7; at Yorktown, 213
Watertown (Mass.), 56
"The Way to Wealth," 144
Webster-Ashburton Treaty, 220
Wells, Peter, 234
Wendel, François, 24

Wentworth, Paul, 216
Wertenbaker, Thomas Jefferson, 141
Wesley, Reverend John, 122, 227
West: Articles of Confederation successful with, 238; disposition of, 239-41; English agree to evacuate, 220; English retain forts in, 222; revolutionary war in, 207; settlement of, 232; status of, 239; survey and sale of lands in, 240
West Indies: assemblies moribund in, 130; closed to United States, 276; and colonial economy, 116; illegal trade to foreign, 147; New England trade with, 73, 111; and Peace of 1763, 137; prosperity of, 131; trade with after 1764, 148; trade with blocked, 244; trade with closed to United States, 221; trade with encouraged by Rockingham, 155; trade with foreign, 138; trade with replaced by privateering, 241; trade with and the revolution, 215
West Point (N.Y.), 208
Westminster Confession, 75
Weston, Thomas, 52
Whigs: ideal of, 80, 224; reluctance of English to attack Americans, 180; sympathetic to American cause, 202
White, Reverend John, 35-37, 53
White, R. J., 234
White Plains (N.Y.), 207
Whitefield, Reverend George, 122-24
Wilcox, William B., 235
Wilkes, John, 164
William and Mary, 131
William of Orange, 94
Williams, Roger, 58-59, 60-62
Wilson, James, 253, 259, 260
Winslow, Ola, 141
Winthrop, John, 54, 56-58
Winthrop, John IV, 118
Wise, Reverend John, 94, 120-21
Wittenberg Church, 4
Woburn (Mass.), 56-57
Wolfe, General James, 136, 179
Wool, 17-18
Woolman, John, 107
Worcester (Mass.), 247
Work, 12-13; *see also* labor, slavery, slaves
Wright, Benjamin, 270
Wright, Esmond, 189, 235
Wright, Louis B., 64, 141
Writs of Assistance, 140, 160, 162; *see also* commerce, Navigation Acts, trade
Wyoming Valley dispute, 164

Yazoo strip, 239
York, James Stuart, Duke of: accession of

to throne, 80; and Carolina charter, 86; and imperial policy, 77; and New Jersey, 82-83; and New Netherland, 32, 82-83; proprietor of New York, 82; and William Penn, 84; and slave trade, 104; *see also* James II

Yorke, Sir Philip, 127

Yorkists, 7

Yorktown (Va.), Battle of: Americans victorious at, 213; and French aid, 213; map of, 212; and peace negotiations, 218; victory at portrayed, 209; victory resulted from French aid, 217